CRITICAL
INSIGHTS

Historical Fiction

CRITICAL
INSIGHTS

Historical Fiction

Editor
Virginia Brackett
Park University, Missouri

SALEM PRESS
A Division of EBSCO Information Services, Inc.
Ipswich, Massachusetts

GREY HOUSE PUBLISHING

Publisher's Cataloging-In-Publication Data
(Prepared by The Donohue Group, Inc.)

Names: Brackett, Virginia, editor.
Title: Historical fiction / editor, Virginia Brackett, Park University, Missouri.
Other Titles: Critical insights.
Description: [First edition]. | Ipswich, Massachusetts : Salem Press, a division
        of EBSCO Information Services, Inc. ; Amenia, NY : Grey
        House Publishing, [2018] | Includes bibliographical references
        and index.
Identifiers: ISBN 9781682177105 (hardcover)
Subjects: LCSH: Historical fiction--History and criticism.
Classification: LCC PN3441 .H57 2018 | DDC 809.381--dc23

First Printing

PRINTED IN THE UNITED STATES OF AMERICA

Contents

About This Volume

Virginia Brackett

A volume that focuses on the subject of historical fiction has, in the parlance of the day, its work cut out for it. So many fiction subgenres exist for children's, young adult, and adult audiences that incorporate elements of historical fiction that one volume would be hard pressed to include enough essays to discuss each. This most paradoxical of genres, one that blends historical "truth" with fiction's "untruth" has provided a welcome venue for almost every type of story told. Fantasy, science fiction, romance, and detective genres have all made use of historical fiction's many storytelling enhancements. Authors find it as irresistible as their readers. And why not? Such tales allow their audience to engage in several ways. Readers may reimagine history in cases where it is reconstructed; become better acquainted with history as it is personalized through specific characters; and, perhaps most important, even question historical "truths" once believed to be inviolable.

Parameters for the works discussed as historical fiction in this volume could be set only after research on the editor's part to determine the most simple yet clearly structured elements to be shared by all essays. As many scholars argue, a definition of historical fiction can be complicated (Hundley et al. 95). What most agree upon, however, is that historical fiction not only reflects fact, or "truth," within a fictional framework, but also allows an enhanced reception of material in which readers can identify continuity between the past and their own present (96). In the end, the novels discussed in this volume as historical fiction had to comply with one simple requirement. Each must focus on characters and/or events in novels published at least fifty years after the characters lived or the events occurred. Given the collection's academic focus, some of the more imaginative popular culture approaches to historical fiction, such as those featuring Abraham Lincoln or Jane Austen embroiled with vampires are avoided, not that such presentations cannot be entertaining.

The contributors do hope to entertain, but also to inform, following the advice of sixteenth-century English poet and scholar Philip Sidney. Sidney wrote that poetry—understood as literature—should entertain but also enlighten. Thus, this volume's contributors find value in the fact that literature can be enjoyable but also educate its readers. The education comes partly through exposure to historical fact, but, as Sidney also pointed out, history deals with particulars, specifics, or simple facts. Literature may take those specifics and insert them into a story line, or plot, that appeals to readers through its more general presentation of knowledge. Literature's general nature allows its readers to see themselves in its characters, its social challenges, its conflicts and its triumphs. Therein dwells the benefit of historical fiction, especially for young adult audiences. Young readers learn not only what to read, but how to read through historical fiction, therefore gaining important tools of understanding to apply to later reading but also to their own lives.

The volume anticipates a diverse reading audience. It intends to support study of historical fiction in the classroom, but also reading apart from a structured teaching agenda, so that any member of the reading public may find it of use. For those in the classroom, both instructors and students, the volume provides a hearty resource in terms of novel titles, but also of discussion of related concepts and the sharing of a plethora of research materials, both print and electronic. Thus, its design will satisfy the needs of the scholar and the nonscholar, teachers, parents, and common readers. Its contributors have broad expertise in the topic, as evident in their brief biographies, and those familiar with research about young adult literature will recognize several contributor names as individuals who follow active writing and publishing agendas. Others bring the expertise of the classroom, both at the secondary and college levels, to bear on their analysis.

In respect to the broad use of history in fiction, the collection offers multiple examples. The novels discussed are united by their incorporation of historical fact, but also diversified in its application.

Readers will be introduced to concepts in historical fiction by the first four essays, all of which focus on Critical Context through exploration of historical nonfiction's background, its critical reception, its view through a select critical lens, and via comparative analysis.

Danielle Barkley reviews the background to the development of historical fiction, a challenging task, because the location of historical fiction has changed over time. While Sir Walter Scott has been traditionally recognized as the father of historical fiction, Barkley challenges that label through a discussion of Gothic novels whose publication predated Scott's *Waverley* series. The reception by readers and critics alike of various genres of fiction often proves crucial to their popularity. Steven T. Bickmore will trace that reception, providing a useful timeline, as well as a number of early examples of historical fiction. Readers will find additional information about several of the novels he includes in other essays within this volume. Mary Warner applies feminist criticism to several works of historical fiction that focus on the American Revolution. Each novel she discussesfeatures a female protagonist seeking freedom from racism, sexism, and oppression prevalent in the male-dominated culture of a young United States. Application of a critical approach, like that offered by feminist criticism, supplies the reader tools to apply to readings in order to understand them from various points of view. Jeffrey S. Kaplan adopts a comparative analysis approach to introduce readers to historical novels about the Holocaust that feature young protagonists. Each provides unique characters and contexts—differing in situational perspective and viewpoint—in their imagined, yet too-real young person's eyewitness to history.

Some of the chapters challenge the audience's concept of historical fiction and its effect on readers. Again, many critics look to Sir Walter Scott and his novels as the birth of the genre, but Christine E. Kozikowski takes a different approach. She compares the elements that make Scott's *Ivanhoe* (1815) fit the definition of historical fiction with works from an earlier era categorized as medieval romance. In addition to introducing readers to literature likely new to them, Kozikowski makes the case that critics should broaden consideration of earlier works to include them in the subgenre of historical fiction. Natalie Neill also looks to the century before that in which Scott wrote to analyze elements of the Gothic romance that align with historical fiction. Neill reveals that Gothic writers experimented with the blending of history and fiction and used historical milieus and fictionalized historical figures in sophisticated ways to achieve a range of goals. While their work would not be considered historical fiction in the accepted sense, readers should keep in mind that no genre ever simply springs forth fully formed from a single writer's pen. Precursors that strongly influenced Scott and other historical fiction writers are important to keep in mind.

Other contributors offer familiar characters in new and/or reconsidered roles. Amanda L. Anderson discusses the familiar story of Maid Marian and Robin Hood and reviews the popular position of Maid Marian as a heroine of historical fiction. As Anderson demonstrates, such a construction is problematic because of a modern tendency to incorrectly revise certain historical details to appeal to modern sensibilities. Thus, works labeled historical fiction may lack the true focus on historical detail that they claim. Chris Crowe also examines the masking of truth by historical fiction, but he sees that filter as a positive, especially in the case of young readers, as he relates via personal narrative. In Crowe's vast experience and that of additional educators and scholars, young and otherwise inexperienced audiences may benefit when historical fiction serves as a lens. It may "translate" history by modifying content perhaps not suited to young readers' level of comprehension. Although historical topics may prove difficult, they should not be hidden from young readers, particularly when they reflect the culture of that audience. While all of the essayists readily admit that historical fiction offers a representation of the truth, not truth itself, they view that representation with differing degrees of acceptance in its application to specific themes and eras.

The development of American culture comes under the lens of historical fiction in several of this collection's essays. LuElla D'Amico examines "contact literature" represented by early American romance writers James Fenimore Cooper and Catharine

Maria Sedgwick. Readers of their day would have been able to justify the colonization of Native Americans through the sympathetic portrayals of the settlers shaped by Cooper and Sedgwick. D'Amico will compare those early American novels to a contemporary novel by popular author Mary Pope Osborne that similarly brings together Native and Anglo Americans. However, Osborne's protagonist learns to accept and value diverse views and backgrounds. D'Amico then analyzes Osborne's success at offering a more nuanced view of the political death of Native Americans in a narrative where friendship becomes a forceful agent of change. Marta María Gutiérrez Rodríguez examines the popular topic of the Salem Witch Trials. She discusses the fact that the "afflicted girls of Salem," long considered the perpetrators of the terror that resulted in death and imprisonment for members of their community, might instead be considered victims of cultural circumstances. Sheng-mei Ma moves beyond American culture to consider three classical Chinese novels, which highlight stories from the third through the sixteenth centuries. He then returns to American culture in his discussion of the legend of Fa-Mu Lan and whether it succeeds as a crossover tale as utilized by Maxine Hong Kingston. Readers will also benefit from an introduction to unfamiliar works featuring various representative crossover characters, male and female, situated between history and fiction, heroism and banditry. They are the material of mythmaking, a process crucial to the development of any culture's values.

Amy Cummins focuses on several novels that portray life for a specific group during the American Civil War (1861-1865). Her essay analyzes fictional portrayals of soldiers in camp and in battle, perspectives on the reasons for the war, and African-American resistance to enslavement and injustice. While these topics might be too challenging or disturbing for young readers when read as history, through the adoption of the lens that Crowe's essay discusses they may be presented in an age-appropriate manner. Jericho Williams also examines the African-American community as represented in novels that depart from the focus of popular pre-Civil War slave narratives. He considers authors who write outside the boundaries of historical narratives that confine African-American resistance to well-known revolts. Instead, each author discussed asserts the primacy of family sacrifice among those denied rights throughout American history. Authors including Toni Morrison and Mildred Taylor wrote historical novels that serve to personalize history, encouraging readers to consider their roles within their communities. Sara Rutkowski turns her focus to the era that produced the Works Progress Administration (WPA) Federal Writers' Project. That project hired unemployed professional and aspiring writers to document the nation during the Great Depression. Federal Writers were tasked with unearthing histories and folklore, interviewing Americans, and gathering their community stories. Many of those writers brought their research and documentary training into the postwar era to produce fictional work that enlightens and invigorates America's past. Rutkowski reminds us that literature may be molded by political, social, and economic currents of society not only as a reaction to those currents, but also as a direct effect of formally structured programs.

Christine De Vinne continues the march along a timeline to the twenty-first century through her discussion of the process of placing real characters within a fictional presentation. She introduces readers to the four Mirabal sisters, underground heroes whose 1960 deaths at the hands of Rafael Trujillo helped bring down one of the bloodiest Central American dictatorships of the twentieth century. De Vinne frames her discussion with the Latin American tradition in which readers agree to a "willing suspension of disbelief" in order to participate in the truth-telling of *testimonio*, a rhetorical approach forcefully adapted to speak back to power.

In combination this volume's chapters open wide a door to discussion of the importance and the joy of historical fiction for readers at all levels. They also invite readers to compare fictional presentations of "true" events and persons to that of traditionally understood historical narratives. Such consideration may result in a clearer understanding of the nature of historical fiction on the part of readers and writers alike.

Works Cited

Hundley, Melanie, et al. "Enhancing the Canon with Historical Fiction and Informational Texts." ALAN *Review*, no. 41, vol. 2, Winter 2014, pp. 95-98.

Sidney, Philip. "Defense of Poesy (1583)." *The Poetry Foundation*, 2017. Accessed 1 June, 2017. https://www.poetryfoundation.org/poets/philip-sidney.

On Historical Fiction

Virginia Brackett

Much debate exists over the value of a certain genre, or more accurately, a subgenre, still in its infancy when one considers that literature began development in classical times. That subgenre is historical fiction, a writing approach birthed by the connection of two sometimes at-odds literary parents. On the one hand, its supporters argue that historical fiction developed as a naturally organic extension of history and fiction, each of which tells a story. On the other hand, historical fiction detractors argue that it not only contorts and exploits historical fact in the name of fantasy, but that it may actually prove detrimental to the absorption of such fact in the classroom, but also beyond that space. Only weaker minds not fit for the rigors of history turn to historical fiction, they might say, or those who deem history unimportant and with little relevance to today, in whatever age that "today" may occur. If one extends the debate to include the topic of the use of historical fiction in the classroom, the voices declaring the dangers of oversimplification and dilution of historical fact may grow even louder. The debate, like most of its type, may never find a definitive resolution.

The participants in, and audience for, such a written debate remain broad and varied. Readers of historical fiction and the debate it stirs may be classroom participants, both teachers and students. They may also be what Virginia Woolf prioritized as common readers, those beyond classrooms or the critic's circle who continue to enjoy the experience of opening a book, whether they pull it from a library collection, from their own shelf, or from their electronic library. Those within the classroom may have a stronger interest in discussing historical fiction's value as it applies to younger readers, as instructors are burdened with the heady responsibility to appropriately "shape young minds." If that final phrase seems anachronistic, in the light of ever-changing educational requirements such as that of the recently invoked (and perhaps soon to be revoked)

Common Core State Standards, we may still hope that within such dictates exists a value of imaginative learning. Whatever the audience leaning, any discussion must begin with as clear as possible a definition of the discussion topic.

Various definitions and descriptions of historical fiction always share basic elements. One element is that of the traditional building blocks of fiction, including plot, setting, character, and conflict. A second element is history as a major focus, historic characters and/or events playing major roles. A third element is a long view. Events and characters featured in historical fiction should have existed at least fifty years in the past. Five decades allows history time to produce the required facts for an author's use and also for the perspective that allows a rich context into which to incorporate those facts. Disagreement may occur over the exact length of time necessary for such authorial perspective, and, more importantly an enriched reader experience. Some argue that novels *written* fifty years in the past may also qualify as historical fiction when applied to the era in which they are read. As is true with most genres, hard and fast boundaries do not always hold. For example, Harper Lee's *To Kill a Mockingbird* (1960) was separated by decades from its historical setting, but not by fifty years. However, the application of the topic of racial inequality proved so important to its author's era that it is accepted by many as historical fiction. As to what historical fiction should seek to achieve, Cristina Mihăescu writes that "the historical novel often tries to provide a broader view of a past society where important events are reflected by the impact they have upon the private lives of fictional characters" (83). While history deals in specifics, a more general presentation of the effect of such specifics on individuals provides readers a means through which to identify with the character and the historic period. She offers novels like Sir Walter Scott's *Waverley* and others published during the nineteenth century as examples (83). Most would agree to that value, but they might not deem such fiction credible. It uses history for a means other than education or enlightenment and eschews the trappings of the historian, such as footnotes and sources that prove accuracy. Tanya Lee Stone goes to great lengths to distinguish narrative nonfiction, which may include dialogue and creative techniques, from historical nonfiction: "If a book is being categorized, labeled, marketed, shelved, or in any other way identified as nonfiction—either keep it untarnished or be sure the reader is made aware of what the author is doing" (87). No "pure" definition of historical fiction exists, but one easily recognizes some of its elements. In addition, it appears in novel form far more often than in short story form.

As scholars have turned their attention to a genre that at one time would not have been thought worthy of scholarly debate, controversy has also arisen as to the origin of historical fiction. While Sir Walter Scott was long credited with "creating" historical fiction, scholars remain aware that no literary form emerges complete and inviolate in a single identifiable use. It is surely inspired and/or affected by literary forms that come before, whether it grows to contrast with or support those forms. Toma Pavel comments on Scott's debt to the eighteenth century for stories "representing the greatness of the soul, the brutality of picaresque adventures, the precision of social details, using the ironic and kind voice of the omniscient narrator" (237). No doubt Scott would agree.

Still, many critics traditionally viewed Scott's century as the golden age of historical fiction. Harry Shaw has developed and revisited three categories to apply to nineteenth-century fiction that utilize historic fact. A novel such as *A Tale of Two Cities* (1859) adopts a historical era "primarily as a source of imaginative energy to fuel what was essentially a timeless story" (175). George Elliott's *Romola* (1863) falls into the second category as a novel "employ[ing] a historical setting primarily as a screen on which to project present concerns" (176). The third category includes Scott's novels, as historical fiction "representing the dynamics of the past and exploring its relationship to the present" (176). Those novels seek to claim "that a representative historical character (Fergus MacIvor in *Waverley*, [for] instance) would have been literally a different person sixty years before or sixty years after a given historical moment" (176). Shaw's point was to explain that fiction could "put us in touch with history" (180), and that is of great value. Historical fiction *can* be true to the past, but in some cases is not.

In the early twenty-first century, some critics claimed that because no new plots were available, historical fiction would disappear (Mihăescu 87). However, with the 1970s and a new focus on previously marginalized ethnicities, as well as on women and children in history, the floodgates opened and proved such claims disingenuous. The opportunity in the later twentieth century to apply historical fiction to the task of re-visioning history through the eyes of those who were invisible in traditional history permitted fresh, exciting, and revealing narratives. A few of hundreds of examples include Barbara Kingsolver's *The Poisonwood Bible*, Louise Erdrich's *The Master Butchers Singing Club*, Julia Alvarez's *In the Time of the Butterflies*, Ernest J. Gaines's *The Autobiography of Miss Jane Pitman*, Toni Morrison's *Beloved*, and Lydia Kang's *A Beautiful Poison*. Contemporary readers' fascination with Diana Gabaldon's Outlander series, Philippa Gregory's *The White Queen* and *The Constant Princess*, Hilary Mantel's Thomas Cromwell Trilogy, and Ken Follett's Pillars of the Earth series, as well as the deconstruction and rebuilding of the past in novels by Stephen King and Philip Roth, to name a scant few, readily prove the public's continuing fascination with historical fiction. Postmodern philosophy, gaining weight by the late twentieth century, holds that truth is contingent, based upon one's private worldview. Thus, we are all conditioned by our culture to bring a certain viewpoint to history, creating perhaps a false, but seemingly true, impression of historical events.

It follows that the so-called facts of history must be viewed with some distrust, or at least be acknowledged to be affected by the individual historian's own values and that of the period on which she may focus. Most readers in centuries past remained unaware of their cultural "training" to read and digest history in a particular manner. In reviewing the opinions of various scholars regarding how history has been received by the common reader over time, Xiaotang Lv writes, "there is no unified, grand history but histories narrated by historians with subjective choice and propensity to satisfy his or her own ideological and political prejudice and preference and nobody can transcend the historical situation" (2016). The appeal of historical fiction tests that statement daily, and has grown stronger over time, despite predictions of its demise.

Perhaps more crucial are the criteria that apply to the quality of historical fiction, beyond those generally seen in quality fiction. After all, historical elements are simply part of the literary recipe unless allowed to *distinguish* plot development, characterization, and, most importantly, reader identification. As with any recipe, a mixture of proper ingredients is not a guarantee of success. Such success is achieved through the care and skill applied to the combination and presentation by its creator. As Cristina Mihăescu points out, a skilled historical novelist must perform the necessary research to bring believable detail to the era and characters featured, yet retain a balance between fact and fiction. Such attention is needed in order that the account does not become a "historical document" (84). The author must also take care not to ignore certain "historical aspects," making the novel "historical only due to the action placement in the past and to the pseudo-historical themes and characters" (84). One pitfall a historical fiction writer must avoid is over emphasis on "truth and objectivity" to the detriment of the well-made tale, as well as dependence upon hyperbole, which can distort facts that "must remain recognizable" (86). In other words, a fictional work must still present information in an authentic and informed manner. Suzannah Lipscomb writes of the author's need to create an "allure of the past" that will create a consistent and dependable readership for historical fiction (45). A "danger" of the genre is that it convinces readers fascinated by its protagonists that they may understand "the nature of an interiority of which we can realistically have no idea" (45). Readers seek a certain experience from historical fiction and trust the quality author to find the perfect blend of fact with fiction.

While adults enjoy historical fiction, so do children and young adults. Few authors have written as well for both audiences as Penelope Lively, winner of both the Carnegie Prize, the British version of the American Caldecott Award, for *The Ghost of Thomas Kempe* (1973) and the Booker Prize for her 1987 adult novel *Moon Tiger*. Lively has often mentioned her fascination with the power of historical coincidence, and that theme appears throughout her fiction. Her novels regularly incorporate historian types to challenge a traditional historical narrative. Those characters emphasize false assumptions and misunderstandings readers have been trained to accept. For instance, in *Moon Tiger* future historian Claudia Hampton describes listening at thirteen to a history lecture. When Claudia questions how Elizabeth I can be characterized as "good" when she ordered her cousin beheaded, her teacher responds that she need not worry: "Just put down what is on the board. Make your headings nice and clear in red ink" (Lively 15). Claudia stops writing to "ponder," later failing history due to a lack of neat headings. Xiaotang Lv writes that Lively "retrieves history from different perspectives of her literary characters" (2018). Hampton, for instance, will write a world history adopting an "emotional tone and . . . chaotic organization to write Cortez, Napoleon, and other historical personages" (2018). Use of a female perspective allows Liveley's "subversion of the grand narration" that is mostly male-centric, generally accepted as truth. Claudia labels history's "voice . . . composite," with some voices "louder than others" (Lively 5). Historical fiction like Lively's offers a believable, enjoyable alternative view of history, as well as characters whose gender, age, or ethnicity is not featured in traditional historic accounts. Finally, historical fiction allows readers to empathize with representative characters that may help them better understand history when read in a nontraditional context.

Historical fiction's various "distortions" of history do cause concern that a young audience may learn an "incorrect" history. That concern became acute as historical fiction moved into the classroom. However, experienced educators and scholars of psychological learning theory do not share such trepidation. Historical fiction enlivens the typical history lesson in most elementary and middle school classrooms. In addition, it may allow young minds to appreciate even on a basic level an era during which violent and inhuman events took place that as a history lesson would challenge their understanding and simply evoke an emotional response, such as fear. For many readers, the classroom provides their introduction to this genre, which eases them into the too-often violent nature of human interaction. This is true, for instance, of Mildred D. Taylor's *Roll of Thunder, Hear My Cry* (1976), winner of the 1977 Newbery Medal and ranked an American Library Association Best of Children's Books 1970-1980. Among the notable modern examples of historical fiction for children, Taylor's novel transported readers into 1930s America. Hers sharply differed from other novels representing the horrors the Depression heaped on the farmer already suffering subsistence living, such as John Steinbeck's *The Grapes of Wrath* (1939). *Roll of Thunder, Hear My Cry* allowed readers to view the effect of that era on an African-American farming family. Told from the viewpoint of nine-year-old Cassie Logan, the novel provided for many children a first exposure to the terror of Southern night riders, racial violence, and the humiliation of discrimination. The family's intimate narrative permitted a first glimpse inside a system that defied the laws of the land and, more importantly, those of simple humanity. Through Cassie's limited understanding of what she witnesses, Taylor's readers learn about inequality, but also about the Logans' empowerment by their own family values. In her Author's Note, Taylor wrote of her father's ability through stories to make her laugh with "happy tears," but also to "shiver and be grateful for my own warm, secure surroundings," adding "splashes of character and dialogue" that made the past as real as the present. She echoes the sentiment of those who value historical fiction that allows individuals silenced by traditional history to tell their stories at last:

> I learned a history not then written in books but one passed from generation to generation on the steps of moonlit porches and beside dying fires in one-room houses, a history of great-grandparents and of slavery and of the days following slavery; of those who lived still not free, yet who would not let their spirits be enslaved . . . I learned to respect the past, to respect my own heritage and myself.

In the introduction to her excellent bibliography, *Experiencing America's Story through Fiction: Historical Novels for Grades 7-12*, Hilary S. Crew reviews elements of historical fiction that support its classroom use for study particularly of American history. She so strongly believes in its value that she developed an annotated collection of 150 historical fiction novels, their setting ranging from the Colonial Period to the Iraq War (this group blurring the fifty-year removal criteria), for use in the classroom. Many of the issues she discusses relate more broadly, although perhaps less urgently, to historical fiction read outside the classroom as well. As Crew notes, debate over the appropriateness of historical fiction to the classroom focuses "on issues of accuracy, authentication, and the definition of historical fiction." In an age where commentators express alarm over the lack of accuracy in common perceptions of history, historical fiction told well may provide some needed shoring up of readers' knowledge. Crew notes that discussions of books such as Edward P. Jones's *The Known World* (2003) "contribute to new ways of understanding the landscape of slavery." She adds that such "novels offer readers opportunities to ask and debate questions regarding authors' interpretations and ideological standpoints in choosing how to tell their stories." Thus, the approaches employed by history and historical fiction reflect upon one another and encourage discussion of their differences and similarities rather than a blanket acceptance of one in lieu of the other.

An appreciation for historical fiction does not rule out one's value of history to inform. As an author who has written both, David O. Stewart values each. In explaining the usefulness of a fictionalized history, Stewart writes of the demands of history that "We never know enough to tell a past story completely." He agrees that history's focus on the particular, the specific, may convince its reader to see its value only during the era of which it tells. With no hint at a manner by which readers might apply history to their own situation, that general truth that fiction provides the reader may not find history useful. Teachers commonly witness that phenomenon, and those contemporary adults hopeful of conversing with a friend or coworker about the similarities between the Iraq War and WWI may be out of luck.

Yet when Stewart writes a biography of a famous person, like all historians, he must resist any embellishment or generalization. Thus, the historian cannot create dialogue if no records of that exact exchange exist. However, the novelist can add to a historical tale character "self-awareness…surroundings…context," demonstrating that "the hush of history" cannot compete with "the cacophony of life as we live it." Unfortunately in the view of the historian, those not keen on learning and recalling incidents and personalities that shape their culture and that of others because they cannot see the relevance may need to turn to fictionalized versions in order to benefit from history's lessons. Stewart is careful to conclude, however that "Writing historical fiction can lead writers of history to powerful backstage moments, but it does not relax the essential requirements of careful documentation and thoughtful, fact-based interpretations. There is no license to pass off even a single detail of the writer's imagination as history" (XXX).

Sabina Murray agrees with Stewart that bias has long been a troubling aspect of historical writing and automatically moves it into the realm of fiction. If the conscientious historian did take the liberty to project thoughts into any historical figure's head or dialogue coming from his mouth, she would utilize phrases such as, "Presumably he believed that," or "He may have told the lieutenant" to clarify the degree of supposition involved. Although the historian bases any constructed thoughts and dialogue on research as to the appropriateness to the specific situation, the result is still generalization and fictionalization and must be identified as such.

Despite their weaknesses in the historian's view, fictionalized historical novels find support from scholars such as Cynthia Mershon. Mershon writes that the use of fiction to transmit important historical facts "breathes life into the dusty past, bringing alive kings and conquistadors, peasants and soldiers." One reason that proves so true in the case of young readers is that they do not often find people of their own age in history texts. Conversely, they are "often at the center of tales of fiction. By teaching this genre, you can expand students' appreciation of history from simply learning facts, names, and dates to understanding real people's emotions, beliefs, and motivations" (XXX). Of course history is also populated with real people, but unless readers find a fact to grasp within the text that seems particularly to apply to them, they may not retain or benefit from history study. Whether we believe that should or should not be, the condition is evident among all reading groups.

Even in historical fiction, facts and dates should be correct, lending authority to the text, but not all historical fictions pay the close attention to detail that the genre demands. Examples applicable to young readers may be found in the narratives that accompanied the original American Girl Doll line. In its beginning, each American Girl Doll—Kirsten, Addy, Felicity, and Samantha—represented a specific time period in America's development. As Fred Nielsen states, educational value was important to the dolls' creator, Pleasant Rowland, who had worked "as an elementary school teacher, a newscaster, and an author of children's textbooks" (85). She founded the company in 1985 as a mail order venture; the stores with which many are familiar appeared years later, along with the high prices for the dolls.

Each American Girl Doll had its own historical narrative about its family and the challenges they faced in the developing nation. Soon the narratives became books based on each doll. *Meet Kirsten* tells the story of Kirsten Larson, the girl the doll represents, first released in 1983 and chronicling America's Western migration. According to Nielsen, "Pleasant Rowland's guiding purpose was to create books and dolls that would bring history alive and provide modern girls with appropriate role models" (87). Although the books often failed in Nielsen's opinion, featuring characters with sharp socioeconomic advantages that distanced them from the typical reader or even from the "normal" girl of their period, historian Gary Cross wrote of their value as compared to most toys that "are detached from nature, from real life, from parents, and from history" (qtd. in Nielsen 85). And while the dolls proved too expensive for many consumers, the books about them remained affordable and available separately.

As Nielsen explains, the books drew their own criticism, most strongly for various errors and misrepresentations, as well as for their "blind eye" approach to some issues. In *Meet Kirsten*, for instance, Native Americans appear in the story but quickly disappear when they must move away, with little explanation. In *Meet Felicity*, Felicity lives in the slave-owning community of Williamsburg, and

African Americans appear in some illustrations, but slavery is never addressed; the black character Marcus is described only as a man who helps Felicity's father. However, each book contains a final essay with clearer focus on social concerns of the day. An African-American doll was eventually introduced, and Pleasant Rowland blamed parents and the schools for any lack of education about slavery (89). Still, critics hold that while toys and books are not responsible for the education of children, they also should not make claims of contributing to that education when not fully vested.

Thus, many critics were concerned when the Pleasant Company began offering teacher guides for use in the classroom in conjunction with the dolls and their stories (www.americangirlpublishing.com/marketing/teachers-guides).The guides prompted varied reactions, and some contained obvious historical errors in the doll narratives that were transferred to the classroom, as discussed by scholars like Daniel Hade in his popular essay, "Lies My Children's Books Taught Me: History Meets Popular Culture in the American Girl Books." The dolls and books have faced various controversies on the score of claimed racial and gender discrimination and gender insensitivity.

According to blogger Alexandra Petri, the Pleasant Company American Girl Dolls at least at first gave children "an entry point to history. Felicity or Samantha or Addy reminded you that, during the Civil War and the Revolutionary War and all the fascinating important times of history, there were Girls Almost But Not Quite Like You. You could see yourself in history! You could engage with the biggest moments of the past!" Those early historical fiction books portrayed girls encountering dangerous surroundings, enduring threats against their family's welfare, and losing loved ones through death. Since purchase by Mattel, the American Girl Dolls no longer have a historical connection. In Petri's opinion, that change greatly weakens the effect of second- and third-generation American Girl Doll stories, which focus on modern challenges, such as the loss of school arts programs.

Perhaps one of the greatest boons to American historical fiction was Shelby Foote's writing about the Civil War. A blatant Southern sympathizer, Foote proved a controversial character neglect of women—black and white, northern and southern, nurses and spies . . . as a 'wasted opportunity' to tell a larger story" (25). And in 2011 "historian Annette Gordon-Reed argued that Foote's three-volume Narrative bears 'the very strong mark of memory as opposed to history'" (Huebner and McGrady 25).

Controversial topics often enjoy long lives, which will surely prove true of historical fiction. Book sales of that genre remain healthy, and its support is visible through groups such as the Historical Novel Society, www.historicalnovelsociety.org. While this genre should never presume to replace history, clearly it will remain firmly ensconced among many as their favorite reading material.

Works Cited and Consulted

Crew, Hilary S. *Experiencing America's Story through Fiction: Historical Novels for Grades 7-12,* Chicago. ALA Editions, 2014. *EBSCOhost.* Accessed 1 July 2017. https://www.ebsco.com/.

Gómez, Sarah Hannah. "Decolonizing Nostalgia: When Historical Fiction Betrays Readers of Color." *Horn Book Magazine*, vol. 92, no. 6, pp. 20-25. *MasterFILE Premier.* Accessed 8 July 2017. https://www.ebsco.com/.

Hade, Daniel. "Lies My Children's Books Taught Me: History Meets Popular Culture in the American Girls Books." *From Inquiry to Academic Writing: A Text and Reader.* Bedford/St. Martin's, 2nd ed. Edited by Stuart Greene and April Kidinsky, pp. 563-73.

Huebner, Timothy S., and Madeleine M. McGrady, editors. "Shelby Foote, Memphis, and the Civil War in American Memory." *Southern Cultures*, vol. 21, no. 4, Winter 2015, pp.13-27. *Humanities International Complete.* Accessed 13 July 2017. https://www.ebsco.com/.

Hundley, Melanie, Steve Bickmore, Jacqueline Bach, and Paul E. Binford, editors. "Enhancing the Canon with Historical Fiction and Informational Texts." *ALAN Review*, vol. 41, no. 2, Winter 2014, pp. 95-98. *Education Source.* Accessed 8 July 2017. https://www.ebsco.com/.

Lipscomb, Suzannah. "Face to Face with History." *History Today*, vol. 66, no. 6, June 2016, p. 45, *Humanities International Complete*. Accessed 14 July 2017. https://www.ebsco.com/.

Lively, Penelope. *Moon Tiger*. Grove, 1988.

Lv, Xiaotang. "Retrieving the Past—the Historical Theme in Penelope Lively's Fictions." *Theory and Practice in Language Studies*, vol. 6, no. 10, Oct. 2016, pp. 2014-18. *Literature Resource Center*. Accessed 14 July 2017. https://www.ebsco.com/.

Lyons, Matthew. "Between Fact and Fiction." *History Today*, vol. 66, no. 1, p. 46. *Humanities International Complete*. Accessed 13 July 2017. https://www.ebsco.com/.

McGrath, Charles. "'A Writer Writes': Penelope Lively's Fiction Defies the Test of Time." *The New York Times Book Review*, 4 May 2017. Accessed 14 July 2017.

Mershon, Cynthia. "Focus on Historical Fiction." *Instructor*, vol. 109, no. 3, Oct. 1999, pp. 49-52.

Mihăescu, Cristina. "The Historical Novel: An Invitation to Know Our Past." *Euromentor*, vol. 6, no. 2, June 2015, pp. 82-88. *Education Source*. Accessed 10 July 2017. https://www.ebsco.com/.

Murray, Sabina. "Literary Imagination and Living History." *Massachusetts Review*, vol. 54, no. 1, Spring, 2013, pp. 41-50. *MasterFILE Premier*. Accessed 10 July 2017. https://www.ebsco.com/.

Nagy, Ladislav. "Historical Fiction as a Mixture of History and Romance: Toward the Genre Definition of the Historical Novel." *Prague Journal of English Studies*, vol. 3, no. 1, 2014, pp. 7-17. *Directory of Open Access Journals*, doi:10.2478/pjes-2014-0014. Accessed 8 July 2017.

Nielsen, Frank. "American History through the Eyes of the American Girls." *Journal of American & Comparative Cultures*, vol. 25, no. 1/2 , spring, 2002, pp.85-93. *EbscoHost*. Accessed June 1, 2017. https://www.ebsco.com/

Pavel, Toma. *Novel Thinking*. Translated by Mihaela Mancaş. Humanitas, 2008.

Petri, Alexandra. "Even More Terrible Things Are Happening to the American Girl Doll Brand Than You Thought." 1 May 2013. *ComPost Blog*. Accessed 11 July 2017. https://www.washingtonpost.

CRITICAL
CONTEXTS

More Than Sixty Years Hence: Historicizing the Historical Novel_____

Danielle Barkley

Understanding the origins of the novel as a literary form is an ongoing challenge for scholars and critics. Thus, unpacking the origins of a particular *type* of novel and its specific fiction topic proves even more difficult. In the case of the subgenre of historical fiction, making sense of how it came to be a recognizable and beloved type of literature involves a kind of metafiction: one must tell a story about how, at a moment sometime in the past, people came to be interested in telling stories about moments sometime in the past.

In order to understand the rise of historical fiction's popularity, one must follow two distinct narratives until they intersect. The first involves understanding how ideas of history changed over time; the second involves understanding how the novel came to be a dominant literary form. Both history and the novel are modes of narrating human experience, and they function in different ways according to the cultural needs of the moment. Understanding how, then, they unfolded alongside of each other, and eventually came to overlap, offers the key to understanding why historical fiction became, and has remained, an important literary genre.

As is usually the case when writing about history, literature, or the history of literature, one cannot know precisely where an account of historical fiction should begin. One appealingly straightforward, traditional answer is with Sir Walter Scott. However, while Scott's novels undoubtedly signify a moment where the genre of historical fiction coalesces into something with recognizable generic boundaries, it would be a mistake of oversimplification to begin there. As literary historians have increasingly noted, his work was preceded by a number of authors and literary movements with profound, if varied, attachments to negotiating representations of the past. In reality, Scott's predecessors laid the groundwork for both what he wrote and the manner by which the public received his fiction.

A number of scholars, most notably Richard Maxwell, locate the key foundations of historical fiction in seventeenth-century France. The writer Madame de Lafayette, a member of the French nobility, lived from 1634 to 1693 amidst the colorful court intrigues of King Louis XIV. She wrote a number of works of long prose fiction at a time when this structure was still relatively uncommon; readers were more likely to consume either poetry (which could take forms ranging from very long to very short) or drama (Cave viii-ix). In two of Lafayette's fictions, the events of the plot take place at recognizable historical moments. *The Princess of Montpensier* (1662) is set in 1572, with plot events taking place prior to, during, and after the St. Bartholomew's Day Massacre. During this violent moment in French history, a large number of Protestants were killed as part of an ongoing conflict between Catholic and Protestant factions. The plot of the novel, however, focuses on a young, married aristocratic woman who loves a man who is not her husband. Lafayette primarily used actual historical figures as characters, but invented the relationships between them (Maxwell, *Historical Novel in Europe* 20), drawing together fact and fiction into a hybrid blend.

In her more well-known work of historical fiction, *The Princess of Cleves* (1678), Lafayette invents a fictional protagonist but places her at the court of an actual French king, Henri II, who reigned from 1547 to 1559. Historical events, such as the king's affair with his mistress Diane de Poitiers, function as backdrop to the adulterous and tragic love affair at the plot's center (Maxwell, *Historical Novel in Europe* 27). *The Princess of Cleves* proved extremely popular, and at least some of that popularity must have stemmed from the novelty of Lafayette's intermingling of the public and the private. The historical events and figures existed in public knowledge, available to anyone with the interest and means to consult relevant historical documentation. The forbidden desires harbored by a virtuous but conflicted young woman were, on the other hand, something that would have been a closely guarded secret. *The Princess of Cleves* is a significant milestone in the development of the novel for the attention it devotes to representing the interior, subjective experiences of its protagonist. Juxtaposing this focus against widely known events serves to heighten the contrast and establishes part of what has helped historical fiction remain so popular.

The intermingling between private life and historical record blurred further as other writers recognized the potential therein. Richard Maxwell argues that the period between 1700 and 1750 was marked by a rise in what he terms "memoir-novels" (*Historical Novel in Europe* 31). These fictional texts were similar to Lafayette's novels in that they took place at specific moments in the past and combined fictional and historical characters. Distinguishing these works was their narrative style, and the manner by which they represented their relationship to history. They tended to be narrated in the first person by a historical, but not well-known, individual. They also did not prioritize any clear boundary between what was factual and what was invented; that is to say, there was at least a fear, if not a reality, that readers would misunderstand a fictional memoir novel as in fact having been authored by the historical individual who functioned as its protagonist.

One of the most important works of this type was written by Antoine Prévost, sometimes known as the Abbé de Prévost, who lived from 1697 to 1763. Prévost was a Frenchman, but he was fascinated by British history, culture, and literature; he would, for example, translate Samuel Richardson's hugely influential epistolary narrative, *Clarissa* (1748), into French. It is not surprising, therefore, that his work of historical fiction, entitled *The History of Mr. Cleveland* (published in 8 volumes between 1731 and 1739) invented a protagonist who was the fictional and illegitimate son of Oliver Cromwell, the leader of anti-Royalist forces during the English Civil War. Cleveland experiences many dramatic upheavals in the aftermath of the Civil War, providing a narrative in which personal turmoil mirrors political unrest (Maxwell *Historical Novel in Europe* 32-34). Prévost's novel shows the further development of literary form by taking full advantage of the potential for using the length of the text to trace personal development and invoke psychological depth.

By the time Prévost wrote in the 1730s, the notion of long prose narratives, usually focusing fairly closely on the life and experiences of a single individual who could readily be identified as the protagonist, was becoming more familiar to readers in both France and England. Daniel Defoe published *The Life and Adventures of Robinson Crusoe* in 1719, describing the adventures of a sailor castaway on a remote island. *Robinson Crusoe* proved extremely popular, and Defoe followed this work with other texts tracing the life and adventures of a single dominant figure, such as *Moll Flanders* (1722) and *Roxana* (1724). While laying much of the groundwork for what readers expected from a novel, these texts did not in fact explicitly present themselves as fiction; if anything, the cover pages and promotion teased readers with the possibility that these were true accounts of the experiences of actual individuals. At least some of Defoe's early readers did not identify his work as fiction. While not being situated in the distant past, these early novels thus also have a role to play in establishing the possibility of historical fiction. That is because they suggest that something that *did not* happen (a fictional event) is not as distinct and separate from something that *did* happen, or *might have* happened, as one might immediately suppose.

By the second half of the eighteenth century, the moment proved ripe for these precursors to take on the recognizable shape of what most readers would identify as historical fiction. Writers such as Richardson, with his *Pamela; or, Virtue Rewarded* (1740) and *Clarissa* as best sellers, had solidified a public appetite for that type of narrative, to the extent that editorials and opinion pieces lamented how readers were consumed by fiction. The form soon labeled *novel* was viewed as exciting and dangerous. Such fiction lacked the historical and intellectual foundations of poetry or drama, both of which could be traced to ancient times. Fiction's tendency to focus on personal responses to events and experiences (whether that be Crusoe's isolation on the island, or the aggressive courtship to which Pamela is subjected) meant they potentially engaged a wider span of the population, including women and working class readers. Cultural critics worried what this meant for both literature and culture in general, but the demand for novels was undeniable.

As novels consumed the attention of a significant portion of the literate population, a burgeoning interest simultaneously grew in history. Anne H. Stevens cites a number of indications that a broad concern with imagining the past marked the mid to late 1700s:

> some of the most celebrated historiographic works of all time appeared, including Edward Gibbon's *Decline and Fall of the Roman Empire*, the works of William Robertson, and of course Hume's own *History of Great Britain* ... New institutions related to the study of history proliferated: antiquarian societies began in London and Edinburgh and the British Museum was founded in 1753. In the realm of popular culture, history was all the rage: David Garrick helped to popularize more historically accurate costumes on the stage, Horace Walpole's gothic revival home at Strawberry Hill became a tourist attraction, and "modern antique" poets like James Macpherson and Thomas Chatterton inspired controversy. (1)

Stevens presents some foundational historical texts as indications of a public fascination with exploring and understanding the past; that is to say, David Hume writing his six-volume *History of Great Britain* (1754, 1756, 1759, and 1761) occurred for the same reasons that led to the founding of a museum, or to the fashion trend to design a new house to appear to be old. However, other writers suggest that the way history was written at this time might more accurately be viewed as the *cause* of those types of cultural trends. Debates about the best method to chronicle history, and what types of events to include or exclude, had raged since the era of Ancient Greece, but for the most part, history tended to be taught and presented with a focus on key political and military events. Eventually, as authors such as Mark Phillips have argued, a shift toward considering the personal as part of the historical began: "it was increasingly hard to think of history as exclusively concerned with the narrative of political action ... the possibilities of political action were shaped in a hundred ways by the often invisible movements of economy, custom, or opinion" (17).

This development of the manner by which history was conceived and presented proved important for the rise of historical fiction in several ways. If history were more than battles, treaties, and royal funerals, then an expanded range of artifacts could be considered part of historical experience. Interest in replicating, or claiming to replicate, clothes and architectural styles from the past could only become possible when one studied or considered the meaning of distant eras, reflecting about what people might have worn, eaten, and how they spent leisure hours. This approach subsequently proved so fundamental to how and why history is studied that one may fail to understand it as a relatively recent mindset.

This line of thought about the past also creates conditions necessary for the development of historical fiction. If history provides simply a record of what happened, and some consideration of why it happened, little need exists to write a novel about it. If, however, history also reflects an imaginative reconstruction of a particular moment's sounds, tastes, and smells in a specific location, then perhaps no artistic form is as well suited to that project as the novel. Simultaneous to the rising vision of a history that spoke to these matters, a literary form arose that made its mark through its ability to notice and record detailed experiences. If, to quote historian David Lowenthal's popular maxim, "the past is a foreign country" (1), then the same literary techniques that made readers feel as though they were being transported to desert islands and shadowy urban underworlds could also move them back through time.

Beyond the novel's ability to imagine and reconstruct past materiality, the potential also exists for it to do the deeper work of reconstructing the subjectivity of the past. Walter Scott's foundational role in the development of the historical novel, as discussed below, depends less on his having been the first person to write about past events (he was not) than on his position as one of the first to significantly imagine ways that people thought and felt differently in the past than in the present. Scott's interest in not simply importing contemporary subjectivities into the past, but in suggesting what it might have felt like to have lived through a particular historical moment, requires a specific relationship to the past. It includes potential difference, and yet sees a deep thread of connection, acknowledging that "we are such people as we are because such things happened in the past, and because we are such people, this is how we imagine the past" (Polhemus 78).

The move to this nuanced and multifaceted representation of history in fictional form did not occur immediately, but by the 1760s, significant milestones in the development of the historical novel had occurred. Two seminal texts were published in this decade: Thomas Leland's *Longsword, Earl of Salisbury* (1762) and Horace Walpole's *The Castle of Otranto* (1764). The former is regularly cited as a contender for the first historical novel in English. Leland sets his novel in twelfth-century England, and chooses the historical figure of William Longsword, the illegitimate son of King Henry II, as protagonist. The plot revolves around Longsword's attempt to return to his estate after fighting in France and draws on historical records. *Longsword*'s representation of the impact of historical events on a range of different characters offers a significant contribution to the development of historical fiction. Firstly, as Stevens points out, "it is significant for taking the misfortunes of a medieval peasant seriously as an object of readerly interest and sympathy. In this way, Leland draws upon growing antiquarian interest in social and cultural history, using his novel as a vehicle for depicting everyday life in the past" (30).

The term antiquarian is significant for revealing the second point of interest. A historian and academic employed at Trinity College Dublin, Leland mainly wrote history (Leland's authorship of *Longsword* is widely accepted but has never been definitively confirmed). Antiquarians could be broadly defined as individuals with a scholarly or amateur interest in the study of the past. The antiquarian could be distinguished from the historian because the latter focused on major historical figures and events, while the former tended to prioritize study of artifacts, buildings and sites, and manuscripts, often with emphasis on the discovery of new sources or objects of historical interest, followed by careful study. Because the antiquarian's methodology was not unlike that of a scientist, the field of study became increasingly popular after the Enlightenment.

The Society of Antiquaries received its official charter from King George II in 1751, and a Society of Antiquaries of Scotland was established in 1780.

Horace Walpole was active in the Society of Antiquaries in the 1750s, and his fascination with the past spilled into hobbies of antique collection and architectural design. It also laid the foundation for his narrative *The Castle of Otranto* (1764), which Walpole presents in its opening pages not as the work of fiction that it is, but as an old manuscript, discovered by an antiquary and being made public. This framing of the text plays with potential confusion between fact and fiction that had animated interest in such narratives throughout the eighteenth century. The setup might also pique the interest of audiences increasingly interested in more personal and immediate encounters with the past, unmediated by construction of a historical record. The idea of a found manuscript created at a time close to that when the events took place suggested it could potentially hold a higher degree of authenticity in its representation, that it could somehow offer a reader a deeper and truer sense of another time period.

This hunger for raw and unmediated encounters with the past played out with particular prominence in the controversy surrounding the Ossian poems. In 1760, the Scottish poet James Macpherson published a manuscript entitled *Fragments of ancient poetry, collected in the Highlands of Scotland, and translated from the Gaelic or Erse language.* The manuscript contained poetry that Macpherson claimed he had heard recounted orally in Gaelic and then written and translated. The poems were supposedly ancient, composed and narrated by a figure named Ossian, recounting epic adventures occurring around the third century BCE. After the initial publication, Macpherson claimed to have discovered more manuscripts, eventually leading to a collected edition of *The Works of Ossian* in 1765. The Ossian poems proved extremely popular and highly controversial. Many doubted their authenticity, while others celebrated them as a window into a lost time.

Walpole understood that the blurred boundary between historical document and fictional composition could entice readers and capitalized on this strategy in the opening of *Otranto*. However, he combined this gesture toward potential authenticity with plot events so outlandish that his narrative famously established an entirely new genre: the Gothic. Walpole understood that a setting in the distant past offers potential for the bizarre, fantastical, and frightening and uses this combination to craft a new kind of story aimed to provoke titillating fear in its audience. As Stevens writes, "Much of what later would become the staples of gothic literature—suits of armor, secret passages, ancient curses, ghosts, and skeletons" (33) had links to the antiquarian practice of exploring the past by investigating its material remains. These Gothic tropes seized the public imagination, and from the 1760s onwards, many Gothic novels adopted these features, as well as an interest in supernatural events, threatening sexuality, and repressed or hidden secrets.

Frequently, Gothic novels were set in medieval time, often in a Continental European location like France, Italy, or Spain. These settings safely distanced outrageous events of Gothic plots for the typical English reader, and especially with the beginning of the French Revolution, offered an indirect way to express a sense of fearfulness and threat. Thus, an eighteenth-century Gothic narrative most likely partially met one of the key criteria for being considered a historical novel (the plot events take place in the past). However, that past often tended to be unspecific; Gothic texts rarely referenced events or dates and could be free with anachronistic (historically inaccurate) details. While often quite groundbreaking in their exploration of psychology, including representations of trauma, repression, and non-normative sexuality, Gothic texts did not usually explore subjectivity as linked to a historical moment or experience. If anything, the historical past was flattened in the Gothic, made to function as a kind of oppressive counterpoint to what was often celebrated as a more enlightened, rational, and egalitarian present.

Alongside the Gothic, other historical fiction narratives became popular in the final years of the eighteenth century and the first decade of the nineteenth century, such that there was a "proliferation of stories set in a determinate historical past" (Ferris 556). Political events from the 1790s onward also spurred both the growth of historical narratives and molded the shape they might take. Georg Lukàcs most explicitly articulated the traditional argument: "It was the French Revolution, the revolutionary wars and the rise and fall of Napoleon which for the first time made history a mass experience … strengthening the feeling first that there is such a thing as history, that it is an uninterrupted process of changes and finally that it has a direct effect upon the life of every individual" (23). Debates about nationhood, and a heightened sense of national consciousness, emerged from widespread political upheaval and military conflict across Europe, leading many to look to the past in order to strengthen a sense of connection to the roots of national identity.

Therefore, only within the context of more than 150 years of literary and cultural evolution may the impact of Walter Scott's historical fiction be properly understood. Such contextual understanding aligns Scott's ability to write the novels he did with the form those novels took. Scott's contribution to historical fiction, and to the development of the novel in general, is often celebrated for its wide-ranging and inclusive vision of how he implicates diverse individuals in the experience of history. This perspective would logically emerge at a moment when different types of literature had, and were still, experimenting with ways to tell stories about the past. As Maxwell explains, "Scott is often seen as an innovator. But he was also a great synthesizer; he knew what everyone before him had done and found a way to put it all together, without losing a purposeful overall direction" ("The Historical Novel" 75).

Nonetheless, when Scott's first novel *Waverley* (1814) appeared, readers sensed that it achieved something new. Already well established as a poet, Scott could have capitalized on the success of poems including "The Lay of the Last Minstrel" (1805) and "Marmion" (1808). Instead, he published *Waverley* anonymously, although his identity as its author rapidly became a kind of playful open secret. Ultimately, Scott did not need to attach his name to the publication for sales purposes, as *Waverley* proved an immediate critical and commercial success. Scott's subsequent novels would be promoted as "By the author of Waverley" and at times be referred to as the *Waverley* novels.

Waverley united many of the features that had marked the development of prose fiction, of a new kind of historical consciousness, and of a type of novel that could contain and combine the two. Scott, like Lafayette, chose well-known political events and actors as backdrop to his narrative, but then invented a fictional protagonist whose personal, inner turmoil becomes a major anchoring point for the reader. The protagonist, Edward Waverley, a young English soldier, journeys to Scotland where he becomes caught up in the 1745 Jacobite uprising, in which supporters of Charles Edward Stuart attempted to restore him to the throne.

Waverley is thus a witness to important and verifiable historical events and interacts with historical figures. He also, however, feels torn by the emotional experience of negotiating his own political loyalties and conflicted over desire for two different women. The novel also invests in reconstructing the tapestry of daily life in eighteenth-century Scotland for diverse groups of people. This orientation reflects the broadened view of history and the antiquarian mindset that had flourished in generations prior to Scott. Scott chooses to make that representation dynamic, not static, signaling to readers "that to live in historical time is to experience time in the participial modality of vanishing and passing, as well as emerging and rising. Alert both to what was on its way in and to what was on its way out, the Waverley Novels embody the understanding that any historical moment is a moment of passage" (Ferris 561).

This ability to represent the past as immersive and simultaneously remind readers that they too are living through a moment of history is perhaps what ultimately brought Scott resounding success. His interest in experimenting with representations of the past continued throughout a wildly successful novelist career. In his "Tales from My Landlord" trilogy, Scott plays with tropes of seemingly "true" stories being handed down, discovered, and then made public by a sort of editor or intermediary. Beginning with *Ivanhoe* in 1820, Scott moves further back to the medieval past and brings to this period an interest in uncovering and documenting experiences of a wide range of characters. The impact of the popularity of his works can hardly be overstated; "During the Romantic period 'the Author of Waverley' sold more novels than all other novelists of the time combined, while sales of the collected editions of the Waverley Novels, which continued to be regularly produced throughout the nineteenth century, had run into the millions by the end of the century" (Ferris 551). Scott's writing shaped the way in which historical and realist fiction would function throughout the nineteenth century and beyond.

With his historical fiction, Scott was able to achieve something that remains difficult for contemporary novelists: he wrote works celebrated for their artistic merit and was regarded as a serious author, and yet he also sold millions of copies and developed a crowd of faithful readers. This particularly desirable convergence of popular and critical success is one of the legacies Scott made available to subsequent authors of historical fiction.

While other clearly recognizable genres such as science fiction or romance are typically taken less seriously as works of literary value, historical fiction can be both respected and beloved; "it is a fictional genre that does not suffer the stigmatizing label of 'genre fiction'" (Stevens 3). Because it emerges from a number of different ways of narrating human experience, each speaking to a different set of desires and expectations, historical fiction offers a particular kind of satisfaction. It can be simultaneously big and small, private and public, individual and universal. And in being all those things, historical fiction continues to have something to tell readers about both other times and their own.

Works Cited

Cave, Terence. Introduction. *The Princesse de Clèves* by Madame de Lafayette. Oxford UP, 1992, pp. vii-xxx.

Ferris, Ina. "Authorizing the Novel: Walter Scott's Historical Fiction." *The Oxford Handbook of the Eighteenth-Century Novel*. Edited by J. A. Downie. Oxford UP, 2016, pp. 551-66.

Lowenthal, David. *The Past is a Foreign Country.* Cambridge UP, 1985.

Lukàcs, Georg. *The Historical Novel.* Merlin, 1962.

Maxwell, Richard. *The Historical Novel in Europe, 1650–1950.* Cambridge UP, 2009.

_____. "The Historical Novel." *The Cambridge Companion to Fiction in the Romantic Period*. Edited by Richard Maxwell and Katie Trumpener. Cambridge UP, 2008, pp. 65-88.

Phillips, Mark. *Society and Sentiment: Genres of Historical Writing in Britain, 1740-1820*. Princeton UP, 2000.

Polhemus, Robert. *Erotic Faith: Being in Love from Jane Austen to D. H. Lawrence*. U of Chicago P, 1990.

Stevens, Anne H. *British Historical Fiction before Scott*. Palgrave Macmillan, 2009.

Historical Fiction and its Critics: From Sir Walter Scott to Contemporary Young Adult Literature_____

Steven Bickmore

While historical fiction remains a popular genre, its quality, to which critics look for evaluation, can be difficult to measure. It is often inaccurate just as, in as many ways, it is accurate. Authors for adult and younger audiences ask readers to reposition themselves in a past setting beyond the lived experience of both writer and reader—fifty years removed is the benchmark. Writers depend on historical accounts—documents such as birth records, court proceedings, interviews, and other histories—but they do not write history. Their readers must willingly suspend disbelief while reading (Coleridge). Authors strive to capture accurate details of the setting, the beliefs, the politics, and the period's daily life. Yet, "an author may not even be aware that the content of his or her novel might suggest a critique of some event or some beliefs pervasive during the period of writing that novel" (Soter 46). Anna O. Soter argues with Stephen Greenbatt that "boundaries between history and literature are blurred rather than clearly defined" (46), a point that critics continue to debate. While authors of historical fiction capture a version of the past, they also comment on current events, ideologies, and social beliefs, actions that may elicit critical skepticism or acclaim. Readers and critics alike demand that historical fiction must meet all criteria for quality fiction, as well as that for truthfulness, if not truth itself.

As an example of quality fiction that meets the goal of truthfulness, Colson Whitehead's historical novel *The Underground Railroad* (2016) set pre-Civil War, reimagines the metaphor as a literal underground railway system with engines and tracks. Because no such physical railroad existed, his narrative varies from historical "truth," yet with undeniable quality and appeal, garnering critical praise and the Pulitzer Prize, the National Book Award, the Carnegie Medal for Fiction, the Heartland Prize, and the Arthur C.

Clarke Award. Although not "true," the novel is truthful in terms of racial conflict, both that of a bygone era and during the era in which Whitehead writes. Thus, the novel encourages readers to contemplate contemporary racial unrest that continues to fuel political protests and has spurred Black Lives Matter and other civil rights movements. Critics acknowledge the novel's grounding in fact, yet do not demand that it reflect only truth. Colson's book receives praise as excellent fiction and also for its quality depiction of previously marginalized or stereotypically represented individuals and situations. His topic resonates so strongly with current events that readers can hardly fail to miss its relationship to their own existence, the hallmark of desirable historical fiction.

Toward a Working Definition of Historical Fiction

Scholar and literary critic Stephen Greenblatt, a twentieth-century founder of New Historicism, drew upon his Shakespearean scholarship to help define his attitude toward historical fiction and provide context using quality, universal literature. Like historical fiction authors, Shakespeare appropriated stories but was unconcerned with accurately portraying any historical moment. Rather than on historical accuracy, he focused in his drama on emotional and motivational accuracy that mirrored contemporary societal concerns. Similarly, politics and contemporary social mores threaded throughout nascent historical fiction narratives, as writers tended to reflect their own cultures onto those from the past, an approach valued by Greenblatt and some fellow critics. To "transcend our own historical situation" (Selden 163) becomes difficult; instead, we seem to constantly reinterpret and reconstruct past narratives through "our personal agendas and concerns" (Soter 47). Such methodology has drawn both critical support and scorn.

Most scholars expect that the decades that remove historical fiction from the events and individuals on which it focuses allow for perspective and accumulation of applicable factual knowledge. H. S. Dalton defines the genre as "a fictional story in which the elements of history, be they persons, events, or settings, play a central role." This definition is useful, but remains too general to satisfy. To be bolder, Dalton adds, "The historian...seeks to answer the question 'What happened?' By contrast, the writer of historical fiction seeks to explain 'What was it like?'" Combining concerns of Dalton, Greenblatt, Raman Selden, and Anna O. Soter, a definition emerges that allows critics several assumptions. They are:

1. The genre captures the mood of the historical moment.
2. Historical fiction carries the burden of ideology, current perceptions, concerns, and interpretations.
3. Authors portray historical elements based on available primary documents and other reliable sources; yet, inaccuracies and anachronisms appear.
4. Writers portray and analyze the past, and in turn the present, through narrative inventions common to their context: romantic aggrandizement, satire, alternate realities, speculative worlds, and alternate endings.

Thus, the term *historical fiction*, and the critical body that reacts to it, allows for the purist striving for accuracy in character, setting, dialogue, context, and also the speculator who wants to focus on "true" emotion while creating alternate historical realities.

The Early Writers and the Embodiment of a Romantic Past

Not surprisingly, critical evaluation may change over time, based on changing criteria that mark the quality of a novel. Sir Walter Scott, long accepted as the father of historical fiction, was among the most widely read authors of his era (Wachtell). His contemporary "reviewers quickly acknowledged Scotts' novels' strengths ... originality, vivid portrayal of history, and lively characters" ("Waverley Critical Essays"). At the time, historical fiction represented a wholly new approach to fictional narrative, and while criteria were in place to measure quality fiction, they had yet to be established for historical fiction. Thus, later critics did "cite certain deficiencies," in Scott's works, especially in the Waverley novels, "including careless construction and prolixity."

Most English majors learn that Mark Twain later spared no quarter in harsh criticism of Scott's work. Twain even cites Scott as the cause of the American Civil War. The idea reoccurs when critics comment on Scott's nostalgia for a noble age when so-called just men met on the battlefield and defended equally noble causes (Wachtell, Munro, Horton). Scott's work survived Twain's attack, although his approach, later labeled Romanticism, battled Realism, a nineteenth-century development in fiction, for several decades. Scott's vision of noble causes in the Waverley novels and in *Ivanhoe* (1820) contrast starkly with the vision of war in Stephen Crane's *Red Badge of Courage* (1895) or Ambrose Bierce's *Occurrence at Owl Creek Bridge* (1890). While it may seem unfair that critics compare the two styles, such comparison became important critical currency.

Although romanticized, Scott's work focused on major historical events—*Ivanhoe*, for instance, on Norman governance in England—and *Waverley* (1814) on the Jacobite rebellion. Following Scott's approach, American writers James Fenimore Cooper, William Gilmore Simms, and Washington Irving also wrote about historic topics with nostalgia, the latter in the short story genre. Cooper especially contributed much to development of the early American historical novel. Most people are familiar with his Leatherstocking Tales, especially *The Last of the Mohicans* (1826). Further, he reflects on the American Revolution with *The Spy* (1821) and *The Pilot* (1823). Cooper captures conflicts and landscape, and his major characters embody the ideals he promotes. For instance, Hawkeye endorses Chingachgook's nobility, but is the only white man to view natives as equals. Critics found Cooper's Hawkeye a romantic, yet his idealism remained largely unembraced in reality, particularly by later generations.

Simms's American Romantic novels include two series. Eight novels focused on the American Revolution set in South Carolina comprise the first. The second series focuses on Western expansion from Georgia to Louisiana. Simms envisioned the "modern-day equivalent to the ancient epic, drawing its inspiration and power from both drama and poetry.... Its characters ... caught up in extraordinary, uncertain, even improbable events" (unknown). His work elicits a mixed critical reaction with his "rehearsal of social issues through the imagery and language of gender. At its center are stylized heroes and heroines who encounter villains and tricksters in highly dialectic conflicts. They are cartoons, but mythic" (Mayfield 487).

While Simms romanticizes achievements of Southerners, frontiersmen, and Native Americans, he is a slavery apologist and became himself a critic of those not supporting his view. According to scholar Alan Henry Rose, Simms's "early novels... present an image of the Negro in which covert associations with demonic and chaotic destructiveness are given full and terrifying expression" (217-18). True to his beliefs, Simms critically assaults *Uncle Tom's Cabin* (1852), accusing Harriett Beecher Stowe of "consistently trac[ing] something 'sinister' in a white character" (Watson 366). Simms objects to Stowe's black characters, finding "the marvelous virtue of Uncle Tom implausible," adding that Stowe "paints the black characters as better than the white. In fact, 'the negro under her brush invariably becomes handsome in person or character, or in both'" (qtd. in Watson, 366). Simms highly idealizes the past when depicting characters he admires, yet is governed by ideology and social mores inherent to his position within South Carolina society. His racist and segregationist views are stereotypical, harsh, and damning, and his personal agenda must be viewed when assessing his critical output.

The Historical Novel Embraces Realism
In departure from fiction by both Cooper and Simms, Nathaniel Hawthorne, familiar to many for his *Scarlet Letter* (1850), while considered a Romantic, is of the dark variety, both in a metaphoric and a literal sense. As Milton R. Stern writes of Hawthorne's fiction, "Moonlight or shadow is the atmosphere of the invisible world of evil, of the past . . . the twilight world is the world of the seeking imagination" (x). Stern notes of *The House of the Seven Gables* that of Hawthorne's Romances, it "illuminates Hawthorne's use of his source materials . . . that reveals his uneasy—but certain—repudiation" of "the basic, pervasive, hackneyed, productive . . . notion of the New

World as the fulfillment of the dreams and longings" characterizing "Western civilization" (vii). Still, Hawthorne's fiction judges the self-righteousness of his Puritan ancestors with an ideological stance more progressive than that characterized in his novels' settings. His work might be viewed as a step toward Realism in fiction.

A divergence from the Romantic to the Realistic developed in historical fiction in which some writers produced idealized characters and themes, while others created more realistic and critical narratives. The Romantics envisioned characters with high ideals and grand actions, while the Realists created heavily lampooned characters. Both groups layered narratives with their current perceptions, concerns, and interpretations. This trend continued through the late nineteenth century and into the early part of the twentieth, but authors in both camps refined their style with subtlety.

As Realism began to prevail and earn critical favor, a movement away from historical fiction took place. Major fiction writers like William Dean Howells, Henry James, Edith Wharton, Stephen Crane, and Theodore Dreiser followed a trend to depict contemporary settings in order to better represent current issues. Their concern was to create characters, dialogue, settings, and themes aligned with the tenets of Realism and Naturalism. Even Louisa May Alcott, often classified as a Romantic writer of women's stories, nods toward Realism in her novel *Work: A Story of Experience* (1873). Alcott attempted to reflect a republic that represented "virtue and loving self-respect" as "an alternative to the prevailing ethos of a competitive market" (Fitzpatrick 30). According to Fitzpatrick, Alcott could not quite depart from her Romantic roots, her sentimental approach preventing literary success. Still, *Work* remains historically focused fiction, offering a bleak depiction of the work world for women who need to sustain themselves or their family. While Alcott's work reflects the critical tension of her day, as enough time passed following major historical events such as war, historical fiction enjoyed resurgence in popularity and critical approval. Interestingly, Geraldine Mark's historical novel *March* would win the 2006 Pulitzer Prize by reimagining Alcott's Civil War novel *Little Women* from the perspective of the absent Mr. March.

The Move to the Twentieth Century and a Preponderance of War

Twentieth-century literature could not escape the influence of war. Its harsh consequences have influenced notable American fiction writers, many of whom wrote based on personal war experience. A few examples of writers influenced by World War I and World War II include John Dos Passos, William Faulkner, Ernest Hemingway, John Hersey, Joseph Heller, and Kurt Vonnegut, but they could not write historical fiction. The war thread could only expand into historical fiction when the fifty years' required separation from events—a criterion established in that century of war—was met. Thus, Joseph Boyden's critically acclaimed award-winning *Three Day Road*, featuring the World War I experiences of two Canadian Creek Indians, could be published in 2005, and Anthony Doerr's *All the Light We Cannot See*, a story of World War II, could in 2017 win the Pulitzer Prize, both as historical fiction. Only in the twenty-first century could James Brady's *The Marines of Autumn* (2000) feature the Korean War, and Dennis Johnson's *Tree of Smoke* (2007) feature the Vietnam War as historical fiction. Authors who participated in war often revealed an impulse to report, critique, and provide ideological commentary about the fallout of military conflict. However, those writing historical fiction are not as likely to be able to provide firsthand witness accounts, and if they do, they will be informed by the necessary perspective that eliminates survivor guilt and/or anger. Although all writers construct narratives with a certain ideology in mind, quality historical fiction simultaneously encourages but also tempers such personal agenda.

By the twentieth century, historical fiction had reached tradition status. Much would be classified as popular fare with limited claims to high literary merit. Best-known might be Margaret Mitchell's romantic *Gone with the Wind* (1936), widely successful, but rarely labeled a literary masterpiece. Nevertheless, authors with strong literary credentials have written well-received historical novels. A group including Willa Cather, James Michener, E. L. Doctorow, Michael Shaara, Larry McMurtry, Toni Morrison, and Charles Frazier demonstrates that esteemed authors can excel in any genre.

Their works do not resemble those of Scott in style, tone, or intent. While they reflect the definition offered earlier for historical fiction, they are further supported by extended research, a process that technology has greatly simplified in recent decades. Critics require contemporary historical fiction authors to

1. capture the emotion of the historical moment,
2. layer current perceptions, concerns, and interpretations in the narrative,
3. represent historical accuracy through research,
4. and portray and analyze the past, and in turn the present, through a variety of narrative inventions.

Focus on particular ethnic groups, previously invisible or existing as stock characters, has led to an enriched array of works that meet these objectives. For example, the re-visioning of Native American society by authors including Joseph Bruchak in *Code Talkers* (2006) and Shelley Pearsall in *Crooked River* (2005) have drawn praise for their portrayal of "intolerance and oppression" (Fuhler). Their popularity reflects the diversity of a readership that has greatly evolved along with historical fiction.

The Historical Novel in an International Context

Scott's work and influence obviously migrated to the United States, but the historical novel is popular in many countries. A critical assessment of historical fiction in any reading community would confirm a trajectory naturally influenced by specific cultural impulses. For example, two Chinese keystone oral heritage tales, *Water Margin: Outlaws of the Marsh* (most recent, 2011) by J. H. Jackson, Edwin Lowe, and Shi Nai'an, originally published by Shiuhu Zhuan as *Outlaws of the Marsh*, and *Romance of the Three Kingdoms* (1925) by Luo Guanzhong (translated by Charles Henry Brewitt-Taylor) are classified as historical fiction in their recent published forms. Homer's two epic poems, *The Iliad* and *The Odyssey*, both widely translated into many languages, serve as historical fiction precursors that prepare readers for the contemporary use of history in fiction. However, in the twentieth-century classroom, exposure to historical fiction was mostly via works written in the Western tradition. While the canon would broaden greatly to embrace international authors in the next century, earlier students may have viewed a single work popular in the canon as thoroughly representative of its author's culture. In some instances, critical reaction encouraged that reception. For example, Nigeria's Chinua Achebe's *Things Fall Apart* (1958) was the first critically acclaimed historical novel written about Africa by a native. Fafa Foofo, writing for the GhanaWeb in the original review, praised the novel for achieving for Africa what European writers like Joseph Conrad could not, as Achebe offers a "blunt and blatant ... defense of the African, his humanity and his culture." Foofo tempers his praise by noting that the labeling of Achebe's protagonist by many critics as a tragic hero, a Western representation, makes clear the lack of a non-Western tradition in which such topics can be discussed. However, representative works like Achebe's opened the gates to the development of new critical points of view in regard to works from cultures that reflect broad diversity.

A mere sampling of quality authors of international historical fiction could include France's Alexander Dumas and Victor Hugo, Russia's Leo Tolstoy and Aleksandr Solzhenitsyn, India's Salman Rushdie and Rushir Gupta, and Eiji Yoshikawa and Yasushi Inoue from Japan. Isabel Allende—perhaps best known in the classroom for her recounting of the Zorro mythology with which many in the United States are familiar—represents Chile. Carlos Fuentes has familiarized US readers with historical fiction of Mexico, and Columbia's Gabriela García Márquez's *One Hundred Years of Solitude* (1967) stands among the most important and influential twentieth-century historical international novels. Styles vary, but these authors' works capture and comment on historical moments of their cultures and countries.

The Growth, Development, and Importance of Young Adult Historical Fiction

Young Adult (YA) historical fiction has a long history preceding establishment of a clear distinction between children's and YA literature. Examples include Harold Keith's *Rifles for Watie* (1957) and Esther Forbes's *Johnny Tremain* (1987). Intended for adolescents, both were published when scholars would have categorized them as children's literature and not as mass market books. Both novels provide examples of serious historical fiction written for adolescents that meet the genre criteria and helped to establish the era of YA literature, generally noted as beginning in 1967. YA literature eventually received serious critical reaction, and literary awards rewarded its quality.

Well-known examples include Mildred D. Taylor's *Roll of Thunder, Hear My Cry* (1976), which continues to be read, taught, and analyzed. As a "social critic," Taylor "marked a huge cultural shift" for many Americans who suffer "the indignities of poverty and racial discrimination" (Davis-Undiano 11). Critics compare Taylor's "tapestry of cross-indexed themes" in her historical fiction series to William Faulkner's rendering of his "Yoknapatawpha" novels (11). Ashley Hope Pérez's *Out of Darkness* (2016) was short-listed for the Walden Award and a 2016 Printz Honor Book. *Booklist*'s Magan Szwarek describes it as "powerful" with "elegant prose and gently escalating action [that] will leave readers gasping for breath" (108).

A smattering of additional YA historical fiction novels nominated for prestigious awards include, most notably, M. T. Anderson's *Octavian Nothing* (2006), which won the National Book Award. Steve Sheinkin's multiple novels—*The Most Dangerous* (2015), *Bomb* (2012), *The Port Chicago 50* (2014)—were nominated for the same award and several others. Also garnering critical attention are Ruta Sepetys's *Salt to the Sea* (2016), which won the British Carnegie Medal for its focus on the 1945 sinking of the German ocean liner Wilhelm Gustloff. Laurie Halse Anderson's *Fever 1793* (2000) garnered twenty-nine awards including the ALA Best Books for Young Adults, and Julie Berry's *Passion of Dolssa* (2016) was a Printz Award Honor book. Scott O'Dell, Jennifer Donnelly,

Ann Rinaldi, Karen Hesse, Gary Paulsen, Lois Lowry, Jane Yolen, Sharon Draper, and Richard Peck represent highly credentialed and crucially acclaimed YA historical fiction authors publishing during the last fifty years.

Despite such acclaim, contentious critical issues that swirl around YA historical fiction include those of accuracy and cultural representation. Such concerns were sparked in the mid-twentieth century by "the growing trend toward the inclusion of a multiplicity of viewpoints and voices in literature for young people" (Travis 80). That positively motivated effort may have negative results if it produces harmful generalizations and damaging stereotypes. For example, Madelyn Travis's study of British children's literature that focused on Jewish characters and topics found that many "contain ambiguous or critical depictions of Jews" (81). Thankfully, exceptions exist. For instance, Elizabeth Laird's *Crusade* (2007) departs from the traditional medieval portrayal to feature "a strong bond between a Muslim boy and the Jewish doctor" with whom the boy apprentices (80). Other YA historical fiction novels, such as David Clement-Davies's *The Telling Pool* (2005), purposely call attention to, and undercut, traditional stereotypes. Clement-Davies's characters Isaac and Rebecca recall Scott's *Ivanhoe* characters of the same names and counter the anti-Semitism prevalent in Scott's time (81-82).

As proves true in any genre, some historical fiction authors are more thorough than others, and are rewarded for being so, although they may have to defend against contention. For example, Laurie Halse Anderson, an Anglo-American, adopts a black female perspective in *Chains* (2008, Seeds of America trilogy), which some readers and critics find problematic. Anderson counters such criticism by beginning each chapter with a quotation from a historical document demonstrating meticulous research methods, while supporting the book's tone and theme. Anderson engaged readers to offer advice and provide the equivalent of a "member check" as to the quality of her representation. However, such efforts will not satisfy all readers and critics.

Like its adult counterpart, YA historical fiction ranges from Romantic to Realistic. Yet one must remember that YA literature is a postmodern phenomenon. Most YA historical fiction authors were born well after Romanticism's fall from favor, the rise of Realism, and concurrently established schools of literary criticism. Critical lenses employed early on included those by New Critics, as seen in John Crowe Ransom's *The New Criticism* (1941) and Cleanth Brooks and Robert Penn Warren's *Understanding Fiction* (1943). New Criticism was followed by a flurry of new politically and culturally based theories, such as feminist theory, queer theory, new historicism, and colonial theory. Those critical approaches and others were utilized to teach critical analysis of YA literature by respected individuals including Kathy Howard Latrobe and Judy Drury, Steven Lynn, Crag Hill, Deborah Appleman, Anna O. Soter, and Antero Garcia. Most of the work they analyze incorporates Realistic historical fiction characteristics and tendencies rather than those of Scott's Romanticism. Contemporary YA historical fiction topics and settings also tend to follow that of their adult counterparts, with focus on war, social unrest, and political conflict. Historical novels written for adolescents may provide a reader's first in-depth exploration of a historical event. As H. S. Dalton notes, they often begin to read what an event felt like—at least from one ideological perspective—before they begin to understand the details of what happened.

Ann Rinaldi provides a strong example, remaining the so-called queen of the YA historical novel. Rinaldi is described as "Dedicated and thorough in her research," and one who "takes pride in making American history resonate with immediacy in her books" ("Ann Rinaldi"). Her novels trace US history by placing adolescents in pivotal moments, including the Salem Witch Trials in *A Break with Charity* (1992), the Boston Massacre in *The Fifth of March* (1993), the American Revolution in *A Ride into Morning* (1991), the Civil War in *Girl in Blue* (2001), and the issue of the effects of slavery in a story of Harriet Hemings—daughter of Sally Hemings and Thomas Jefferson—*Wolf by the Ears* (2000). The latter was considered "to be one of the best novels of the preceding twenty-five years, and later of the last one hundred years" (https://en.wikipedia.org/wiki/ Ann_Rinaldi). Rinaldi's prolific contributions provide a view of historical events that proves more complicated than that furnished by a few history book paragraphs.

Historical young adult fiction reflects almost every American war. Both *Johnny Tremain* and *My Brother Sam Is Dead*, the latter by James Lincoln Collier and Christopher Collier, reflect on the Revolutionary war from two distinct perspectives: that of the Rebels and that of the Tories. A search in goodreads.com reveals more than a hundred titles heading YA historical fiction set in colonial and Revolutionary America. YA novels about the Civil War also abound. *Rifles for Watie* and Irene Hunt's *Across Five Aprils* (1964) established a strong early tradition that other authors followed. Writers who emerged to focus on teen conflict during that era include Walter Dean Myers, Joseph Bruchac, and Gary Paulsen. Perhaps the most common war-related focus of historical fiction in the period is slavery, which produced award-winning novels such as Draper's *Copper Sun* (2006), Julius Lester's *Day of Tears* (2005), and Mosley's *47*.

Most frequently represented is the World War II era, with special focus on events and effects of the Holocaust. Many might think to begin with Anne Frank's *The Diary of a Young Girl* (1947); however, it is a memoir, rather than historical fiction. Such works provide valuable views of the period, but do not fit the historical fiction definition. Instead, they provide firsthand accounts. Noteworthy YA fiction authors who have written about this time period include Lois Lowry, *Number the Stars* (1989), Elizabeth Wein, *Code Name Verity* (2012), Jane Yolen, *The Devil's Arithmetic* (1988), Han Nolan, *If I Should Die Before I Wake* (1994), and Jerry Spinelli, *Milkweed* (2003). The popularity of such fiction is so intense that works written for adults have been co-opted by teachers, students, and some critics. These authors and works include Marcus Zusak, *The Book Thief* (2005), John Boyne, *The Boy in the Striped Pajamas* (2006), and Jonathan Safran Foer, *Everything is Illuminated* (2002).

Travis, Madelyn. "'Heritage Anti-Semitism' in Modern Times? Representations of Jews and Judaism in Twenty-first-century British Historical Fiction for Children." *European Judaism*, vol. 43, no. 1, pp. 78-92.

Twain, Mark. *Life on the Mississippi*. Osgood, 1883.

Unknown. "William Gilmore Simms—William Gilmore Simms Long Fiction Analysis." *Survey of Novels and Novellas. eNotes.com*. 2010. Accessed 15 Aug. 2017.

Wachtell, Cynthia. "The Author of the Civil War." *The New York Times*, 6 July 2012. Accessed 1 Aug. 2017.

Walker, Warren S., and James Fenimore Cooper. *Leatherstocking and the Critics*. Scott, 1965.

Watson, Charles S. "Simms's Review of Uncle Tom's Cabin." *American Literature*, vol. 48, no. 3, 1976, pp. 365-68.

"Waverley Critical Essays: Sir Walter Scott." *Enotes*, 2017, https://wwwenotes.com/topics/waverley/critical-essays. Accessed 9 Sept. 2017.

Imagining the Other: Female Protagonists of YA Historical Fiction Voicing Alternative Perspectives

Mary Warner

Readers may use various critical tools to better understand any work of literature. While many critical approaches can be applied to any work of historical fiction, feminist criticism allows readers to adopt a point of view that helps them best understand historical patriarchal hegemony, or the power structure generally controlled by males. Helpful activities inherent to that critical approach include an examination of the "other" based on gender, race, and class that privilege the dominant socioeconomic group, often the only group featured in traditional history narratives. In addition, an application of the feminist lens to historical fiction helps readers identify objectification and dehumanization in historical events. Such application can support robust classroom or other group discussion, or may offer the individual reader insight into historical cultural power structures and the effects on those not a member of the group in power.

The historical fiction genre offers readers the potential to connect with humans and stories from another era. Those connections are crucial to the reader personally identifying with figures and events that may seem irrelevant when read in traditional historical accounts. According to Harvard Professor Elaine Scarry, a crucial component to such connection is

> the imagination: The human capacity to injure other people has always been much greater than its ability to imagine other people. Or perhaps we should say, *the human capacity to injure other people is very great precisely because our capacity to imagine other people is very small.* (103, italics in original)

Although Scarry acknowledges that story, even great literature, might not be enough to lead to greater empathy, novels like the ones discussed below do challenge reader imagination with a goal to develop an emotional bridge between eras. That bridge may be strengthened when elements of feminist criticism are applied, helping readers better understand the motivations of characters and/or the moving forces behind powerful historic events.

The books *Chains* (2008) and *Ashes* (2016) by Laurie Halse Anderson, *Witness* (2001) by Karen Hesse, and *Sold* (2006) by Patricia McCormick offer stories in which the "other" is deeply violated by objectification. Those who view humans—females specifically—as objects do so in order to deny them basic freedoms. *Chains* and *Ashes*, books one and three of Anderson's Seeds of America trilogy, chronicle five years of the American Revolution. They provide the most extensive coverage of a historical event of the four novels, and therefore will be analyzed at the most length. The latter two novels, formatted as free-verse vignettes, convey the narrative more compactly through dramatic monologues. Additionally, all the books, while of interest to adult readers as well, are classified as Young Adult (YA) historical fiction with the added potency of featuring teenage protagonists.

This discussion capitalizes on the potential of viewing the situation of the "other" through an alternate perspective via feminist criticism to that brought to the traditional reading. To illustrate the idea of perspective, Deborah Appleman brings high school students into the complexity of literary criticism through the use of RayBan sunglasses containing lenses specially ground for driving. She asks students to look through the glasses and comment on what they see; they explain that colors appear brighter and sharper. One student comments, "They just seem to bring out what's already there… so you won't miss it" (Appleman xvi). Feminist criticism offers such a perspective of what one *cannot* afford *not* to see or imagine, particularly "the essential quality of other visions: how they shape and inform the way we read texts, how we respond to others, how we live our lives" (75).

Feminist criticism examines political, social, cultural, geographical, and historical contexts, frequently centering on the gender, race, nationality, and social class of the writer, the reader, or characters within a work (Nichols). "The feminist literary tradition," asserts Elaine Showalter, "comes from the still-evolving relationship between women and their society" (12). Thus, use of the feminist lens as one that recognizes those emerging from a place of dominance—usually patriarchal control—challenges objectification and promotes examination of political, gender, moral, and cultural relationships and realities. Because of their marginal position, women have contributed to identifying oppressions in addition to gender—especially those of race and class. In the context of "imagining rather than injuring others," Anderson's, Hesse's, and McCormick's works display what cannot afford not to be imagined. Specifically, their female protagonists relay historical events through symbols, metaphors, epigraphs, and images that privilege the physical, spiritual, and tangible aspects of human existence. Use of the feminist perspective clarifies how the rational, philosophical, and abstract, which mark the masculine vision, make the objectification of others much easier.

Feminist critic and author Alice Walker writes, "It is, in the end, the saving of lives that we writers are about. Whether we are 'minority' writers or 'majority.' It is simply in our power to do this. We do it because we care...We care because we know this: *The life we save is our own*" (31). Anderson is a "majority" writer, but her sensitivity to dehumanization, particularly in slavery, drives her works of historical fiction. In *Chains* and also in *Ashes*, thirteen-year-old Isabel Finch is legally freed from slavery through instructions in her mistress's will. However, Isabel and her younger sister Ruth are sold to a Tory couple, their freedom denied. Isabel's desperate attempts to regain freedom for herself and Ruth unveil the deep pain of slave dehumanization, placing them on the lowest social rung in Colonial America. They willingly fight on either side—that of the Tories or the Colonists—not because of political philosophy, but to achieve basic human liberties. These novels detail the history of the American Revolution through Isabel's experience, offering an alternative perspective to that of a free male-dominated narrative.

Chains opens on May 27, 1776, as Isabel, primary narrator of both books, and her five-year-old sister, Ruth, attend their former mistress's funeral. Ruth is described as "simple" because she suffers from seizures due to a disability. Although legally granted independence by the will, because they are female, black, and slaves, the girls have no legal voice. In response to Isabel's assertion about the intent to grant them freedom, their new owner, Robert Finch, relies upon their slave status to rebut the claim, saying, "Slaves don't read ... I should beat you for lying, girl" (9). Finch's words serve as hallmarks of a typical patriarchal perspective. When he sells Isabel and Ruth to a Tory couple, Isabel comments that "Mr. Robert dropped the heavy coins into a worn velvet bag. The thudding sound they made . . . reminded me of clods of dirt raining down on a fresh coffin" (23). She voices one of many feminist images—a coffin, emblem of death and the enclosed, restrictive world females faced—explicitly expressing her objectification as chattel and her experience of otherness.

Anderson's chapter epigraphs illumine Isabel's plight and that of her black American slave peers. The epigraph for the chapter referenced above offers lines from poetry by Phillis Wheatley. Wheatley, the first published African-American female poet, was sold into slavery at age seven or eight:

> I, young in life, by seeming cruel fate
> Was snatch'd from Afric's fancyied happy seat: ...
> ...That from a father seiz'd his babe belov'd:
> Such, such my case. And can I then but pray
> Others may never feel tyrannic sway?
> (Phillis Wheatley, "To the Right Honourable William, Earl of Dartmouth," in *Chains* 8)

Not only was Wheatley literate, taught to read by her owner, she was also literary, a rare combination for a female African slave. Thus, the use of this epigraph reflects concerns of feminist critics, but also of humanists in general.

The novel *Ashes* continues the story of Ruth and Isabel. Through their eyes, Anderson starkly depicts violence inflicted on their fellow slaves. British General Alexander Leslie writes a letter to Lord Cornwallis about the decision to spread smallpox in the Virginia countryside a few months before the siege of Yorktown: "About 700 Negroes are come down the river [with] the smallpox. I shall distribute them about the rebel plantations" (160). As Ruth and Isabel are walking the woods on the road to Yorktown as they travel home to Rhode Island, Ruth repeatedly hesitates, complaining of "not liking the woods," and later simply saying aloud, "Dead." Haunted by the smell of death as they discover five dead slaves, Isabel explains:

> These were children of Africa, like me. Like my sister, and our
> mother, and our father. Like Curzon, Aberdeen, Serafina, Walter…
> like the countless souls, some in their natural state of freedom, many,
> many, many more kidnapped, stolen, and forced into the unnatural
> state of slavery. (164)

Isabel's comment exemplifies the compassion of the feminine, of one who has been objectified, her personal freedom violated, but also of the African, who remembers and calls on ancestors from a rich African tradition. She reflects that if she only knew names of the dead, she might "speak them out loud in quiet moments, in beautiful places, and in so doing, keep a part of them alive…Your true name was one of the few things they could not take away from you…" (164). While Isabel reflects on the humiliation of dead slaves, the theme of loss of her personal identity also provides a feminist focus.

Images of female endurance and tradition dominate both novels. From the beginning of *Chains* and the early days of the Revolution, Isabel is driven by her mother's admonitions to persevere and to care for Ruth. As she dwells in the captivity of the Locktons Tory household, Isabel desperately tries to design a route to freedom. Another former slave named Curzon offers the solution. Isabel, while serving Elihu Lockton, can spy for the Patriots, subverting her objectification to transform it into a tool against the enemy. Curzon explains, "You are a small black girl… You are a slave, not a person. They'll say things in front of you they won't say in front of white servants. 'Cause you don't count to them..." (Anderson, *Chains* 41). The conversion of a traditional weakness into power remains a feminist criticism focus. It demonstrates for readers how the oppressed may exchange roles with their oppressors.

While trapped in her slave existence, Isabel witnesses backstories of the Revolution to which many are not privy. They include the plot to kill General Washington and Tory treachery and lies. Although the Tories had promised both land and freedom to slaves and indentured servants, and had the power to fulfill such promises, they never intended to do so. Betrayed by those with whom she shares information, Isabel describes to Curzon, who is "a firm believer in the Patriot cause," her reality, which is that of "otherness." Marginalization as the Other becomes a crucial part of her identity: "I was forever reminding him that we'd been enslaved by both Patriots and Loyalists, and that neither side was talking about freedom for people who looked like us" (Anderson, *Chains* 123). That particular reality lingers late into the War. In another of Curzon and Isabel's arguments, Isabel allows that some men, even whites, who are committed to freedom do exist. However, she knows the harsh reality: "... there were more white people . . . who looked at me and mine and saw not people, but tools that would earn them money. They did not see us for the people that we were, people just the same as them" (217). Objectification as property of the dominant class remains a fact of life for slaves in any culture.

As demonstrated by these novels, gender provides no guarantee of compassion for the "other." Anne Lockton, a woman who brutally abuses Isabel and Ruth, represents the antithesis of the feminine stereotype. She operates from a dispassionate utilitarian, classist position, using her femininity to manipulate and gain power and representing patriarchy at its most brutal in her gender role reversal. After heartlessly selling Ruth, she orders Isabel branded with an "I" for insolence. Isabel thinks "The fire in my face burned on . . . deep through my flesh, searing my soul ... momma and poppa appeared from the shadows. . . and wrapped their arms around me and cooled my face with their ghost tears" (Anderson,

Chains 148). The branding further emphasizes Isabel's loss of identity, ironically through use of her own initial. However, that particular act of cruelty has an unpredicted effect that undermines control of the dominant group. Isabel's maternal instincts toward Ruth, another hallmark of the "feminine," further strengthen her resolve. Isabel draws power from her natural instincts, a power that her patriarchal environment attempts to destroy. Throughout the five years of war, Isabel survives solely to find Ruth, to gain freedom, and to go home. Feminist criticism celebrates instances in literature where women overcome limitations and make choices based on private values, such as that of family.

In *Ashes*, which opens on June 25, 1781, Anderson continues Isabel's journey, further emphasizing the importance of power inherent in feminine strength. Isabel's underlying power flows from her African ancestors, but is rooted especially in her mother and the surrogate mothers she and Ruth meet. Serafina, who mothered Ruth in Charleston, voices the wisdom of maternal figures that recognizes strength in various guises:

> Strong starts out being the right thing. Your hands grow strong enough for your work. Your back strengthens under your burdens. Soon your mind becomes strongest of all; … Don't forget how to be gentle… Don't let the hardness of the world steal the softness of your heart. The greatest strength of all is daring to love. (Anderson, *Ashes* 39)

French feminist Viviane Forrester discusses the importance of women's ability to see multiple perspectives as opposed to the traditional masculine binary perspective. She suggests that "… this blindness to women's vision, which in fact prohibits any global vision of the world, any vision of the human species, has been fashioned by men for our mutual impoverishment" (35). In discussing Hesse's *Witness*, one recognizes historical fiction that undermines such "blindness." It presents through multiple perspectives a 1920s act of violence by the Vermont Ku Klux Klan. While eleven characters share their perspectives, the two most vulnerable targets of Klan violence, twelve-year-old Leonora Sutter who is black and six-year-old Esther Hirsh who is Jewish, voice the most poignant narratives.

Hesse exposes the KKK's blatant racism and bigotry toward any "other" and reveals the ongoing limitations women face in a male-dominated society. *Witness* is set historically nearly 150 years after the American Revolution. In the ensuing years, the 1870 Fifteenth Amendment to the Constitution granted African-American men the right to vote. Though the 1840s marked the onset of the women's suffrage movement, not until August 26, 1920, did the Nineteenth Amendment give women this right. Although that Amendment legally included African-American women, their cultural rights and recognition were achieved even later.

One level of the feminist perspective in *Witness* comes through the characters of Iris Weaver, a rumrunner in the era of Prohibition, and Sara Chickering, an independent farmer. Iris rationalizes her illegal actions, rooted in her prioritization of the altruistic, life-engendering feminine:

> i know i shouldn't be running liquor[.]
> and maybe i'll end up in jail [.]
> but i paid for this restaurant
> by transporting hooch
> and i've made enough
> to fork out tuition for two of my brothers
> and my baby sister, who is smart as sateen,
> and would have been trapped in this valley forever. (46)

Existing under strict gender restrictions, Iris combats life's challenges through an application of simple logic to reach a solution, too often characterized by patriarchy as *feminine wiles*.

In another vignette, Iris comments on the letter of Senator Greene urging votes for Coolidge and Dawes: "…i would have cast my vote without being told. —women have waited too long for the right to vote—. . . but i'll vote for the man i choose…" (Hesse 144). Iris also must defend her choice where a white male would not. An additional example of gender and racial discrimination may be seen in the views of Johnny Reeves, a local clergyman who champions the Klan's causes. Hesse elucidates the dominance of males through Reeves's remarks: "he said we'd all be better off if we—got the family—out of the restaurant—and back to the dinner table. —he said the average woman, —she loves her home and family first. —she might have got distracted—when she was earning wages—while her man fought in the great war…" (44). American women could be wage earners, enjoying a sense of accomplishment and independence, but only as they filled absences left by males who fought in World War I. Although equal to *the work*, they are not equally eligible *to work* in a patriarchal society. Hesse adds another layer of discrimination against women through Reeves who claims the authority of religion, another common tool of patriarchy, to restrict women's actions.

Sara Chickering exemplifies multiple feminist perspectives. She chooses to remain single and practice farming, but feels pressured to defend that choice. Such a decision "betrays" the stereotypical role of women, again countering gender discrimination. She watched her mother prioritizing the family, never getting a holiday, while her father did little in the home:

> that's why i moved out and came to work on the farm.
> soon as i could i bought it for my own.
> all these years i've managed fine without a man.
> i may work as hard as my mother,
> but i'm drudge to no one. (Hesse 30)

Still, Sara's independence represents an anomaly. For instance, Esther Hirsh, a Jewish girl whose mother has died, moves with her father to Vermont from New York City as one of many "fresh air" children escaping the city; Sara invites the Hirshes to live on her farm. Sara connects to her maternal nature, and Esther's vulnerability to the Klan's wrath opens Sara's eyes to a new reality, founded not only upon gender but upon religious and ethnic discrimination:

> i think a lot about it these days.
> the klan says they don't stand against anyone.
> but a catholic, a jew, a negro,
> if they got arrested,

and the judge was klan,
and the jury was klan,

. . .

it took having the hirshes here
to see straight through
to the end of it. (59)

The motherless girls, Esther and her twelve-year-old sister, Leanora, suffer the most injury. Their innocence and racial and religious vulnerability allow Hesse to shape her strongest critique of the Klan and its sympathizers. At school Leanora's classmate, Willie Pettibone, shows her a newspaper clipping describing a minstrel show, "a night of fun brought to you by 22 genuine/black-faced 'coons'" (Hesse 7). Leanora responds that she "felt like skidding on ice … felt like twisting steel" (7). Readers may be willing to blame Willie's actions on adolescent ignorance. However, the feminist lens refuses to grant his words tolerance. Willie represents violation and dehumanization and a patriarchal inheritance. Leanora reacts by expressing anguish, but she also takes action to resist his jibes.

Later Willie tells Leanora that at a Klan meeting, "the dragons talked about lighting you—and your daddy up—. . . -- you'd be cheap fuel, they said. —they liked the smell of barbecue…" (Hesse 10). Leanora walks out of school into the cold without coat, hat, or boots. Her description of the experience highlights the juxtaposition of physical warmth and psychological cold that mark feminist criticism with its emphasis on the corporeal and the spiritual: "i didn't feel the cold, —i was that scorched" (10). Her classmate's words have the power to make Leanora's spirit burn.

One section of *Witness* powerfully details multiple responses to a cross burning. While Johnny Reeves, the Klan sycophant preacher, speaks of the cross blazing "perfect" (Hesse 52), Leanora hides in the closet amid her mamma's cotton dresses, using imagery that counters that of Reeves as her child's perception converts the cross into a monster. She reveals that "in that dark and narrow place, —i opened a hole for myself—but no matter how i turned, —the light from the cross—curled its bright claws under the door" (54). Leanora transforms a scene that she is unable to rationally process into myth in order to seek meaning from the terror. Unlike members of the Klan, who hypocritically claim the authority of patriotism to validate acts of terror, Leonora puts her imagination to use in order to shape a tolerable world.

When the Klan threatens the Hirshes for polluting Sara, a Christian woman, Mr. Hirsh suggests they move on. Sara cannot imagine life without Esther: "damn klan. —to think of what they could drive from my life—with their filthy—little—minds" (Hesse 61). The limited vision, the binary perspective, and the lack of ability to imagine the other, dominate the mindset of the Klan. Their surface level appeal to patriotism can only be challenged by those who can see and imagine diversity and plurality.

Readers may link the treatment of Isabel and Ruth, of Leonora and Esther to the emblematic violence done to Patricia McCormick's protagonist in the novel *Sold*. As McCormick's thirteen-year-old Nepali narrator, Lakshmi represents every victim of child prostitution. The history of violence against prostitutes is described by self-declared feminist author Tillie Olsen as "Unclean; taboo. The Devil's Gateway…Buried alive with the lord, burned alive on the funeral pyre, burned as a witch at the stake. Stoned to death for adultery. Beaten, raped. Bartered. Bought and sold…" (53). An application of feminist criticism to those phrases reveals the dehumanization, fetishization, and objectification that are perhaps the worst elements of patriarchal power.

Through Lakshmi, McCormick brutally depicts the destruction of innocence and the human spirit. Lakshmi believes she can help her family by going to India to be a maid where she will instead enter the world of child prostitution. She remains unaware of reality until foisted onto her first client. *Sold* graphically envisions human trafficking as not isolated to any one historical event or period.

The enslavement inherent to sex trafficking includes that of the body and the psyche, encompassing every level of degradation and objectification. *Sold*'s poignancy comes from numerous stark realities, but above all through Lakshmi's age. At thirteen, she is still a child. McCormick's closing author note reveals that annually "nearly 12,000 Nepali girls are sold by their families…

into a life of sexual slavery in the brothels of India. Worldwide, the US State Department estimates that nearly half a million children are trafficked into the sex trade annually" (265). Children become property, sacrificing physically and spiritually for the sake of their families.

Child sex traffickers are not always male. In the second transaction of Lakshmi's sale, a tragic gender role reversal is revealed as the child's Auntie Bimla barters with "Uncle Husband." Lakshmi recounts,

> ...the man gives Auntie a roll of
> rupee notes.
> I do not know what they have agreed to.
> But I do know this:
> he gives her nearly enough money to buy a water buffalo.
> (McCormick 75)

The only way for females to gain power in such transactions is to assume the traditionally male role, as does Auntie. Lakshmi has already realized the powerless position of the female: "A son will always be a son, they say. But a girl is like a goat. Good as long as she gives you milk and butter. But not worth crying over when it's time to make stew" (8). Seeking to understand why women must suffer, Lakshmi asks her ama (mother) why women must suffer. Her ama responds, "This has always been our fate... Simply to endure is to triumph" (16).

At first, Lakshmi does not participate in her own degradation. She believes she will be performing physical labor and wonders why it matters that she "has no hips" and is "plain as porridge" (McCormick 53), phrases she has overheard. An innocent victim of poverty and gender, Lakshmi wants to work to help her family to purchase a tin roof to protect their house against the Nepali mountain monsoons. Her innocence makes her sale especially appalling, because she will soon transform into an unimaginative cynic, like her Auntie. Auntie Bimla has lost the power to envision even her own family member as more than an object of gratification, in this case, of her own financial benefit. She can boost herself out of her own lower class status only by victimizing younger versions of herself.

Additional examples in *Sold* emphasize that gender does not solely account for one's actions and treatment of others; class status is crucial. The female brothel owner, Mumtaz, like Lakshmi's Auntie, undermines gender stereotypes as she assumes the role of patriarch, dominating her sex slaves. She runs the ironically named Happiness House where she metes out as much physical abuse as any male. Mumtaz threatens, cheats, betrays, and manipulates everyone, bribing police for their cooperation and destroying hope of rescue for her slaves. For instance, she forces Lakshmi on her first client. Lakshmi comments, "She grabs me by the hair and drags me across the room. She flings me onto the bed next to the old man" (McCormick 103).

This infliction of brutality results, however, in the unexpected. Lakshmi understands that among the admirable qualities of the feminine is stoic endurance, but then she realizes that imagination may trump endurance. Together they provide her means of survival. She says of the customer rapes, "I pretend it is a TV show that I am watching from far, far away. I pretend I have a button I press to make everything go quiet. And another one that makes me disappear" (157). The feminine privileging of the spiritual is Lakshmi's key to endurance. Through its power, she converts infliction of silence and anonymity into a survival tool, undermining another patriarchal edict. The attempt by others to erase her self-awareness fails as Lakshmi negotiates her own disappearance into a world of safety, just as Hesse's Leonora transforms fire to a dragon as a self-defense mechanism.

This is not to claim that Lakshmi does not face destruction. As she endures multiple assaults, the girl's dramatic monologues reveal her emotional vulnerability. The rare presence of kindness, of any act of compassion, or the appearance of anyone able to imagine her humanness, threatens to "undo her." Lakshmi describes the toll she pays for her victimization:

I have been beaten here,
locked away,
violated a hundred times
and a hundred times more.
I have been starved
and cheated
tricked
and disgraced.
How odd it is that I am undone by the simple kindness
of a small boy with a yellow pencil. (McCormick 182-83)

Lakshmi is at first "undone" by the son of another victim. He teaches
her English, thereby opening the doors to a world of literacy, which
she must find the strength to embrace. Should Americans attempt to
rescue the slaves of Happiness House, the power to communicate
could prove crucial. Lakshmi must also overcome her distrust of
Americans, having been told by the other women of their treachery.
She has also witnessed those who unsuccessfully attempt escape; they
must endure having their heads shaved, being stripped naked, and
being stoned by others, who call them "dirty women" (McCormick
204). The propaganda provides another hurdle for the powerless.

Through powerful narratives of historical fiction, Laurie Halse
Anderson, Karen Hesse, and Patricia McCormick offer compelling
critiques that demonstrate how some humans are more capable
of injuring others than imagining them. In their rich depictions,
the voices of their young adult protagonists compel readers to
view historic events through alternative perspectives. In addition,
application of feminist criticism allows readers to question the
motivations of those who objectify others, particularly females.

Echoing Elaine Scarry's claim that opened this essay, feminist
historian Rebecca Solnit stresses the critical role of imagination for
re-visioning not just history, but the real people that inhabit it:

When you don't hear others, you don't imagine them, they become
unreal, and you are left in the wasteland of a world with only yourself
in it, and that surely makes you starving, though you know not for

what, if you have ceased to imagine others exist in any true deep way that matters.

Solnit understands the potency of the feminist perspective. Her words reinforce the vision for a better existence of the characters Isabel, Leanora, Esther, Sara, Iris, and Lakshmi and the real individuals they represent. Solnit suggests that without hearing and imagining others, a person remains in a "wasteland of a world."

Works Cited

Anderson, Laurie Halse. *Ashes*. Atheneum Books for Young Readers, 2016.

_____. *Chains*. Simon & Schuster, 2008.

Appleman, Deborah. *Critical Encounters in High School English: Teaching Literary Theory to Adolescents*. Teachers College, 2009.

Forrester, Viviane. "What Women's Eyes See". *Feminist Literary Theory: A Reader*. Edited by Mary Eagleton. Blackwell, 1990, pp.34-35.

Hesse, Karen. *Witness*. Scholastic, 2001.

McCormick, Patricia. *Sold*. Hyperion, 2008.

Nichols, Cindy. "Feminist Literary Criticism." https://www.ndsu.edu/pubweb/~cinichol/271/FeministCriticism.htm. 4 April 2017.

Olsen, Tillie. *Silences. Feminist Literary Theory: A Reader.* Edited by Mary Eagleton. Blackwell, 1990, pp. 53-57.

Scarry, Elaine. "The Difficulty of Imagining Other People." *For Love of Country: Debating the Limits of Patriotism*. Edited by Martha Craven Nussbaum and Joshua Cohen. Beacon, 2002, pp. 98-110.

Showalter, Elaine. "A Literature of Their Own." *Feminist Literary Theory: A Reader*. Edited by Mary Eagleton. Blackwell, 1990, pp. 11-15.

Solnit, Rebecca. "The Loneliness of Donald Trump: On the Corrosive Privilege of the Most Mocked Man in the World." Blog post. 30 May 2017. http://lithub.com/. Accessed 3 June 2017.

Walker, Alice. "Saving the Life That Is Your Own: The Importance of Models in the Artist's Life." *Feminist Literary Theory: A Reader*. Edited by Mary Eagleton. Blackwell, 1990, pp. 28-31.

Identity Formation in Young Adult Holocaust Historical Fiction: Comparative Analysis of Lois Lowry's *Number the Stars* and Jerry Spinelli's *Milkweed*

> "Through fictionalized accounts, often told through a child's point of view, children today can take on, for a moment, the perspective of a child who lived during the Holocaust and perhaps begin to address their own questions of what it was like and how it could have happened." (Jordan 200)

In young adult historical fiction about the Holocaust, two seminal works are the most discussed in American secondary schools: Lois Lowry's *Number the Stars* (1989) and Jerry Spinelli's *Milkweed* (2003). Both works capture the point of view of adolescents living during the Nazis' World War II takeover of Europe. Both speak in clear, defined language about the impressions and historical understandings of innocent youngsters as they shoulder enormous burdens and sacrifices. And both bring to life the emotional and situational search for identity in the face of devastating and far-reaching consequences.

Number the Stars and *Milkweed* could not be more different. True, they each feature the Holocaust, are works of historical fiction, and introduce adolescent protagonists, but from there, they differ. *Number the Stars* is written in the present tense—all action happens to the central characters in real time—while in *Milkweed*, the story's narrator recalls his life as a young boy. Moreover, *Number the Stars* is from the perspective of a young person who is not Jewish, yet displays great empathy and courage for people who are, while *Milkweed* tells of a young boy with no religious and ethnic identity at a time and place in history when one's identity means everything.

To be sure, the search for identity as a literary theme predominates many works of literature, whether based on historical

Identity Formation in Young Adult Holocaust Historical Fiction   47 and/or imagined contexts. Critical and comparative analyses of literary endeavors most often touch upon such relevant ideas and fiction stalwarts as theme analysis, character development, and understanding of the story's setting. This approach proves especially beneficial when one discusses historical fiction. Each literary element contributes to reader understanding of literary meaning, as opposed to historical meaning, in a more broadly defined context. Each also illustrates how the author demonstrates her narrative's significance. The author is, then, challenged to represent history in a realistic rather than real manner, presenting stories that might be true, not allowing documentable truth to dominate the fiction narrative.

Written for and about adolescents, these two captivating novels are compelling, primarily because they involve the central characters' search for and demonstration of their own newly formed and evolving identity. Through the authors' skill, young readers may identify with historically representative characters from an event as far removed from their personal existence as the Holocaust. Although history provides the framework, these novels succeed by offering a vivid creative telling of how two innocent young people, caught in the throes of an inexplicable, undeniable horror, manage not only to survive but also to thrive in their self-discovery.

Lois Lowry: *Number the Stars*

Lois Lowry's *Number the Stars* (1989) received the Newbery Medal in 1990 for its distinguished contribution to American literature for children. "Lowry draws on extensive historical research and interviews to make real this harrowing true-to life adventure. Its subtle, poignant title refers both to Psalm 147:4, a psalm that recalls how God has numbered all the stars and named each one of them, and to the Star of David, a symbol of Jewish devotion. Lowry's acclaimed novel features one Jewish family's escape from Denmark during World War II" ("Number the Stars"). Ten-year-old Annemarie Johansen narrates this tale of befriending a Jewish family and helping them escape from the Nazis. She and her Christian family rescue and relocate hundreds of other Danish Jews from the invading and conquering Nazi military regime.

The story begins in 1943, the third year of the Nazi occupation of Denmark. Two ten-year-old girls, Annemarie and Ellen, live in Copenhagen. Their families exist in fear and despair, a desperation heightened by the country's shortage of food and electricity. After a brief and terrifying encounter with two German soldiers, Annemarie and Ellen resolve to remain constantly on guard, especially because Ellen is Jewish. Later, though, they learn that Germans are relocating Denmark's Jewish population. Quickly, Ellen's parents flee Denmark with a Danish resistance fighter named Peter. They leave Ellen to stay behind with Annemarie and her family, the Johansens.

In Annemarie's home, Ellen pretends to be Lise, Ellen's deceased older sister. The Johansens think Ellen is safe until one day, at four in the morning, Nazis burst into their apartment, looking for Ellen and her family. Terrified, Annemarie realizes what is happening and quickly does what she can to hide Ellen's identity; she rips off Ellen's necklace, which is a Star of David. Annemarie knows that if the Nazis see Ellen wearing her Star of David, they will discover she is Jewish. The Nazis still become suspicious because of Ellen's dark hair, which contrasts with the blond hair of Annemarie and her family. Mr. Johansen, Annemarie's father, thinks quickly and shows the Nazi intruders a picture of their baby Lise, who had brown hair as an infant. Convinced Ellen is Lise, the Nazis leave.

The next morning Annemarie, her mother, her five-year-old sister, and Ellen travel to their Uncle Henrik's house. A Danish fisherman, Uncle Henrik has a house by the sea within close range of Sweden. Sweden is a desirable destination because at that point, it remains Nazi-free. Upon their arrival at Uncle Henrik's, Ellen reunites with her father and mother who have been taken to the same home by Peter, the Danish resistance fighter who also happens to have been the fiancé of Annemarie's deceased sister, Lise.

That same evening, Annemarie sees a huge casket in her uncle's living room. Naturally, she is puzzled. Uncle Henrik tells everyone that Great-Aunt Birte has just died, which leaves Annemarie even more puzzled. Annemarie knows there is no Great-Aunt Birte. When she questions her uncle in private, Uncle Henrik says that it is best for him not to explain: "It is much easier to be brave if you do not know everything. And so your mama does not know everything. Neither do I. We know only what we need to know" (Lowry 82).

Slowly but surely mourners fill Uncle Henrik's house, all there to pay respects to Great-Aunt Birte. Annemarie's puzzlement turns to fear when, suddenly, Nazis enter her Uncle's home. They had noticed lights on past curfew, and, finding a house full of people, question the reason for the gathering. Uncle Henrik explains that their Great-Aunt Birte has died, and they are carrying out traditional Danish rituals in respect for the dead. When the Nazis demand the casket be opened to prove that Great Aunt Birte is really lying inside, Annemarie's mother explains that the deceased had typhus. According to the doctor, Great-Aunt Birte, even in death, remains contagious. Annemarie's mother does lay her hand on the casket, signaling that she will open it, only to have one of the Nazis slap her, saying she should keep it closed.

After the Nazis leave, Annemarie learns the true meaning of the casket. It is concealing warm clothing and blankets, all meant to help Ellen, her family and other Danish Jews escape from Uncle Henrik's home on the Danish border. The supplies will provide warmth and concealment, as the refugees flee by boat to Sweden. Uncle Henrik is part of the Danish Resistance, a group of Danish people rescuing Danish Jews. Along with Annemarie's mother, he leads Ellen, her family, and other Jewish people to his fishing boat in the dark of night. There, Henrik will hide them, as he takes them across the sea to Sweden for their immediate safety.

Later that morning, Annemarie watches in horror as her mother crawls back to Uncle Henrik's home. While helping people escape, her mother has accidentally fallen and broken her ankle. Quickly, Annemarie helps her mother back to the house whereupon she discovers a packet that Ellen's father had dropped when he accidentally tripped on a flight of stairs. Realizing the importance of the packet to the Danish Resistance movement, Annemarie's mother tells her daughter to fill a basket with food, including the packet, and to run as fast as she can to catch up with Uncle Henrik's boat. Heading through the northern Danish forest toward her uncle's boat, Annemarie is halted by Nazi soldiers and their ever-present German shepherds. When the soldiers demand to know what she is doing in the woods so early, Annemarie says she is taking food to her uncle who lives nearby. The Nazis do not believe her, searching her basket and discovering the package. Yet, to their dismay, the package only contains a handkerchief. Satisfied, the Nazis let Annemarie go, and she reaches her uncle's boat just in the nick of time.

That evening Uncle Henrik is safe at home after having transported the Danish Jews to Sweden. After dinner, Uncle Henrik thanks Annemarie for bringing the handkerchief. Sensing her puzzlement, Henrik explains that the scent of the handkerchief (laced with rabbit's blood and cocaine) served as a decoy that prevented the German dogs from smelling the human cargo hidden below. Relieved, Uncle Henrik praises Annemarie for her bravery while reassuring her that she will meet her friend Ellen again.

Two years later, in May of 1945, World War II ends. The reader finds Annemarie and her family watching from their balcony as people joyously parade in the streets of Copenhagen. Annemarie thinks of her friend Ellen, hoping her family will soon return home. All is not well, however. Peter, Lise's fiancé, has died, shot in the public square for his involvement in the Danish Resistance. Then Annemarie learns the truth about Lise's death. She had believed that Lise died in an accident. However, because she was also part of the Danish Resistance she was murdered by the Nazis who deliberately struck her with an automobile.

Saddened but still hopeful, Annemarie enters her home, rummages through her belongings, and finds the Star of David. It is the necklace she had ripped from Ellen's neck when the Nazis first invaded her home. She holds it in the palm of her hand, promising to wear the necklace until Ellen returns.

Jerry Spinelli: *Milkweed*

Milkweed (2003) grew of out Jerry Spinelli's personal obsession to "understand" the Holocaust. Spinelli has no immediate personal connections with the Holocaust other than a personal sense of social justice and human compassion. As an author writing for young adults, he felt compelled to write what the Nazi reign of terror must have looked like to a child. The title of his novel—*Milkweed*—refers to a plant that hosts monarch butterflies. Ultimately, the milkweed seeds are scattered by the wind, reseeding the earth both near and far. Like the story itself, milkweed pods symbolize the fragility of life, the impermanence of existence, and the willingness to endure.

The novel presents the story of a young boy suffering through the Holocaust in Warsaw, Poland. Orphaned and alone, he lives with a group of street urchins, struggling to avoid Nazis, or "Jackboots" (Spinelli 2). Narrating the novel as an adult in America, he recalls his Polish childhood during Hitler's reign.

The story begins in 1939 in the Warsaw Ghetto. The central figure—a young boy—has no identity, except for a noticeable yellow stone that he wears around his neck. Living at a time in Europe when having an identity means the difference between life and death, the young protagonist adopts a determined attitude to survive at all costs. Readers become engaged in the experiences of a child—lost, alone, and unworldly—who does not fully comprehend what is happening around him. In fact, the unnamed boy acquires multiple names throughout the narrative: Jew, Gypsy, even Stopthief, because as child he often steals bread. Someone is always chasing him and shouting, "Stop! Thief!" (Spinelli 1). When the boy attaches himself to a band of thieves, he meets Uri, a fellow thief and vagabond, who quickly becomes his protector. Uri names his new protégé Misha Pilsudski. Young, naïve, and unassuming, Misha becomes Uri's partner, learning to steal, like his newly found compatriots. He also admires the strength and uniforms of the German soldiers.

Soon, Uri creates a false identity for Misha, so no one will think of him as a Jew. Uri spins a tale of how Misha is really a Gypsy, born to a large Russian Gypsy family. Misha's mother, Uri declares, was a talented Gypsy fortune-teller who gave birth to seven sons and five daughters. They all lived together until the war intruded on their idyllic Polish countryside life, leaving Misha separated from his family and alone on the streets of Warsaw. One day, Misha is thieving and smuggling confiscated goods whereupon he meets a girl named Janina. Janina reveals to Misha that she is Jewish and that she is celebrating her seventh birthday. Invited to attend her party, Misha sees something he has never seen before: a cake lit with candles. Thinking that Janina's family is trying to burn down the cake, Misha blows out the candles, leaving Janina and her family shocked and bewildered.

Roaming the streets of Warsaw following the party, Misha finds himself out after the Nazi-enforced curfew. When Nazi guards spot him and warn him to stop, Misha takes off, only to have shots fired at him. Both of his earlobes are destroyed by the whizzing bullets. Dismayed and distraught, Misha wonders why an honored and loyal Jackboot would shoot a young child such as him. Soon, though, Misha witnesses at first hand exploding shops, random beatings, and deliberate torture of Polish citizens. Gradually, he begins "to understand the German soldiers' real purpose" (Fiske 80).

As Nazis close in on marginalized Warsaw citizens, they are forced to live inside the segmented and walled-off ghetto. Determined to survive, Misha doubles down on his stealing. Each night he slips through a hole—a space about two bricks wide—in a wall that separates him and his fellow orphans from the outside world. Gradually, Janina and her Jewish family realize they have no choice but to move into the ghetto as well, joining Misha and his orphaned gang in hiding. In order to survive, Janina joins Misha in his stealing, as food is a rare commodity and starvation is the order of the day. Sadly, Janina's mother becomes a victim, dying almost immediately upon her arrival inside the ghetto. Uri, his mentor and fellow thief, warns Misha that the Jackboots are deadly serious, and that everyone living in the ghetto will go to concentration camps where they will inevitably die.

Fearing the end, Janina's father tells Misha that when he and his daughter steal, they should run away. Misha agrees, but when Misha tries to force Janina to escape, Janina refuses to leave. In fact, Janina drags Misha back into the ghetto, only to discover that the room where she was living with her father is now empty. A crazed Janina searches for her father, disappearing into a crowd of people. Misha runs to catch up to her, only to spot Janina tossed into a railway boxcar by a Nazi soldier. Misha tries to rescue her. Before he can, his mentor Uri appears, dressed as a Nazi. Uri proceeds to shoot him in the ear, taking off the rest of his earlobes. Misha nearly dies only to awaken all alone, lying near the railway tracks that have taken Janina away. Misha can only vaguely recall what has happened. Fate intervenes, and a nearby farmer rescues him. For the next three years, Misha stays with the farmer, working the fields, tending his animals, and sleeping in the barn. Eventually, Misha tires of his new life and once again runs away.

Catching trains as he passes through the Polish countryside, Misha eventually winds up in Warsaw, by now a city in complete rubble. There, Misha wanders the streets, stopping everyone he sees to regale them with his adventures as a child thief. His stories go unnoticed until a young woman named Vivian grows fond of him, and soon the two decide to marry. Their marriage, though, does not progress well, and after five months, with Vivian pregnant, she decides to leave Misha and venture out on her own. Once again, Misha finds himself left alone.

Many years pass, and Misha, now known as Jack, is living in America where he works as a supermarket clerk. By chance, his daughter and his granddaughter—the offspring of his long-ago marriage to Vivian—enter his supermarket, and to his surprise, introduce themselves to him. Naturally, Misha is astounded. He learns that Vivian has died, but his family has relocated to America, and now, are eager to begin anew. His daughter also suggests that Misha choose his granddaughter's middle name. He decides to call her Janina in honor of the Jewish girl he knew long ago in Warsaw.

The Search for Identity: A Comparative Analysis

In *Number the Stars* and *Milkweed*, the central theme is the search for identity. Two young people—both coming of age during World War II—face the difficulty of growing up in the midst of unspeakable circumstances. For both protagonists, the central question is, whether Annemarie and Misha belong to the world of children or to the world of adults. After all, the fine line between assuming responsibilities as a child and as an adult is difficult to define. Particularly in times of war, the line between childhood and adulthood is often tenuous at best.

As young people, Annemarie and Misha assume both child and adult roles. Their active presence in their fight for survival, and their intimate roles in suffering at the hands of the Nazi regime, demonstrates vividly how confusing the distinction between childhood and adulthood can be. Because of the war—because they are both heroes and victims as result of their involvement in helping others escape the brutality of Nazi oppression—both Annemarie and Misha are vulnerable to the same injustices, mental and physical, that one usually experiences later in life.

Annemarie and Misha differ, though, from other characters in their respective stories. In *Number the Stars*, Annemarie is juxtaposed with Kirsti, her five-year-old younger sister, a child in a complete state of innocence and happiness. In *Milkweed*, Misha stands in direct contrast to Janina, his Jewish friend, a fellow ten-year-old he meets just outside the Warsaw ghetto. Janina is aware that she is Jewish, but, unlike Misha, she does not have a growing sense of danger for her family and herself until it is too late. Misha, however, comes to terms with the horrors of life under Nazi oppression as he slowly immerses himself in the realities of everyday life in the Warsaw ghetto. His acceptance eventually saves his life. According to Rachel Dean-Ruzicka, "from the very early moments in the book readers are introduced to a person who is defined and described by his interaction with Jewish characters, rather than self-determined" (216).

Moreover, these two stories remind us that in Nazi Germany identity was always subject to victimization. The Nazis systematically killed an estimated six million Jews and an additional eleven million people during World War II. As Sally M. Rogow writes, "Nazi victimization of vulnerable people was unique in its organization, its mercilessness, and its bureaucratic efficiency and serves as a lasting reminder of the peril of making value judgements on the worth of human lives" (83).

Identity and Innocence

Innocence, perhaps the most salient feature of childhood, is no longer a possibility for Annemarie and Misha. In *Number the Stars*,

Annemarie does not really want to be an adult; she would rather remain a child playing with friends. In the beginning of the story, Annemarie clearly prefers make-believe (fairy tales and happy bedtime stories) to the true stories happening around her (Walter 126). Yet, when Nazis enter her home looking for Jews, Annemarie spontaneously rips off Ellen's Star of David necklace. She knows that if the Nazis see Ellen's Jewish star, they will take her away. Similarly, in *Milkweed*, Misha at first assumes that Nazis on parade with their shiny boots and rhythmic marching are the heroes he wants to be. Only later, when he recognizes their brutality toward him, his fellow orphans, and Janina and her Jewish family, does he come to grips with the horrors of who they are.

Both Annemarie and Misha take their rightful, if unwilling, place in the world of adults. Although both make it clear they do not feel like adults, they know that they must be brave and that feeling brave makes them feel mature. Annemarie feels brave and mature when she assists Ellen and her family's departure from Denmark. That is especially true when she confronts suspicious Nazis, both in her Copenhagen home and on her way through the forest to her Uncle Henrik's fishing boat. Similarly, Misha feels brave and mature when he races after his friend Janina as she searches for her father as he boards a train headed to a Nazi concentration camp—until he is suddenly stopped and brutalized by his former mentor, Uri, now a Nazi Jackboot.

Identity and Curiosity

Additionally, Annemarie and Misha's curiosity plays a fundamental role in forming their sense of self. Annemarie knows that is not appropriate for a child—especially for her five-year-old sister, Kirsti—to be told certain things, particularly concerning war. Yet, in order for Annemarie to process what is happening around her, she wants to know more. Annemarie wants to know why Nazis persecute Jews and why her parents must lie and conceal the Rosens' whereabouts.

Similarly, Misha wants to know the truth about what he experiences living in the Warsaw ghetto, but he knows better than to

Rogow, Sally M. "Child Victims in Nazi Germany." *Journal of Holocaust Education,* vol. 8, no. 3, 1999, pp. 71-86.

Spinelli, Jerry. *Milkweed.* Knopf, 2003.

Walter, Virginia A. "Metaphor and Mantra: The Function of Stories in *Number the Stars*," *Children's Literature in Education*, vol. 27, no., 2, 1996, pp. 123-30.

CRITICAL
READINGS

Historical Fiction: A Comparative Analysis of Medieval Romance and Scott's *Ivanhoe*_____

Christine E. Kozikowski

As one of the earliest historical novels written, *Ivanhoe* by Sir Walter Scott presents a rich and romanticized picture of the Middle Ages. Stylized in the fashion of a medieval romance, *Ivanhoe* combines nationalism, tournaments, witch trials, and other stock romance tropes, adding to the growing popularity of medievalism in the nineteenth century. Through these elements, Scott romanticizes an already romanticized landscape, depicting a medieval England that never existed in an attempt to connect the past to the present. While *Ivanhoe* and medieval romances are centuries apart in creation, comparing their romantic elements and their presentation of the past provides a useful frame for analysis. Historical fiction often says more about the present in which it is created than it illustrates a concretely historical past. Alternatively, as Chris Ferns states, it works "not merely to explain the past but also to make it possible to rethink the present" (134). Furthermore, since historical fiction has become intertwined with the modern form of the novel, critics have often ignored its earlier forms. Although Scott has been credited with the popularization of historical fiction, the earlier form of fictional narrative that he drew on, medieval romance, had already proven extremely popular. Medieval romance served as a model for Scott primarily in its demonstration of the blurred lines between history and fiction.

Broadly defined, medieval romances are tales of high adventure, written in verse or prose, in which a knight with superhuman abilities undertakes a journey in order to gain fame and skill. Along the way, he defeats enemies and monsters and rescues and/or wins the love of a lady in order to bring about a resolved, hierarchical social order. To achieve success, this knight must learn and maintain values of courtesy, chivalry, and Christianity in the face of adversity. In addition, the conclusion of the tale generally serves as reclamation of patrimony or a return from exile. While love is important to the hero's journey in many medieval romances, marriage is not always necessary to the knight's denouement; the successful attainment of fame, skills, and courtesy—in other words the actual adventure—proves most important. Although many medieval romances depict similar tropes, texts in the genre reflect a broad range of subject matter. They spanned almost four hundred years of intense popularity and were produced throughout the reaches of medieval Europe. Medieval romances have been essential to the development of fiction in their content and their form, influencing major writers from William Shakespeare and Edmund Spenser to Matthew Lewis, Alfred Tennyson, J. R. R. Tolkien, and of course, Sir Walter Scott. Likewise, the romance genre itself has shifted and changed with time, and love has taken a more central role; little remains the same in today's historical romance novels set in the Middle Age when they are compared to their medieval predecessors.

Middle English romances are a form of medieval romance produced in England broadly spanning from the thirteenth century to the end of the fifteenth century. Scholars disagree about the purpose of these texts—whether they were didactic or intended for entertainment—and most settle on a purpose that is a combination of the two. Middle English romances entertained aristocratic audiences while teaching the listeners of both sexes about etiquette, manners, and, most importantly, courtesy. The medieval concept of courtesy can be equated with chivalry. Courtesy was a set type of behavior practiced by aristocratic men and women in their interactions with other people of the same status. Between men, courtesy, or chivalry, meant behaving in a respectful manner toward other men of the same social status, religious ideology, and martial skill level. It meant practicing mercy in the field toward enemies. Between men and women, courtesy was a game of flirtation between individuals of the same class that might or might not end in consummation. Eighteenth-century French antiquarian Gaston Paris named this game "courtly love"; as an actual practice, however, courtly love did not exist.

In addition to these other characteristics and most important to this study, Middle English romances are historical fiction. Even though most discussions of historical fiction examine it as part of the development of the novel, the genre itself seems difficult to define. Dean Rehberger argues, "Historical novels seem to borrow from all fictive conventions, cannibalizing any new territory opened up by literary developments. They consume not only the forms of tragedy, comedy, and epic, but they extend into conventions of the gothic, the romance, and the melodrama—all the time borrowing from realism and naturalism to create the texture of history" (59). While this statement only refers to novels, medieval romances written in both poetry and prose borrowed liberally in form and/or content from other texts and tales as well. In fact, medieval romances could even be considered proto-novels. Thus for this chapter, historical fiction refers to any text set in a clearly recognized time and place with either historical characters or other "real" characteristics; this definition remains purposely broad in order to encompass writing that existed prior to the novel's appearance on the literature scene.

One of the characteristics of historical fiction is the manner by which it combines history (facts) and imagination (fiction). Brian Hamnett argues that "A distinction between the romance and history had existed at least since the Renaissance humanists' criticism of romance as shapeless, fantastic, and a corrupting influence, contrasting it with the Classical epic" (25), but it is clear that medieval writers also understood that there was a distinction between romance and history. For example, the fourteenth-century verse romance *Richard Coer de Lyon* describes the deeds of Richard I (1156-1199) during the Third Crusade. Not only is the romance imbued with the weight of real and imagined figures from the beginning, but its action takes place during an actual historical event, the Third Crusade, and focuses on historical figures such as Richard and Saladin (1137-1193), the first Sultan of Egypt. Peter Larkin, editor of the newly updated edition of *Richard Coer de Lyon* comments,

Indeed, all manuscripts and printings of *Richard*, even those characterized by fabulous interpolations, present historically traceable, albeit embellished details of Richard's crusade. With notable geographic specificity, each describes Richard's preparations, his adventures in Sicily, including the pillage of Messina, his conquest of Cyprus, the capture of Acre and massacre of Muslim prisoners, the march to Jaffa, Saladin's (Salâh al-Dîn) destruction of castles and poisoning of wells, Richard's victory at Arsuf and rebuilding of Ascalon, his celebrated defense of Jaffa, his truce with Saladin, his return to England to deal with his brother John's intrigues, and finally, his death on the continent while laying siege to a vassal's castle.

As a historically based document, the romance's featuring real places and the actions of war would have been familiar to readers who had experienced wave after wave of crusader fervor. Richard's deeds during the Third Crusade were known throughout England; he had already become a hero during his own lifetime. Furthermore, battle scenes, such as that featured in the following excerpt from *Richard*, would have been commonly drawn from other romances or real life:

> Thoo myghte men see many wyght man,
> Hasteyly to hys armes ran
> And wenten quykly to the dyke,
> And defendyd hem hastelyke.
> There was many gentyl heved
> Quykly fro the body weved;
> Scheldes, many schorn in twoo,
> And many stede stykyd alsoo. (3015-22)

> [Though men might see many a brave man
> Hastily run to his arms
> And go quickly to the duke,
> And defend themselves with haste.
> There was many a genteel head
> Quickly from the body severed;
> Shields, many shorn in two,
> And many steeds stabbed also.]

The narrator accurately describes the trauma of war: dead horses, decapitated soldiers, and broken weapons.

However, as historical fiction, the creative license to revise the past or to embellish details is just as significant in the romance as is historical realism. In *Richard*, depictions of the king range from courteous knight to savage warrior. Larkin concedes,

> But the poem's representation of Richard is not always "historical," diverging not only from chronicle sources but also from the conventions of *chansons de geste*, an epic genre often considered historical in nature. And while the violent, fearless, and aggressive warrior found in the poem frequently resembles the historical figure, on a number of occasions, *Richard* presents the king as uncourtly and unchivalric, and it frequently identifies him as a devil. Some texts even depict Richard as a demonic cannibal. Of course, the historical Richard was no cannibal, nor was he uncourtly or unchivalric. Despite these distortions and despite the poem's extreme, even savage, Christian militancy. . . *Richard* became one of the most popular romances in medieval England.

It is these moments that add to the entertainment value of the text— the creative license by which the poet provides a new dimension to the character. In addition, a number of these unhistorical depictions have parallels in yet other romances and chronicles that were produced during and after crusades. As Larkin points out, *Richard* portrays King Richard as a cannibal; in the more popularized version of the romance, the king eats Saracen flesh not just once but twice. In the first scene, Richard is sick and craves pork; however, due to the Muslim prohibition against pork, there is none available. Instead, an old man advises that he be fed a "yonge and fat" (3088) ["young and fat"] Saracen, cooked in saffron and spices. The text describes in gruesome detail the king's consumption: "Before Kyng Rychard karf a knyghte; / He eet fastere than he kerve myghte. / The kyng eet the flesch and gnew the bones" (3109-3111). [Before King Richard carved a knight; / he ate faster than he might carve. / The king ate flesh and gnawed on the bones."] The next day, Richard is healed and fights like "the devyl" (3166) ["the devil"] but in the evening becomes exhausted; fearing a relapse, he demands that his supper be made from the head of the swine. After the deception is revealed, Richard "gan to lawghe as he were wood" (3215) ["began to laugh as if he were mad"], crying that they would never starve with such a food supply. Scholars such as Geraldine Heng and Suzanne Conklin Akbari argue respectively that these acts of cannibalism serve to reinforce his Englishness and remind readers of his eastern origin (Heng 98-99, and 150, and Akbari 199-200). But beyond that, this scene and the later episode of cannibalism where Richard is fully aware of his actions, underpin the savagery of war and question the values of chivalry and courtesy that have been attributed to Richard previously. Historically Richard was not a cannibal; however, links to cannibalism during the crusades have been made to chronicles and other romance characters. The poet of *Richard* combined elements from other texts into this romance to create a more dramatic figure.

Criticism of historical fiction has associated the genre with nationalism and national identity as early as the beginning of the twentieth century. Herbert Butterfield and Georg Lukács wrote some of the earliest criticism on historical fiction. Butterfield contends that historical fiction "becomes the consciousness of belonging to a place and a tradition. Even where it seems most local and confined, even where it contains no sounding of the trumpets of nationalism, and where its author holds no patriotic motive, the historical novel cannot help reminding men of their heritage in the soil" (42). Like historical novels, Middle English romances remind readers of their own identity either overtly or more subtly. In the introduction of *Richard Coer de Lyon*, the narrator compares Richard I to both real and fictional characters:

> Lord Jhesu, kyng of glorye,
> Whyche grace and vyctorye
> Thou sente to Kyng Rychard,
> That nevere was founde coward!
> It is ful good to here in jeste
> Of his prowess and hys conqueste.
> Fele romaunces men maken newe,
> Of goode knyghtes, stronge and trewe.

Of here dedys men rede romaunce,
Both in Engeland and in Franse:
Of Rowelond and of Olyver,
And of every doseper;
Of Alisaundre and Charlemayn,
Of Kyng Arthour and of Gawayn,
How they were knyghtes goode and curteys;
Of Turpyn and Oger Daneys.
Of Troy men rede in ryme,
What werre ther was in olde tyme;
Of Ector and of Achylles,
What folk they slowe in that pres. (1-20)

[Lord Jesus, king of glory
Which grace and victory
You sent to King Richard
Who was considered a coward!
It is good to hear the jest
Of his conquest.
Such romances that men make anew
Of good knights, strong and true.
Of their deeds men read in romance,
Both in England and in France:
Of Roland and of Oliver,
And of all of the twelve peers;
Of Alexander and Charlemagne
Of King Arthur and of Gawain
How they were knights good and courteous
Of Turpin and Ogier the Dane.
Of Troy men read about in rhyme,
What war there was in ancient time;
Of Hector and Achilles,
What people they slew in that place.]

By connecting Richard to each character, the narrator relates the English king to those characters' historical relevance, characteristics, reputation, and fictional identity. In addition, each pair reflects one of the three subsets of Middle English romance: the Matter of Britain (Arthur), the Matter of France (Charlemagne), and the Matter of

Rome (Alexander). In *Middle English Romance and the Craft of Memory*, Jamie McKinstry argues that "the mere mention of these characters' names was enough to re-create the narrative whence they emerged, thereby establishing a connection" with the new tale (60-61); the story must carry the weight of its own subject as well as the weight of the references. In this example, the connection of Richard to Roland and Oliver recalls the *Song of Roland* and an emphasis on loyalty, oaths, and Christianity; Arthur and Gawain tie him further to the foundations of an English national identity, as well as the reputation for courtesy and martial prowess of Arthur's court. Finally, each character represents his own historical time and place—English, Frankish, Roman, and Greek—and connects Richard, and therefore all of Britain, to each of these classical traditions. While the concept of English nationhood did not exist in the same way it does now, in part because England did not exist in the way it does now, *Richard* indicates that Richard I created a uniformly governed society: "The kyng comaundyd thorwgh the lond, / At London to make a parlement" (1258-59). [The king commanded throughout the land / at London to have a parliament.] Along with the monarchy, the parliament formed the core government, which became part of a national identity.

Unlike medieval romance whose position as historical fiction must be proven, Scott and *Ivanhoe*, in particular, have held court as the inspiration for the genre in its modern form. The novel received immediate fame but has since fallen in both critics' and readers' esteem, partly because it is historical fiction and partly because of its subject matter. Critics of the genre complain that "Borrowing its form from the aesthetic conventions of the novel and its content from the pages of history books, historical fiction appears as both history and literature, information and entertainment; however, neither the discipline of History nor English accepts this impure and mixed form as a legitimate expression of its discipline's demands" (Rehberger 59). Critics of the novel contend that it "executes the fatal turn in Scott's career from a once influential historical realism . . . to a tinsel-and-tushery medievalism" (Duncan ix). Georg Lukács, who is still considered one of the preeminent critics of historical fiction, argues that Scott's novels inspired his audience to the possibilities associated with combining history and creativity, spurring a new form. Even decades after Lukács's commentary, Richard J. Bourcier concurs: "As for Scott's contribution to the novel, he renovated, as mentioned, content and technique. He popularized history as a source of inspiration for the novel. History was not just a setting, but was seen on a grand scale as the mainspring of the action. The historical interest became the novelist's primary concern instead of the sentimental" (153).

Ivanhoe presents a marked departure from Scott's previous novels such as *Waverley* (1814), *The Bride of Lammermoor* (1819), and *The Heart of Midlothian* (1818), all of which focused on moments of conflict in Scottish history. Fearing an audience bored with current events, Scott turned his attentions to the past. In *Ivanhoe*, Scott tackles post-conquest England in the twelfth century, weaving threads from a variety of historical and fictional roots into a single cohesive tale. Aware of the line between history and literature, Scott addresses in his "Dedicatory Epistle" the concern about where the novel falls into history or romance. Kenneth M. Sroka comments that it reveals "Scott's understanding of the organic intricacy of literary form as it expresses itself in the symbiotic relationship between history and fiction, between the realistic and the romantic" (657). Scott writes, "Still the severer antiquary may think, that, by thus intermingling fiction with truth, I am polluting the well of history with modern inventions, and impressing upon the rising generation false ideas of the age which I describe. I cannot but in some sense admit the force of this reasoning, which I yet hope to traverse by the following considerations" (17). Scott then justifies his intermingling by arguing that although he attempts to follow history as faithfully as possible, he must also attend to the entertainment of his audience. He can neither tell from historical documents what his characters were thinking nor can he write in the language of twelfth-century England; instead he must create the thoughts and write in such a way as to use "the language and sentiments which are common to ourselves and our forefathers" (21) but still completely understandable.

Scott was no stranger to medieval romance literature. A review of his library by Jerome Mitchell indicates that he had read, transcribed, and owned copies of most of the major and minor romances. Mitchell explains,

> We shall see that Scott was immensely indebted to Chaucer and the romances in his narrative poems and in the Waverley Novels. Sometimes he mentions the particular romance he has in mind; when he does not, it is not always easy to catch him in the act of borrowing. I say *borrowing,* not blatant stealing, of which some of his contemporaries (he avers) were guilty. (38)

Scott's interest in the Middle Ages grew out of the medieval revival that had begun with German and French seventeenth-century antiquarians. Eventually spreading to England, scholarly interest in the Middle Ages inspired texts such as Horace Walpole's Gothic *Castle of Otranto* (1764), Bishop Percy's *Reliques of Ancient English Poetry* (1765), Matthew Lewis's *The Monk: A Romance* (1796), and William Godwin's *Life of Chaucer* (1803). Throughout Scott's life, both amateurs and scholars created transcriptions or translations of many medieval texts (Mitchell 3); Scott himself is also included in this group. He produced an edition of *Sir Tristrem* (1804), which contains the romance of Tristan and Isolde.

Ivanhoe is set at a volatile time in England's past, somewhere in the years 1193-94. The Third Crusade had just ended in 1192; Richard I was being held for ransom on the Continent, and there was a power vacuum among England's leaders. Apart from international affairs, domestically, England was struggling with its own identity. In 1066, William the Conqueror, Duke of Normandy, successfully invaded Britain and claimed the throne, bringing with him Norman French language, customs, and law. As with any society that has been conquered and colonized, the old, in this case the Anglo-Saxon, struggles against the new social order. It is in this climate that Scott sets his story.

The conflict of identity politics presents itself in *Ivanhoe* through the relationship between father and son, Saxon and Norman, and king and vassal. In each of these narratives, the question of power is overarching. Wilfred, Knight of Ivanhoe and Disinherited Knight, disagrees with his father, Cedric the Saxon, on matters of state. Cedric states unabashedly that he will always be Saxon, rejecting repeatedly anything even close to Norman. He greets his guests in the beginning, Prior Aymer and Templar Brian de Bois-Guilbert, in his own language and requires them to converse in kind as a show of power. Bois-Guilbert, however, rejects this ploy: "I speak ever French, the language of King Richard and his nobles, but I understand English sufficiently to communicate with the natives of the country" (Scott 57). Throughout the novel, Cedric does his best to negate, to reject, and to reconfigure the power dynamics regardless of his own position at any time. As he watches the tournament at Ashby, he sees each competition as "a repeated triumph over the honour of England" (105). It is only at the end, when King Richard reveals his identity, that Cedric finds himself neatly trapped by his own admissions.

Identity politics in *Ivanhoe* also reinforce a national English identity. Like the romance *Richard Coer de Lyon*, King Richard in Scott's novel drives forward nationalism; however, Scott's Richard does this by uniting disparate factions and ousting traitors. In addition to the grudging loyalty of Cedric the Saxon by the text's end, the yeoman Locksley, the Robin Hood character, rejects rulership by Prince John who has been unduly influenced by his Norman and Catholic companions: "I have vowed, that if ever I take service, it should be with your royal brother King Richard" (Scott 160). Locksley and his men serve as the middle ground throughout the story; they do not reject the conqueror's right to rule but will only follow the true king. In addition, Scott distances Richard from the Normans, and therefore from his French background, throughout the text. He does so first through Richard's anonymity as the Black Knight, and second through his proclamation at the end: "Richard of Anjou!" exclaimed Cedric, stepping backward with the utmost astonishment. "No, noble Cedric—Richard of England!—whose deepest interest—whose deepest wish, is to see her sons united with each other" (470). The king's disavowal of his ancestry reinforces a common identity.

The resolution of the novel is the restoration of order, an essential characteristic of romance literature. Enemies of the state—the Catholic Church and its representatives, unruly Saxons, and rebel yeomen—have all been conquered or subdued, or have accepted the new social order; likewise, the feudal state, the reconciliation of father and son, the son's reclamation of his patrimony, and the acceptance of two previously separated lovers, achieves order as well. Alice Chandler argues:

> The idea of order is particularly important in *Ivanhoe*, Scott's fullest attempt to interpret medieval society in accordance with his social philosophy. He works in that novel with a wide range of cultural levels: from Urfrieda, the demented Saxon hag who calls upon Wotan and Zernebock for vengeance, to Brian de Bois-Guilbert, who has so far outgrown chivalry and Christianity as to think honor and religion mere superstitions. . . Bois-Guilbert is specifically stated to be false in his oaths, faithless to women, hypocritical in his religion. Unwilling to fulfill his feudal responsibilities to the weak and oppressed, he thinks only of his own freedom and ambition. (324)

Medieval society was hierarchical and each group had a specific position within society. It was difficult for people to shift from one level of society to the next. Gurth's rise to freeman status demonstrates the idealism present in romantic texts; as a loyal supporter of his overlord, Gurth is rewarded for his service. Kenneth M. Sroka, however, argues that the restoration of order is less than ideal. He contends:

> However, closer readings reveal that Scott's fidelity to the conventional romance form is tempered by altered conventions and deflations of idealistic imaginative elements—variations which create a more realistic romance. Although the English nation is delivered finally from the power of the usurping Norman rulers by the accession of King Richard in union with the formerly oppressed Saxon people, the conventional romance pattern is much qualified in *Ivanhoe*: the heroes are not ideal; the maiden's rescue is due more to chance than to valor; the titular hero marries a second, less attractive heroine; and the new social order falls far short of a wish-fulfillment ideal. (645)

Much has been said about Wilfred's union with Rowena instead of Rebecca; however, the rigid social order of the Middle Ages rejects any marriage between them unless Rebecca converts. Therefore, while there may have been attraction between the two, their future together would have never been a foregone conclusion. In addition, Ivanhoe's triumph over Brian de Bois-Guilbert, chance that it may be, also upholds the social order; even in his weakened state, Richard proves to be the heaven-chosen victor.

In the comparison of such vastly different texts, a number of issues about genre become clear. As may be expected, the difference in genre form, verse romance versus novel, has been a factor of this analysis. Middle English verse romances are generally episodic in nature and much shorter than novels. This disparity in length then required Scott to pull content from a variety of romances instead of following the plot of a single tale. The trope of the exiled hero returning home and restoring order is an integral part of the medieval romance genre and one that Scott applies as well; in the end, Wilfred is reunited with his father and Cedric grudgingly accepts Richard as king. Medieval outlaw poems about Robin Hood are not romances but folktales, and Robin appears only in an occasional reference. Regardless of the range of source material used, medieval romance tradition provided an intertextual bond between *Ivanhoe* and romances such as *Richard Coer de Lyon*. Aside from the differences in form, both *Ivanhoe* and medieval romances like *Richard* are definitively historical fiction. Although historical fiction has mostly been assessed as novels, fiction before the novel cannot be ignored either. Though broad, defining historical fiction as a text about a recognizable place and time with recognizable characters allows medieval literature to join the ranks of historical fiction.

Works Cited

Akbari, Suzanne Conklin. "The Hunger for National Identity in *Richard Coer de Lion*." *Reading Medieval Culture: Essays in Honor of Robert W. Hanning*. Edited by Robert M. Stein and Sandra Pierson Prior. U Notre Dame P, 2005, pp. 198-227.

Bourcier, Richard J. "Scott and Historical Fiction: The Case of *Ivanhoe.*" *Selected Papers on Medievalism*, 1-2 II, 1986-87, pp. 150-59.

Butterfield, Herbert. *The Historical Novel: An Essay.* Cambridge UP, 1924.

Chandler, Alice. "Sir Walter Scott and the Medieval Revival." *Nineteenth Century Fiction*, vol. 19, no. 4, 1965, pp. 315-32.

Duncan, Ian. Introduction. *Ivanhoe*, Oxford UP, 1996, pp. vii-xxvi.

Ferns, Chris. "Walter Scott, J. G. Farrell, and the Dialogics of Historical Fiction." *J. G. Farrell: The Critical Grip.* Edited by Ralph J. Crane, Four Courts, 1999, pp. 128-45.

Hamnett, Brian. *The Historical Novel in Nineteenth-Century Europe: Representations of Reality in History and Fiction.* Oxford, 2012.

Heng, Geraldine. *Empire of Magic*, Columbia UP, 2004. pp. 98–99, and 150.

Larkin, Peter. Introduction. *Richard Coer de Lyon*, Medieval Institute, 2015. http://d.lib.rochester.edu/teams/text/larkin-richard-coer-de-lyon-introduction. Accessed 23 July 2017.

Lukács, Georg. *The Historical Novel.* Translated by Hannah and Stanley Mitchell, Beacon, 1962.

McKinstry, Jamie. *Middle English Romance and the Craft of Memory.* Brewer, 2015.

Mitchell, Jerome. *Scott, Chaucer, and Medieval Romance: A Study in Sir Walter Scott's Indebtedness to the Literature of the Middle Ages.* UP of Kentucky, 1987.

Rehberger, Dean. "Vulgar Fiction, Impure History: The Neglect of Historical Fiction." *Journal of American Culture*, vol. 18, no. 4, 1995, pp. 59-66.

Richard Coer de Lyon, Medieval Institute, 2015, http://d.lib.rochester.edu/teams/text/larkin-richard-coer-de-lyon. Accessed 23 July 2017.

Scott, Walter. *Ivanhoe.* 1819. Edited by Ian Duncan. Oxford UP, 1996.

Sroka, Kenneth M. "Function of Form: *Ivanhoe* as Romance." *Studies in English Literature, 1500-1900*, vol. 19, no. 4, 1965, pp. 645-60.

Tales of Other Times: The Gothic Novel as Historical Fiction

Natalie Neill

In 1764, Horace Walpole wrote a tale of feudal tyranny and supernaturalism—*The Castle of Otranto: A Gothic Story*—which he tried to pass off as a true story obtained from a twelfth-century manuscript. In the preface to the second edition, Walpole admitted the hoax and defended his book as a work of the imagination. The historical settings of eighteenth-century Gothic novels afforded writers like Walpole a space in which to engage in literary experimentation and explore the relationship between the past and present. Yet the historical novel in Britain is usually said to have originated in the early nineteenth century with Sir Walter Scott. Unsurprisingly, Georg Lukács excludes Gothic fiction from his account of the historical novel because, he argues, in works like *The Castle of Otranto* "history is treated as mere costumery" (19), whereas Scott's works "grasp [...] the historical peculiarity of characters and events" (20). This chapter offers an overview of several influential historical Gothic novels to demonstrate that, although the novels typically lacked the historical realism of later historical fictions, the settings are not incidental.

Crucial Gothic conventions, including ghosts, graveyards, ancestral piles, family curses, moldering manuscripts, and long-buried secrets, reflect the genre's inherent fascination with the past. The Gothic writers portrayed historical milieus and characters in various ways to achieve a wide range of effects. They used representations of past times to entertain readers, intervene in debates about the novel, re-evaluate official history, comment on present events and recent history, and forge ideas of nationhood. This chapter concludes with a discussion of how Scott, the supposed progenitor of historical fiction, benefited from the experimentations of the Gothic writers. In particular, *Waverley* (1814) is considered in terms of Scott's acknowledged debts to specific texts. The object of the essay is to show that the Gothic novels of the eighteenth century should not be a footnote in the history of the historical novel in Britain, but rather an important early chapter in the development of the genre.

Although *The Castle of Otranto* is usually cited as the first Gothic novel, that honor should perhaps belong to *Longsword: Earl of Salisbury: An Historical Romance* (1762), by Irish historian Thomas Leland. Leland's book appeared one year after the completion of David Hume's successful multivolume work, *The History of England* (1754-61), and the popular interest in history that Hume inspired may have prompted Leland to write his only work of historical fiction. Set during the reign of Henry III of England (1216-72), the novel gives an account of William Longesprée (Longsword), Third Earl of Salisbury, illegitimate son of Henry II. Longsword returns home from the war in France to discover that his castle in Cornwall has been seized and his wife Ela taken prisoner by Raymond de Burgh (the nephew of Henry III's advisor). Longsword's adventures in France and the perfidious seizure and eventual return of his castle are recounted over two volumes through a series of interlocking first-person narratives by various characters including the titular earl. The work is part history, part legend, and part chivalric romance. Leland also draws from his era's novels of sensibility, as many later Gothic novelists would do. In relocating the highly sensitive hero, the wicked rake, and the long-suffering heroine of sensibility fiction to a medieval castle setting, Leland creates prototypes for the Gothic hero, villain, and persecuted heroine. Ela of Salisbury is a picture of distressed virtue, imprisoned and nearly forced to commit bigamy by marrying Raymond in a secret ceremony presided over by a vicious Catholic monk. Leland embellishes official history and draws on lore about Longesprée and his wife. There are no supernatural horrors of the kind found in later Gothic works, yet Leland's readers are never permitted to forget that they are engaged with fiction as opposed to true history. In the notice to readers, the author observes,

women were just as capable of being rational as men were, and that women should cultivate their reason. Emily is confronted with one apparently supernatural occurrence after the other, but in every case, she discovers a natural explanation. Anachronistically, Emily acquires a rationalist world*view*. The development of her reason enables her to withstand her uncle's trickery, maintain her autonomy, and retain possession of her property. When Montoni tries to trick her into signing away her inheritance, she stands her ground: "I am not so ignorant, Signor, of the laws on this subject, as to be misled by the assertion of any person. The law, in the present instance, gives me the estates in question, and my own hand shall never betray me" (Radcliffe 380-81). Ultimately, Emily wins her freedom, marries the man of her choice, and returns to her peaceful abode in France.

Charlotte Smith's *The Old Manor House* differs from the previous texts in that it is a novel of the recent past, a fact that would disqualify it as historical fiction, according to traditional descriptions of that genre. Set in the 1770s, it tells the story of a young Englishman, Orlando Somerive; his controlling ancient relative, Mrs. Rayland, whose estate he hopes to inherit; and the beautiful orphan, Monimia, whom he loves. To please Mrs. Rayland—whose ancestors sided with the Royalists during the English Civil War (Smith 160)—Orlando leaves England to fight in the American War of Independence. Near the close of Smith's book, Orlando returns from America to find that Mrs. Rayland has died; he inherits Rayland Hall and marries Monimia—the expected romance resolution.

Like Radcliffe, Smith uses a historical setting to defamiliarize present-day realities. In Smith's hands, historical fiction is a vehicle for expressing subversive political views. Smith supported the French Revolution and often incorporated libertarian sentiments in her fiction. In the 1790s, there was real fear in Britain that the unrest in France might inspire unrest at home, and so repressive measures were taken to silence radicals. Jacqueline M. Labbe observes that Smith had received "strong criticism" for her novel *Desmond* (1792), which "had been openly sympathetic to the Revolution." The 1770s setting of *The Old Manor House* enabled Smith "to factor in a liberal politics without being overtly political" (Labbe 13). Smith uses odious upper class characters to attack aristocratic power. The tendency of her work is to "express sympathy for the rebels and to urge change" (London 218). Mrs. Rayland disparages Americans, calling them the "descendants of the Regicides" (Smith 13) and "round-heads" (336). Another dishonourable character, the novel's villainous General Tracy, speaks contemptuously of the "chimerical liberty" of the "insolent colonialists" (160, 261). However, admirable characters look upon the rebels with sympathy: for his part, Orlando feels "a pity not unmixed with respect" for the Americans and comes to question the justness of the British cause, asking himself *"what all this was for?"* "He sometimes [...] endeavoured to persuade himself that it was for glory" but was then "induced [...] to enquire if it was not from a mistaken point of honour" or the "wickedness of governments, or the sanguinary ambition or revenge of monarchs" (353). In such moments, Smith's republican principles are on display, and yet her novel escaped censure. By using tropes of Gothic fiction and engaging contemporary politics at an historical remove, Smith drew attention away from the incendiary ideas in her work. *The Old Manor House* "was read as a romance, rather than as a political novel" (Labbe 27).

Like Smith, the Irish writer Maria Edgeworth eschews medievalism in favour of more recent history. However, Edgeworth's *Castle Rackrent* (1800) is a work very different in kind from *The Old Manor House*. Edgeworth's text is a parody of the historical Gothic novel. It was written on the eve of the Act of Union (1801) and is set in the period before Ireland's Parliament gained legislative independence in 1782. The story presents the amusing history of the Rackrents, a family of Anglo-Irish landlords, as told by their "illiterate old steward," Thady Quirk, "in his vernacular idiom" (Edgeworth, Preface 62). Edgeworth supported the Union, and her comical treatment of the lives of the Irish gentry is framed as a tongue-in-cheek guide to English readers. As Scott asserted in his general preface to *Waverley*, "[Edgeworth's] Irish characters have gone so far to make the English familiar with the character of their gay and kind-hearted neighbours of Ireland, that she may be truly said to have done more towards completing the Union, than perhaps all the legislative enactments by which it was followed up" (7).

Castle Rackrent is important because in satirizing earlier historical Gothic works it encourages a more innovative approach to historical fiction. Edgeworth treats Gothic conventions with irony, including the stock characters of the heroine and the villain. In Edgeworth's tale, one of the Lady Rackrents is "shut up for seven years" in a barrack room (*Castle Rackrent* 81) after her husband is unsuccessful in using "all his arts" to compel her to relinquish her diamond necklace (*Castle Rackrent* 80). Edgeworth includes footnotes and an entertaining glossary at the end of *Castle Rackrent* to explain local customs "[f]or the information of the *ignorant* English reader" (Preface, 63). The notes and glossary parody the kinds of "antiquarian [...] paratextual features" often found in eighteenth-century historical novels (Stevens 102). Edgeworth also mocks another conventional feature of historical novels, namely the use of first-person interpolated narratives, through her unreliable "historian" Thady. Thady purports to be truthful, but his account is based on questionable family lore. He concludes his narration as follows: "As for all I have set down from memory and hearsay of the family, there's nothing but truth in it from beginning to end" (Edgeworth, *Castle Rackrent* 121). Edgeworth makes fun of the spurious truth claims found in many Gothic texts and situates her mock history within the tradition of the tall tale, even as she calls for realism in historical fiction. The genre's lack of realism is addressed in Edgeworth's preface:

> The heroes of history are so decked out by the fine fancy of the professed historian; they talk in such measured prose, and act from such sublime or such diabolical motives, that few have sufficient taste, wickedness, or heroism to sympathize with their fate. (61)

By contrast, Edgeworth's fiction is marked by greater social realism and historical specificity; it manages, however ironically, to provide a "specimen of [the] manners and characters" of Ireland (*Castle Rackrent* 121). In focusing on a particular locality and using Irish demotic language (i.e., Thady's colloquial narrating voice), Edgeworth set a precedent for nineteenth-century historical novelists, especially Scott.

Although Scott is customarily credited with the invention of the historical novel, Stevens, in her study of eighteenth-century historical fiction, lists "eighty-five British novels with historical settings published between 1762 and 1813" (that is, before the publication of *Waverley* in 1814) (15; 16-18, Table 1.1). Evidently, Scott's important contributions to the genre did not emerge out of a vacuum. Scott did not invent the historical novel; however, it could be argued that our modern understanding of the historical novel as a work that presents an "artistically faithful image of a concrete historical epoch" (Lukács 19) emerges as a result of Scott's borrowings from, and reworking of, the Gothic novels.

Scott departs from the Gothic novelists in using recent Scottish history rather than a remote historical and geographical setting. Moreover, *Waverley* has a precise setting: Edward Waverley is a quixotic English soldier who travels through the Scottish Lowlands to the Highlands, where he takes part in the Jacobite Rebellion of 1745 (specifically, the Battle of Prestonpans). As in the works by Leland, Reeve, and Lee, Scott's fictional characters intermingle with historical figures. After Waverley deserts the army, his adventures take him to Holyrood Castle, where he meets the Jacobite pretender, Charles Edward Stuart himself. Waverley is so taken with the "royal Adventurer," "whose form and manners, as well as the spirit which he displayed [...], answered his ideas of a hero of romance" (289), that he pledges his support for the Stuart cause (Scott 290).

Scott did not conceal what he owed to earlier historical writers. In his general preface, he suggests that the idea for *Waverley* originated in Walpole's Gothic text; Scott explains that he had long "nourished the ambitious desire of composing a tale of chivalry, which was to be in the style of the *Castle of Otranto*, with plenty of Border characters" (6). In the preface, and throughout his oeuvre, Scott also alludes to Radcliffe. Again, Scott's references suggest that her historical fiction inspired him, yet he also wished to modify her approach by using a setting closer to home. Scott defends his choice of setting and subtitle ("'Tis Sixty Years Since") in the first chapter:

> Had I [...] announced in my frontispiece 'Waverley, a Tale of Other Days,' must not every novel-reader have anticipated a castle scarce less than that of Udolpho [...]? Would not the owl have shrieked and the cricket cried in my very title-page? (53-4)

Here, Scott playfully disassociates his work from earlier wild Gothic tales, suggesting that his novel will be more authentic, more historically realistic, than *The Mysteries of Udolpho* because the setting is more familiar. As Scott discusses in his preface, he emulated Edgeworth's method (8-9). Like Edgeworth, he tells a tale of local color, uses regional dialects, and sets his work in living memory. Yet, Edgeworth's comical work was not granted the same importance as *Waverley*. Scott's novel was immediately recognized as a more artistic alternative to the popular, yet critically maligned, Gothic novels of the day. The influential reviewer Francis Jeffrey found some faults in the book (for example, he complained that "[half of it was] composed [...] in a dialect unintelligible to four-fifths of the reading population of the country"), but Jeffrey also acknowledged that because of the "truth and vivacity of its colouring, [*Waverley* was] already casting the whole tribe of ordinary novels into the shade" (208). It is important to note, however, that *Waverley* is not, strictly speaking, a realistic novel; it is a romance. Scott's readers are encouraged to find Waverley's Highland adventures as romantic as he does himself. Radcliffe had earned the sobriquet "The Great Enchantress" for her historical romances; similarly, Scott was called "The Wizard of the North." As these epithets suggest, the difference between his approach and that of his predecessors is not so stark after all.

To conclude, the Gothic writers deploy history in a range of sophisticated ways. Some present the Middle Ages as the dark "other" of the Enlightened present to explore the supernatural and the irrational and other topics that were sidelined during the Age of Reason. Others use depictions of the past (medieval and more recent) to comment on the present; their "Tales of Other Times" intervene in debates about literature, women's rights, politics, and even history writing itself. According to Dent, "history was considered one of the noblest forms of literature" in the eighteenth century (4); the novel, on the other hand, especially the Gothic novel, was still new, experimental, and suspect. Writers like Reeve, Radcliffe, and Scott incorporate historical details to elevate their works. Meanwhile, Lee and Edgeworth call attention to the subjectivity of history; their texts suggest that the line separating imaginative literature and history is blurry. In short, history is more than a backdrop in the works that have been discussed in this chapter. The Gothic novel is not merely an "antecedent" of the nineteenth-century historical novel (De Groot 11); Gothic novels *are* historical novels. Recognizing them as such helps readers to broaden their definition of historical fiction and to better understand the canonical historical works that they helped to inspire.

Works Cited

De Groot, Jerome. *The Historical Novel*. Routledge, 2010.

Dent, Jonathan. *Sinister Histories: Gothic Novels and Representations of the Past*. Manchester UP, 2016.

Edgeworth, Maria. *Castle Rackrent*. 1800. *Castle Rackrent and Ennui*. Edited by Marilyn Butler, Penguin, 1992, 65-138.

_____. "Preface." *Castle Rackrent*. 1800. *Castle Rackrent and Ennui*. Edited by Marilyn Butler, Penguin, 1992, pp. 61-63."

Hurd, Richard. *Letters on Chivalry and Romance*. 1762, Edited by Edith J. Morley. Frowde, 1911.

Jeffrey, Francis. Review of *Waverley*, by Walter Scott. *Edinburgh Review*, vol. 24, Nov. 1814, pp. 208-13.

Labbe, Jacqueline M. Introduction. *The Old Manor House*. 1794. Edited by Jacqueline M. Labbe, Broadview, 2002, pp. 9-29.

Lee, Sophia. *The Recess: A Tale of Other Times*. 1785, Edited by April Alliston. U of Kentucky P, 2000.

Leland, Thomas. *Longsword, Earl of Salisbury*. 2 volumes. W. Johnston, 1762. *Eighteenth Century Collections Online*. Gale. York University Library, http://find.galegroup.com.ezproxy.library.yorku.ca/ecco/infomark.do?&source=gale&prodId=ECCO&userGroupName=yorku_main&tabID=T001&docId=CW3309534296&type=multipag

e&contentSet=ECCOArticles&version=1.0&docLevel=FASCIMI LE. Accessed 14 Dec. 2017.

London, April. *The Cambridge Introduction to the Eighteenth-Century Novel.* Cambridge UP, 2012.

Lukács, Georg. *The Historical Novel.* U of Nebraska P, 1983.

Moers, Ellen. *Literary Women.* Women's, 1978.

Radcliffe, Ann. *The Mysteries of Udolpho.* 1794. Edited by Jacqueline Howard. Penguin, 2001.

Reeve, Clara. *The Old English Baron.* 1777. Edited by James Trainer. Oxford UP, 2008.

_____. Preface to the Second Edition. *The Old English Baron.* 1777. Edited by James Trainer. Oxford UP, 2008, pp. 2-4.

Scott, Walter. *Waverley.* 1814. Penguin, 2012.

_____. General Preface. *Waverley.* 1814. Penguin, 2012, pp. 3-18.

Smith, Charlotte. *The Old Manor House.* 1794. Edited by Jacqueline M. Labbe. Broadview, 2002.

Stevens, Anne H. *British Historical Fiction Before Scott.* Palgrave, 2010.

Tompkins, J. M. S. "James White, Esq.: A Forgotten Humourist." *Review of English Studies*, vol. 3, no. 10, 1927, pp. 146-56.

Wallace, Diana. *Female Gothic Histories: Gender, History, and the Gothic.* U of Chicago P, 2013.

Walpole, Horace. *The Castle of Otranto.* 1764. Edited by Nick Groom. Oxford UP, 2014.

_____. Preface to the First Edition. *The Castle of Otranto.* 1764. Edited by Nick Groom. Oxford UP, 2014, pp. 5-8.

_____. Preface to the Second Edition. *The Castle of Otranto.* 1764. Edited by Nick Groom. Oxford UP, 2014, pp. 9-14.

Watt, James. Introduction. *The Old English Baron.* 1777. Edited by James Trainer, Oxford UP, 2008, pp. vii-xxiv.

Made of Legend and History: The Robin Hood Tradition in Young Adult Literature_____

Amanda L. Anderson

The legend of Robin Hood and his band of outlaws exists at the juncture of folklore and history. The persistent belief that Robin Hood was a real person (Holt 40) and the adventures of Robin Hood take place in tales in Sherwood Forest in Nottingham, England, during the reign of King Richard I causes many readers to assume Robin Hood novels are historical fiction. However, while the legend has a certain historical verisimilitude, the retellings often lack the historical and sociocultural authenticity that historical fiction demands. Unlike historical fiction, which seeks to explore a historical social system by presenting plausible events and characters based on fixed evidence, legends, like all folkloric material, operate within a cultural framework that is constantly in flux. Therefore, while it is certainly possible to use the legend of Robin Hood as the inspiration for a work of historical fiction, a novel based on Robin Hood is not necessarily historical fiction.

A skilled author of historical fiction will be able to expose the inherent conflict in social values between the past and the present without imposing modern values upon the setting or characters. As Rebecca Barnhouse notes in *Recasting the Past The Middle Ages in Young Adult Literature*, "when contemporary novelists do include medieval texts within their works, they have a responsibility to give their medieval characters reactions befitting their own times, not ours" (29). In contrast, an author re-visioning folk material must bring to it the values and ideologies of the current generation. Therefore, the legend of Robin Hood, though it may have historical antecedents, also often contains glaring historical contradictions. However, this subjective re-visionary process is essential to the survival of folk material, for it is only through a continual process of renewal that a legend can remain culturally relevant. As a result, re-visioning folkloric material, including retelling legends, does not require the same strict adherence to fact as writing historical fiction. In fact, in the process of re-visioning a legend like Robin Hood many authors either inadvertently or deliberately distort the historical facts surrounding the legend by embellishing, changing, or adapting the facts surrounding the tale to restore and renew it for consumption by the current generation.

The tension between conservation and innovation inherent in retelling legends has resulted in a multitude of adaptations of the Robin Hood tradition ranging from historical fiction to fantasy. Exploring how novelizations of the Robin Hood legend fall onto this spectrum allows one to identify the difference between historical presentations of Robin Hood and presentations of the legend. Furthermore, this enables one to understand how the anachronistic discrepancies function, and why they are important to identify. This chapter aims to examine three adaptations of the Robin Hood legend that show a range from historical fiction to fantasy. Michael Cadnum's *In a Dark Wood* represents historical fiction, Robin McKinley's *The Outlaws of Sherwood* represents a retelling of the legend within the context of folklore, and Kathryn Lasky's *Hawksmaid: The Untold Story of Robin Hood and Maid Marian* represents a fantasy adaptation that is misclassified as historical fiction. Misreading a legend as historical fiction can result in a distorted perception of history that, particularly for young readers, is problematic.

Legend versus Historical Fiction

Distinguishing between a retelling of a legend anchored in history and a work of historical fiction can be quite difficult, as they tend to share similar characteristics. For instance, most retellings of the Robin Hood tradition may meet all Barnhouse's criteria for historical fiction set in the Middle Ages:

- The setting is a recognizable time period and place, although a particular village or town might be invented.
- Historical figures or events may be referred to.
- Christianity probably plays a role in characters' lives.

- Fantastic creatures (unicorns, dwarves, elves) are not characters, although the novel might refer to the belief in such creatures.
- Events do not happen because of magic, although characters might accept magic as real.
- The novel conforms to social and cultural aspects of the medieval period. (85)

One can apply these criteria to most of the novelized adaptations of the Robin Hood legend and see that these novels meet these basic criteria. For instance, most retellings are set in Sherwood Forest during the reign of King Richard I and, as a result, reference historical figures that may appear as characters, like King Richard, Count (or Prince) John, and Queen Eleanor. Furthermore, Christianity frequently plays a notable part in the characters' lives, either through Friar Tuck's presence, or through Robin's or another's faith, particularly in the Virgin Mary. Finally, the retellings conform to the basic social and cultural aspects of the Middle Ages, at least on the surface (Barnhouse 85). The one quality that Barnhouse establishes as a criterion for distinguishing historical novels from fantasy novels that is not explicitly met is the role of magic in these retellings. While there are no fantastic creatures as characters and fantastic magic of the fairy-tale variety rarely occurs, a common theme in retellings of the Robin Hood legend is a supernatural affinity for nature. However, this nature affinity is generally not declared magic as such, and it is left to the reader to decide if it is within the realm of possibility. Therefore, based solely on these criteria, most Robin Hood adaptations qualify as historical fiction. This would be a disservice to the Robin Hood tradition and to historical fiction, for such classification leads to a distortion of the past that cannot be fully explained by an author's lack of rigor or understanding of the period.

So, how does one differentiate a legend from history? The difference is not in the subject matter or in the setting; it is in the author's approach to telling the story. In his study of the Robin Hood tradition, J. C. Holt says that the legend of Robin Hood is always what society needed to be at that time. Adaptations that work to reinvent a legend like Robin Hood for the current age do so often by subverting the expectations of the reader by violating the standard model of the legend. However, by exploring these so-called violations of the traditional legend it becomes clear that those tales that defamiliarize the story have the greatest potential both to support and to subvert the ideology of the producing culture while simultaneously ensuring the legend's survival.

As one seeks to understand the social values portrayed in Robin Hood adaptations, it is most illuminating to examine how an author constructs the characters, as they often clearly reflect, parrot, and convey cultural mores. Characters from folklore and legend provide a unique opportunity to analyze this effect. The legendary character is simultaneously a blank canvas upon which the writer can superimpose his or her mores and values, but is also instantly recognizable by the reader as uniquely present in the narrative fabric of culture. Accordingly, the characters within the Robin Hood legend are familiar within the context of the story and its historical setting. They possess what the current readership perceives as "truths," to use Robin McKinley's term (281), which are certain characteristics of the tale fixed within the producing culture's imagination.

These characters are so familiar that readers may mistakenly assume that the characters from legends like Robin Hood reflect the beliefs, values, and social customs of the actual Middle Ages, even when the characters flagrantly contradict known facts about the time. This makes distinguishing between characters in historical fiction and legend important. Retellings of the Robin Hood story that meet the needs of the society that produced it may do so at the expense of historical accuracy, and so may contain historic anachronisms to favor the social and cultural needs that the author perceives. Such retellings serve the folkloric tradition rather than serving a historical purpose. Therefore, to identify a retelling of Robin Hood as historical fiction, legend, or fantasy one must use an interdisciplinary lens that considers history, culture, and the audience.

In a Dark Wood

If one imagines a scale for adaptations of the Robin Hood legend with pure historical fiction on the left and fantasy on the right, Michael Cadnum's *In a Dark Wood* would be as close to the left as possible. One of the remarkable aspects of Cadnum's *In a Dark Wood* is that while it draws from medieval source materials, and therefore follows the traditional narrative arc of Robin Hood, the novel focuses not on the famed outlaw, but on Geoffrey, the Sheriff of Nottingham. Cadnum's portrayal of the sheriff depicts him very clearly as a product of both his culture and his time: "He knew that a man had no choice in what he did. His father had chosen his wife, and his father had chosen his profession. The type of clothes he wore, the sort of thoughts he had were all prescribed, and happily so. There were no uncertainties" (35). Cadnum's characterization, therefore, reflects the inevitability of Geoffrey's character and choices.

By telling the tale from Geoffrey's point of view, *In a Dark Wood* provides a historically nuanced representation of Middle Ages while drawing from the Robin Hood tradition. To create such a comprehensive portrait of the Middle Ages, Cadnum draws from medieval literature, including some of the source material for the legend, but also from more widely read texts, such as Chaucer's *Canterbury Tales* (Barnhouse 38-39). Cadnum provides linguistic details to show how language was evolving around the shifting notions of culture and class. Additionally, as Barnhouse observes, Cadnum's frequent use of literary allusion helps to create a both richly detailed and convincing portrait of medieval times (41). Therefore, even though Cadnum draws from the Robin Hood tradition, his novel conveys the realities of life in the Middle Ages in a way that honors and illuminates the past.

Another notable difference between *In a Dark Wood* and other adaptations of the Robin Hood tradition is that Cadnum's novel lacks any reference to Maid Marian. Cadnum's choice to exclude Robin's famed love interest reflects his adherence to the medieval source material. However, her absence from both medieval texts and Cadnum's novel speaks to the lack of opportunities and limited value placed upon women during the medieval period. Consequently, the medieval source material lacked strong female figures like Marian (Holt 37). Marian's absence, and indeed the lack of any lover for Robin Hood, is also indicative of the deep-seated misogyny that was common in the medieval period. Barnhouse asserts most convincingly that "Medieval anti-feminism…is an undeniable fact, no matter how unpalatable it is to us" (32). In fact, there are few women of consequence in Cadnum's novel at all. And while this may not sit well with modern readers, it is a statement about how medieval English society viewed women. Therefore, the few women who do appear in Cadnum's novel, such as the abbess and the sheriff's wife, Eleanor, deserve careful analysis. These women also reflect the misogynistic attitudes that were commonplace in the Middle Ages.

Cadnum's abbess, the lady Emily, is the embodiment of medieval hypocritical gender construction. As the abbess, she can be seen as a Madonna figure, but as Geoffrey's illicit lover, she is also a woman of sin. Furthermore, Cadnum's abbess, like Chaucer's prioress, is interested not in the love of God or of Christ but in carnal desires: "He [the sheriff] would come to her…Love did, it was true, conquer all" (32). This is in keeping with much of the misogynistic attitudes of women for, as Barnhouse notes, women were seen as more susceptible to sin and even responsible for it (32). Cadnum makes it clear that not only is their relationship illicit, it was clearly sin: "It was another blot upon his soul" (32). Barnhouse provides an excellent analysis of the abbess in which she draws a parallel between Cadnum's description of the abbess and Chaucer's description of the prioress (39), revealing how closely Cadnum's character resembles Chaucer's character. Drawing upon Chaucer's medieval text allows Cadnum to create a character using medieval material. The abbess feels realistic in her construction because she draws so heavily upon source material.

Eleanor shares many qualities with the abbess. She too takes illicit lovers (Cadnum 35). However, what is revealing about Cadnum's description of the sherriff's wife's intelligence, particularly her ability to produce original thoughts, is quite revealing: "she

[Eleanor] had not been trained to have original thoughts" (41). Eleanor is a reflection of the medieval belief of women's intellectual inferiority. This is in alignment with the medieval construction of female intelligence (Barnhouse 32). Consequently, while Cadnum's novel lacks a strong female protagonist, the lack of prominent or strong women accurately represents the medieval attitude toward women.

Cadnum's novel is not without bias. For example, even though people in the medieval period had misgivings about the written word, and, according to Barnhouse would privilege oral accounts over written documentation (2), our modern bias toward literacy often supersedes historical prejudices. In fact, Barnhouse writes, "Our bias in favor of literacy is so strong that we often overlook or look down upon other ways of learning, ways that can be equally valid" (1). This is true in Cadnum's construction of the Middle Ages, for not only is Geoffrey highly educated, he trusts and believes in written documentation to a point that reflects a more modern sensibility: "Geoffrey felt at home with lists of numbers, with calculations like the ones in his hand...He could imagine the activities of the world round him from lists of figures" (42). Yet Cadnum provides this bias without overtly contradicting the historical realities of the medieval period. Based on Geoffrey's social class and occupation his reliance on literacy fits within the social structure of the Middle Ages.

In a Dark Wood can be considered true historical fiction based on both content and construction of the period. The characters depicted in Cadnum's novel are not necessarily likable by modern standards, but they do provide an interesting and revealing insight into life in the Middle Ages. What Cadnum is able to do is "to give their medieval characters reactions befitting their own times, not ours" (Barnhouse 29). His novel does not distort gender roles or expectations by presenting a woman with equal status to Robin Hood. It does not distort the medieval concepts of love and romance although it does deal with the issue of marriage in contrast to the issue of lust.

The Outlaws of Sherwood

In contrast to Cadnum's use of historical detail and literary allusion to enhance the Robin Hood story, author Robin McKinley's presentation of the Robin Hood legend reflects the effects of folklore in the oral tradition, which enriches and contextualizes the reader's understanding of the legend and its cultural evolution. Consequently, McKinley creates only a superficial medieval setting that provides the reader with a limited context to understand the culture or experiences of life in medieval times. However, as McKinley makes it clear that she is working with the folkloric material rather than with the historical material, the novel effectively represents the cultural, if not historical significance of the Robin Hood legend. Within the novel, the figure of Robin Hood is perceived as "more than man" (McKinley 182). Furthermore, it is the gravitas of the persona that allows the outlaws the freedom to act: "Part of why we've survived this long is because the foresters themselves half-believe this elemental stuff—and half want to, as it excuses them" (McKinley 183). Consequently, McKinley's novel is self-aware of how legend serves a cultural purpose.

Furthermore, McKinley identifies her own inspiration and bias in creating the story. She acknowledges Howard Pyle's influence and then extrapolates that for her: "There were several things that simply were the *truth* about Robin Hood." (281, italics in the original). These truths remain even when research reveals their historical inaccuracy or that they contradict each other. However, so long as the author remains within the framework of "truths," she can adjust the nonfixed characteristics of the characters to meet perceived cultural needs.

McKinley's presentation of the Robin Hood legend is then a study of contradictions. The truths that McKinley identifies do not fix the story, but rather provide her a framework to re-vision the legend. This process of re-vision is essential to the survival of legends like Robin Hood, for, as Betsy Hearne notes, "folklore is not frozen in the past but either survives in a changing context or lives not at all…" (210). Consequently, within the framework of the Robin Hood legend, McKinley recreates the story for a late twentieth-century young adult audience, and in doing so recreates the ideologies present within the tale.

In McKinley's adaptation, it is Marian who faces the sheriff's challenge and wins the prize of the archery contest. Marian's actions contribute to Robin Hood's reputation, for, when pressed, Little John tells those who saw the contest that "The shooting you saw today was Robin Hood's shooting" (203). Consequently, Marian, then, becomes the archer facet of the Robin Hood figure, while Robin himself is relegated to a role as the leader and organizer of the outlaw band. This division of Robin Hood reveals how perceived truth is subjective and leads to an escalation of the legendary figure.

However, while dividing the figure of Robin honors the folkloric archetypes that created a legendary figure, it also paints a distorted picture of the medieval period, and for this reason *The Outlaws of Sherwood* is not historical fiction. Within the context of folklore and legend, the gender distortion in the Robin Hood legend seems innocuous, even justified, as the legends themselves are not fixed historical points and are, therefore, open to interpretation and revision. However, if one mistakes this text for historical fiction, it could drastically distorted one's perception of medieval gender norms and accepted gender roles. McKinley's adaptation depicts the male Robin Hood as the less athletic and more emotional of the two halves that make up the legend. It also portrays Marian as outside of the cultural conventions of medieval society that were nearly universally imposed upon women in Europe during the medieval period.

Despite Marian's freedom from gender norms, *The Outlaws of Sherwood* does reflect the misogyny inherent in the medieval mindset. Throughout the story several female characters find themselves victimized by the patriarchal system, either by unwanted arranged marriages or by a lack of opportunity to marry. Moreover, while there are women in the band of outlaws, Little John openly objects to them and with only a few exceptions, Robin Hood relocates those women back into society. Cecily confronts Robin and Little John, asking them directly, "Would you so freely have taught me to use a staff, and to throw larger opponents, and to leap out of

Critical Insights

trees upon them, had I been Cecily—Lady Cecily of Norwell...?" (McKinley 169). As response to her confrontation Robin says: "I cannot answer that honestly...there is some truth to what you say" (171). The male outlaws are thus forced to acknowledge their own sexist assumptions.

While medieval patriarchal limitations are imposed upon the other female characters of *The Outlaws of Sherwood*, Marian, who is "equal to anything the boys might do, equal as if she gave it no thought" (McKinley 203), not only defies but transcends gender expectations, which enables her to enlighten her male comrades. In "Transgressive Transformations: Representations of Maid Marian in Robin Hood Retellings," Lorinda B. Cohoon convincingly argues that Maid Marian is herself a transgressive site, where authors can play with and expose social and cultural inequalities (209). Consequently, Marian's transgressions allow her to function outside of social conventions, but also to educate both men and women about gender equality. She taught Little John "that a lady could shoot straight, or not mind the calluses on her fingers—or learn to stand guard duty, and handle a staff" (178). She also enlightens King Richard, arguably the embodiment of medieval patriarchy. Upon their first meeting, Richard seeks to reassert Marian within patriarchal society by calling her "breaker of your proper obedience to your lord your father..." and demanding her sworn fealty (269). Still, he does not force her to conform to patriarchal gender conventions.

While King Richard recognizes Marian's defiance of the law and gender expectations, instead of penalizing her, he offers to make Marian the new sheriff. He acknowledges the difficulty this poses, while also acknowledging that there is a plausible way within the medieval social system to appoint Marian as sheriff, "if I ordered you married to the present sheriff, had him quietly assassinated, and ignored the resulting situation while his relict took capably over" (McKinley 276). However, Richard rejects this plausible scheme, because it would give Marian a "distaste for the job" (277). Consequently, rather than insert Marian back into the patriarchal order, Richard proposes reinventing the social system to accommodate a strong woman.

Ultimately, McKinley's adaptation of the Robin Hood legend takes on a modern feminist bias that is a clear distortion of the medieval historical period and in so doing recreates the legend for a new generation of readers. Both J. C. Holt and Betsy Hearne agree that shifts in social values are essential to the survival of folkloric material (Hearne 214, Holt 7). So, McKinley's take on the Robin Hood legend undermines the patriarchal conception of woman and replaces it with a new ideal. While she does not present an accurate portrayal of the medieval period, her retelling accurately reflects the cultural truths within the Robin Hood legend.

Hawksmaid

Kathryn Lasky's *Hawksmaid: The Untold Story of Robin Hood and Maid Marian* reinvents the traditional narrative arc of the Robin Hood legend, and, though it is treated like historical fiction, it is not. The novel chronicles the adventures of Matilda "Matty / Marian" Fitzwilliam, a noble girl whose family fall victim to Prince John's tyranny. While Lasky sets her novel in Sherwood during the reign of King Richard I, she only loosely addresses the realities of the late twelfth century. Consequently, the novel does not offer the reader a faithful glimpse into the past. Furthermore, while many of the Robin Hood legends present a strong affinity with nature, this affinity is not magical. However, in Lasky's *Hawksmaid*, Matty grows increasingly close to her birds of prey. Eventually she learns to speak to them as if they were human, until finally she shares a body with her hawks. Her supernatural abilities are not addressed or explained outside of the context of her bond with the birds. Therefore, while it draws loosely from the Robin Hood legend, Lasky's retelling could more accurately be described as fantasy.

Hawksmaid is problematic because while presenting a distorted view of the Middle Ages, it also includes "proof" provided by the author and publisher that justify or gloss over the historical inaccuracies in the novel. One of the most troublesome addenda to the novel is the epilogue, which reads:

More than four hundred years later a book was found in the ruins of an ancient castle's library, a book from medieval times. The title was *The Art of Falconry: A Complete Guide to the Principles and Practices of Hawking*. It is thought to be the first book ever written on hawking by a woman. The author's name was Marian Greenleaf. The book was dedicated 'To Moss, Marigold, Ulysses, Lyra, Morgana, my greatest teachers, and to Robin, my greatest love.' (283)

The epilogue sounds probable, and because the novel is intended for young audiences, it is unfair to assume a young reader could recognize that the title and the dedication follow modern rather than medieval writing styles and formats. Thus the epilogue gives historical legitimacy to *Hawksmaid*.

In addition to the problematic epilogue, the novel also includes seven pseudoeducational inserts: a glossary, notes (supposedly "taken by Matty Fitzwalter daughter of Lord William Fitzwalter during her recovery in the winter of 1187"), "Author's note," "A Q&A with Kathryn Lasky," "The Real Sherwood Forest," and "The Life of a Young Noble Girl." The superabundance of educational documents, which follow the model popularized by the American Girl Doll series, function in two ways: first they offer legitimacy to the novel as historical fiction, and second, they gloss over many of the realities of the medieval period and present an optimistic and oversimplified presentation of the past (Hade 158). This presentation as historical fiction is extremely problematic because the anachronisms in the novel are too numerous to catalog, even though Lasky claims to have done "an immense amount of research" particularly "about medieval life in England at that time." (Q&A 3). Despite Lasky's research there are errors in her presentation of the period, including the construction of childhood, the inequalities in gender roles, and education, specifically literacy.

The supplemental documents attempt to explain away these anachronisms and frame *Hawksmaid* as historical fiction. For instance, in "The Life of a Young Noble Girl," Lasky's twenty-first-century bias regarding the rearing of children, particularly girls, is justified: "In addition to her ability to communicate with her father's birds, Matty grew up in very special circumstances. When her father lost all his wealth, she was able to avoid some of the harsher realities that came with being a young noble woman in the Middle Ages" (6). This explanation does not accurately represent the period, for it implies that the patriarchal construction of gender only applied to wealthy noblewomen. This, of course, is a gross inaccuracy. As Barnhouse points out, "Women [in the Middle Ages] did not enjoy the same status men did" (32). Consequently, women and girls were severely limited in their employment opportunities, education, and social standing. To suggest otherwise would be to distort history.

While "The Life of a Young Noble Girl" does acknowledge that girls and boys were educated differently, it strongly implies that girls were commonly taught to read and write Latin alongside their sewing and dancing (Lasky 6). This, however, perpetuates the fallacy that literacy in the Middle Ages was common and taught to both girls and boys in equal measure (Barnhouse 1-2). To further perpetuate this misconception several of Matty's "notes" on falconry are included at the end of the novel. Especially in light of her reversal of fortune, it would have been far more likely for Matty to memorize these details than to take notes like a modern school child would (Barnhouse 2). Further muddying Lasky's presentation of literacy in the Middle Ages is the fact that the village boys, Much, Will, and Robert / Robin can comment on standardized spelling: "'Scarlet—one T please. Never fancied that second one hanging off the end'" (136). Finally, all of the children are literate enough to encode messages and then translate the codes back into English (Lasky 156). Engaging in even the simplest level of code work suggests a level of literacy that would have been extremely unlikely for children during the Middle Ages.

The problem is not that Lasky deviates from the conventions of the legend or that she introduces a supernatural element into the story. In fact, historical distortion is not a result of the fantastic elements but of the mundane details. The problem is that *Hawksmaid* is clearly packaged, reviewed, and treated as historical fiction. However, even ignoring the fantastic aspects of the novel, which even young readers are likely to realize are not factual, *Hawksmaid* cannot be considered historical fiction. In attempting to promote this novel as a work of historical fiction, the author and publishers "underestimate their readers' ability to comprehend and learn from such differences, condescending therefore to both the past and the present" (Barnhouse 10). No amount of supplementary material can transform fantasy into historical fiction.

Conclusion

While the legend of Robin Hood is anchored in the past, in retelling the legend authors may present a romanticized and selective representation of that period. Therefore, many Robin Hood retellings serve as a vehicle of social and cultural insight into their producing period rather than into the historical period. Furthermore, using any Robin Hood adaptation as an educational tool without fully understanding its purpose would be to misuse it. As J. C. Holt writes, "Legend is fact of a very peculiar kind. At one and the same time it illuminates and distorts" (190). This distortion of history can be minimized if readers recognize that authorial changes to the characters, symbols, and motifs of the Robin Hood legend functionally create a new story within the confines of the old. As the legend of Robin Hood is made new again and again, it forces readers to refresh themselves with the traditional models, preserving the precursor text in the cultural imagination and capturing the attention of a new readership. However, without careful construction and attention to historical detail, such retellings will not accurately reflect the historical period. Therefore, misidentifying adaptations of Robin Hood as historical fiction is not just a matter of legitimizing fiction as fact, it distorts the concept of history for readers, particularly young readers. Rather than help readers learn about the past, it misinforms and panders to the way they may wish things were.

Works Cited

Barnhouse, Rebecca. *Recasting the Past: The Middle Ages in Young Adult Literature*. Boynton/Cook, 2000.

Brown, Joanne, and Nancy St. Clair. *The Distant Mirror: Reflections on Young Adult Historical Fiction*. Scarecrow, 2006.

Cadnum, Michael. *In a Dark Wood: A Novel*. 1998. Puffin, 1999.

Cohoon, Lorinda B. "Transgressive Transformations: Representations of Maid Marian in Robin Hood Retellings." *The Lion and the Unicorn*. vol. 31, no. 3, Sept. 2007, pp. 209-31.

Hade, Daniel. "Lies My Children's Books Taught Me." *Voices of the Other: Children's Literature and the Postcolonial Context*. Edited by Roderick McGillis. Routledge, 2000, pp. 153-64.

Hearne, Betsy. "Folklore in Children's Literature: Contents and Discontents." *Handbook of Research on Children's and Young Adult Literature*. Edited by Shelby Anne Wolf et al. Routledge, 2011, pp. 209–23.

Holt, J. C. *Robin Hood*. London, Thames & Hudson, 1982.

Lasky, Kathryn. *Hawksmaid: The Untold Story of Robin Hood and Maid Marian*. Harper, 2011.

McKinley, Robin. *The Outlaws of Sherwood*. 1988. Firebird, 2003.

Through a Glass, Lightly: Translating History for Young Readers

Chris Crowe

I am neither a scholar of history nor a translator, but I am a passionate reader and supporter of books for young readers, and I write books, usually books about some aspect of American history, for children and young adults. So although I have a real interest in history, and have, years ago, assisted in the translation of a few projects, I can't claim any sort of theoretical or scholarly background in either area.

My chapter derives its title from a verse in the New Testament: "For now we see through a glass, darkly" (1 Cor. 13.13); The apostle Paul suggested that, in time and changed circumstances, we will come to see things more clearly than we do now. Paul's use of "glass" suggests a lens, a filter of some kind that partially obscures a clearer vision, that prevents the viewer from seeing things as they truly are. When I think about this particular verse, I'm reminded of how material for children—not only books, but most forms of media—are presented through a filtered glass, a lens that blocks or modifies content that might not be suitable for a child. Though this filtering—or translation—process can be difficult and time-consuming, it's not necessarily unpleasant work. Elizabeth George Speare, historical novelist and two-time winner of the Newbery Medal, once said, "It is a very exciting thing to use the magical magnifying glass that is called historical research—a glass with the added perspective of Time" (267).

Coincidentally, Paul's first epistle to the Corinthians contains at least two other well-known references that allude to suitability of reading material for children, and the two I'm thinking of—"When I was a child, I spake as a child, I understood as a child, I thought as a child: but when I became a man, I put away childish things" (1 Cor. 13.11) and "I have fed you with milk, and not with meat: for hitherto ye were not able to bear it" (1 Cor. 3.2) relate better to a general discussion of children's literature than they do to a discussion of how authors translate—or mediate—history for young readers. But more on those biblical metaphors later.

The most dedicated historical researcher I know shares my interest in the Emmett Till case, a notorious lynching/murder in the state of Mississippi in 1955 that triggered the modern civil rights movement. My friend is the world's leading authority on this case, and for nearly two decades, he worked on the most comprehensive account of the case ever written. He knows my two teen books on the case, and our mutual interest in this historical moment has led to many conversations over the years. Five years ago, he mentioned that he was going to be in town and asked if he could swing by my house to drop off a copy of his manuscript; he wanted me to read it and offer feedback, and late one Saturday evening in July, he showed up at my door. I invited him in, and we sat around for an hour discussing his project and his potential leads with publishers and agents.

When I asked about the manuscript, he pulled out a prodigious stack of papers, nearly 700 pages, and dropped it on my table. My colleague is a historical genius but overly humble, and when I looked, stunned, at the stack of paper, he misread my reaction and quickly apologized that this represented only the first nine chapters of his book. He still had five more to write, but would I mind giving these a read and offering my most candid feedback on what he had produced so far?

I consider myself far more interested in the Emmett Till case than the great majority of Americans, but that pile of pages intimidated me. It took me several days to start reading because the manuscript gave every appearance of being, quite literally, an exhaustive treatment of the case. Even before turning one page, I knew what my primary feedback would be: his project needed to be distilled, translated for a more general audience.

Experienced historians and historical novelists know that a great deal of their research will not survive to a manuscript's final form. The late Ray Bradbury pointed out that all writers, not just historians, must learn to sort the wheat from the chaff in their own writing: "[The writer's] greatest art," he said, "will often be what he does not say, what he leaves out . . ." (145), but this ability to know what to keep and what to cut is especially important in historical fiction and nonfiction. Speare explained that, for her, writing a historical novel was like putting together a Chinese puzzle that has many beautiful pieces that can be assembled into a number of interesting designs. But, she said,

> some of the pieces, lovely and intriguing as they appear, must be discarded, and this can be just as difficult and heart-rending as having to leave one child at home from a picnic. Not only must every piece that is chosen be shaped to fit the final design, but to be most effective it must also be colored to blend with every other piece. (269)

The UK's grande dame of children's historical fiction, Rosemary Sutcliff, echoed this sentiment. She said that authors, including those like my Emmett Till friend, must be careful not to cram all their historical research into their stories. "Nothing is worse for a book than to be clotted with too much and too obvious knowledge, which will stick out like the lumps in a badly made porridge" (qtd. in Martin 103).

The sorting and sifting of historical information is a task that *all* historical writers must embrace, but writing and translating history for children requires that history passes through two lenses, or filters, before it reaches its intended audience. The first is the filter applied by authors or historians when they collect historical information to compose a history. Most scholars and writers would agree with critic Anne Scott MacLeod when she says that "Writers of history select, describe, and explain historical evidence—and thereby interpret" (26). No history account can be all-inclusive— if someone were to produce such a record, the information load would be overwhelming. Critic Marc Aronson sees the necessary winnowing of historical information as a kind of translation. "Real events take place, and then human beings interpret them. History is both the effort to recover those events, and the play of mind as we try to make sense of ourselves through the semireflective mirror of the past" (108). It's the job of historians and historical novelists to study historical records and select the relevant details to use to create their version of a historical event; after reviewing all the evidence, they must sift through their material and present their best interpretation of a particular historical figure or moment.

A similar sort of translation occurs in books written for children. Though many established writers for children and teens (Madeleine L'Engle, Katherine Paterson, E. B. White, C. S. Lewis, P. L. Travers, to name a few) deny that they are conscious of audience as they write, nearly all who write for young people, whether or not they admit it, make conscious or unconscious moves to accommodate their readers. The American poet Emily Dickinson probably wasn't thinking about writing for children when she recommended "Tell all the Truth but tell it slant," but she apparently knew that there are times when even adults are not ready to hear "all the Truth" at once because she concluded her poem with the observation that "The Truth must dazzle gradually/Or every man be blind—." If truth must be "slanted" in order for adults to digest it, it must be slanted even more for young readers.

As an author of books for adults and children, Sutcliff admitted that "there are problems in writing officially for children, certain subjects that have to be treated carefully even when they are not altogether tabu, for the sake of publishers, librarians and parents rather than for the children themselves" (qtd. in Townsend 201). This consideration of audience has less to do with a child's intelligence than it does with their maturity and experience. I agree with Jill Paton Walsh that "Children are not less intelligent than adults, or less serious, or less sensitive, or less disposed to laugh or cry. But they do unquestionably stand in a different relationship to the flow of time" ("The Lords of Time" 111). It is that different relationship to the flow of time that requires children's literature in general and children's historical fiction and nonfiction in particular, to be mediated—or translated—for its readers. Children's literature advocate Margery Fisher also felt this way, saying that people who write for children "must be aware of the age and aptitude of his readers in a broad way, just as a teacher or a parent selecting books must take into account in a relative way a writer's choice of vocabulary and of facts, as well as the illustration and design of a book as a whole" (qtd. in Haviland 313).

Unlike those who write for adults, children's authors share a sense of responsibility to their audience, something akin to a physician's pledge, "First do no harm." In his essay, "On Three Ways of Writing for Children," C. S. Lewis stated that he did consider content when writing children's books, and though he was committed to truth and realism, he did not want to add to any child's trauma: "I suffered too much," he said, "from night-fears myself in childhood to undervalue this objection. I would not wish to heat the fires of that private hell for any child" (25). A quick review of some of today's YA novels might suggest that times have changed; some popular books seem explicitly designed to instill night-fears in their readers, but after all is said and done, most people who write for children and teenagers strive to inspire hope in their readers. Katherine Paterson has said many times that she will not write a book that ends in despair. "I cannot, will not, withhold from my young readers the harsh realities of human hunger and suffering and loss, but neither will I neglect to plant that stubborn seed of hope that has enabled our race to outlast wars and famines and the destruction of death" (48-49). This commitment to a children's audience requires that authors filter their work for their readers.

Historical fiction and nonfiction undergoes a second layer of translation. As with all historical writing, "For both the novelist and the historian, meaning lies not in a chain of events themselves but in each writer's interpretation of those events" (Brown and St Clair 33). That interpretation, that translation of historical sources and information into book form requires a winnowing similar to the audience considerations that all children's authors make, but interpreting history can be a delicate operation. Walsh once warned that sugarcoating the crusts of history can harm readers just as much as brutalizing them might ("The Lords of Time" 110). A noted historian put it this way: "A good historical novelist has the same obligation as a good historian: to convey a truthful history, not to perpetuate pretty myths" (Thom 15). Authors of children's historical fiction and nonfiction therefore have the double duty of first translating the historical information and then filtering it again to make it suitable for their readers.

Children's novelist Hester Burton knows that children are vulnerable to some of the terrifying aspects of history. She wants her books to be accurate, but she doesn't want to scar sensitive young readers. She realizes that historical novelists must find ways to present history authentically *and* interestingly to their readers while at the same time leaving on a light, however dim, to glow in the darker shadows of the past. Mary Volmer framed this challenge as a question: "How do we navigate, and then translate, the past's lost and often foreign landscape in a way that engages readers and conveys a sense of immediacy and authenticity?"

Another challenge facing children's historical authors is their readers' lack of historical background knowledge, which may require writers to embed more historical context than adult authors might. Burton said that she strives "to give the historical setting of one's story and to impart the necessary historical facts without appearing to teach or preach and—what is more important— without slowing up the pace of the narrative" (qtd. in Haviland 303). Blending historical fact with fiction can be difficult because fiction sometimes has its own head, a head that resists being reined in by the constraints of what really happened. Authors deal with this conflict in various ways, and most insist on holding as close as possible to what is known to be true historically, but even writers as talented as Rosemary Sutcliff sometimes sacrifice a bit of history for a better story. In a 1986 interview, she confessed that "if it comes down to a crunch, I will choose a good story over absolute historical accuracy" (qtd. in Thompson). While noted historian David M. Kennedy may feel queasy about a novelist sacrificing historical accuracy, he himself admitted that good history must also be a good story, a story that relies on characterization, conflict, change, and catharsis as much as fiction might (465).

Most historical novelists would agree with Walsh's goal, "to enshrine in the heart of the novel, in the very center of its being, a truly historical insight" ("History is Fiction" 19), and that can be accomplished by holding fast to the historical record while also using historical detail to create a readable story. Like historians, historical novelists sometimes deal with an incomplete record, but novelists are fortunate in that they're able to conjure up likely material to fill those gaps. Walsh had a personal experience that helped her frame an apt metaphor for this filling-in process. After seeing some restored ancient frescoes in Crete, she realized that only tiny bits and fragments remained from the original, but using *all* those fragments and his own artistic research and insight, the restorer had recreated a beautiful, full fresco ("History is Fiction" 22). Walsh likened that process to her own work as a historical novelist: using bits of history as much as possible, but using her own imagination, based on her historical research, to fill in gaps. In discussing her historical novel *Alias Grace* (1996), Margaret Atwood articulated a similar approach:

> I devised the following set of guidelines for myself: when there was solid fact, I could not alter it . . . Also, every major element in the book had to be suggested by something in the writing about Grace and her times, however dubious such writing might be; but in the parts left unexplained—the gaps left unfilled—I was free to invent. (1515)

Unfortunately, some sloppy novelists rely on history solely to provide setting, character, or costume. They care little for historical accuracy and produce what Walsh called "costume novels" ("History is Fiction" 19), where little more than the historical setting—clothing, transportation, customs—is important to the novel.

Another concern for the writer of historical fiction or nonfiction is finding a way to avoid using a contemporary or politically correct lens to view the past. Historians have labeled this problem *presentism*, and it has drawn the attention of historians and literary critics. Walsh considered it unethical to "frame the past and soften it, to show it as somehow appearing to characters in the present." Such an approach, she said, "is simply to fail to confront its horror" ("The Lords of Time" 110). Writing more recently, MacLeod complained about some historical YA novels that were tainted by presentism. The problem, she said, is that these novels "evade the common realities of the societies they write about. . . . They set aside the social mores of the past as though they were minor afflictions, small obstacles—and painless—for an independent mind to overcome" (31). Young readers are especially susceptible to presentism, and well written historical fiction and nonfiction can help them see the past and understand it as authentically as possible.

As a writer, I'm keenly aware of these issues. I often talk with my students about how much of children's and teen literature functions as "milk before meat" for young readers, providing them suitably nourishing reading to sustain them until they're mature enough to digest the tougher stuff of adult books. We also discuss the nature of young readers who cannot help but "speak as a child, understand as a child, and think as a child." These classroom discussions and my own reading of children's literature and criticism influence me as a writer.

So I've been thinking a lot about the best metaphor to describe how I translate history for my readers. Because most of my books deal with the civil rights movement, I've had to work with some horrible historical events, and I've felt obligated to present that ugliness as accurately and contextually as I can—without inflicting night-fear inducing trauma. Some metaphors that may be apt comparisons for the translation tools I use include funneling, sifting, trimming, filtering, mining, smelting and refining, and distilling.

As a researcher and writer, I sometimes serve as a funnel for my readers, scooping up a wide swath of history and narrowing it through a small spout suitable for their reading. Or sometimes I sift through primary documents and varying, sometimes oppositional, historical accounts to create an accurate account for my readers. And sometimes, after considering my readers' background knowledge, I've trimmed the scope of my historical narrative. For example, when I first outlined my nonfiction book, *Getting Away with Murder: The True Story of the Emmett Till Case,* I wanted to start at the beginning, to show that the murder of Emmett Till would not have happened if European settlers hadn't brought slavery with them to the New World. After considering my audience, however, I realized they wouldn't want to wade through an account of three centuries of abuse and racial discrimination before getting to the story of Emmett Till. So, instead of starting the book in 1619, I began in 1954. It was a wise move.

Many times in the writing process, I serve as a filter of history. My most recent historical novel, *Death Coming Up the Hill* (2015), is set in 1968, a tumultuous year politically and socially. Even before starting the book, I knew it would be impossible to present everything that happened in 1968, so I chose instead to present events and attitudes that today's teen reader would understand and relate to. That meant that many things that took place that year appear faintly in the background while the real-life and complex trauma of the Vietnam War dominates the story.

As a historical researcher, I sometimes feel like a gold miner digging through the wide vein of history, looking for that thin, shiny golden glint that signals treasure in otherwise worthless rock, or, to move the metaphor closer to my home in the American West, I feel like a prospector panning for gold, looking for sparkling nuggets sliding through the sluice of history. My goal is to find nuggets that have been overlooked by other historians and writers, golden stories that beg to be told. My prospecting has led me to the story, which I've yet to finish, of William Mariner, an eighteenth-century teen who sailed on a British privateer; to Emmett Till, a lynch victim whose death triggered America's civil rights movement; and to Larry Doby, an African-American professional baseball player who, as much as Jackie Robinson, changed the color of Major League baseball.

My last set of metaphors is mixed. The first pair, smelting and refining, follows the mining imagery I've just explained. Smelting uses heating and melting to extract metal from its ore. Once extracted, that metal must be refined, processed in such a way as to remove impurities and unwanted elements. This suggests that my work in history is related to Bradbury's notion that the most important thing a writer does is to decide what to leave out. History overflows with information, interesting and boring, relevant and irrelevant, and my job as an author is to smelt and refine that information into a narrative that shines like a precious metal.

The process of distillation is nearly identical to that of smelting and refining, but is typically applied to liquids, not ores or metals, and while smelting and refining result in a more valuable product, distillation results in a more potent product. A good example of the refining, distilling process resulting in a short but powerful historical story is Deborah Wiles's children's book, *Freedom Summer*. Historical picture books are extremely difficult to write because they must tell a full story in fewer than 1,000 words. Wiles successfully translated a big historical moment into a story appropriate for elementary readers.

In the front matter, Wiles provides essential background information by using a foreword and "A Note about the Text" to present an overview of American racism and the stranglehold Jim Crow had on Southern states. She also explains the impact the freedom workers had on voter registration, especially in Mississippi, and the powerful positive and negative reactions people had to the Civil Rights Act of 1964.

The text itself, though, filters out all that historical detail and context and simply tells the story of two young boys, one white, one black, and the fun they've planned for the summer of 1964. Joe, the white boy, explains why they swim in the creek instead of the town pool:

> "[John Henry] doesn't swim in the town pool with me. He's not allowed." (n. pag.)

A few pages later, Joe relates another Jim Crow detail:

> "John Henry doesn't come with me through the front door of Mr. Mason's General Store. He's not allowed" (n. pag.).

Significantly, the only direct reference to the Civil Rights Act of 1964 comes during a dinner at Joe's house.

> "Daddy stirs his ice tea and says, 'The town pool opens tomorrow to everyone under the sun, no matter what color.'
> "'That's the new law,' Mama tells me" (n. pag.).

Mama goes on to explain how the new law will change things: "It's the way it's going to be now—Everybody Together—lunch counters, rest rooms, drinking fountains, too" (n. pag.). Hearing that, Joe assumes that the change will be simple and immediate: Jim Crow rules will disappear, making John Henry allowed wherever he wants to be allowed.

The climax of the story comes the next morning when Joe and John Henry, filled with anticipation, rush to the town pool only to arrive and see it being filled in with asphalt. The simplicity of the moment, the boys' expectations dashed because of senseless Jim Crow resistance, conveys the frustration and humiliation that was ever-present in the South, and despite providing very little historical context, the story communicates to young readers a very personal sense of what racial discrimination looked and felt like.

In her Newbery Medal-winning novel, *Roll of Thunder, Hear My Cry,* Mildred D. Taylor used a different sort of lens to translate history for her story. To begin with, rather than focusing on a single historical moment, she set her story in 1933 during the depth of the Great Depression. No major historical event is central to the novel; instead, the narrator, nine-year-old Cassie, and her family endure the poverty and discrimination that had existed for decades in the deep South and that is exacerbated by the Depression. The novel includes general historical details like sharecropping, Jim Crow laws, and KKK-like night riders, but the overall story is, for Cassie, about coming of age, moving from a sheltered, naïve experience to learning firsthand about the realities of institutional racism.

By filtering out historical details that don't directly affect Cassie and her story, Taylor creates something more personal and intimate for her readers. When Cassie and her brother are offended by having to use worn-out textbooks discarded by the white schools, readers can also feel the injustice and outrage, even without knowing the fuller background of segregated education. Other key moments in the novel provoke similar personal outrage that transfers from Cassie to her readers: when Cassie is humiliated by racist Lillian Jean Simms, when Cassie and her siblings huddle in fear as night riders roam the roads, and when T. J. Avery is brutally beaten by white men.

These scenes, distilled from the larger history of African Americans and delivered without historical exposition and background, have a powerful effect on young readers and their emerging understanding of what it must have felt like to endure racism.

Much of the history in *Roll of Thunder* comes from stories Taylor heard from her father and other relatives. By using a personal lens to filter history, Taylor created a story that connects with readers who can recall their own coming-of-age experiences. Taylor's novel is free from distracting expository dialogue where characters provide historical context or inform readers of historical facts in the story's background. By leaving that nod to history out of her book, Taylor brings her readers closer to a personal brush with history.

My historical novel *Mississippi Trial* is like Wile's *Mississippi Summer* in that it is tied to a singular historical event, the murder of Emmett Till. The burden of research was great, and I felt obligated to read everything I could about the case and also about African-American history, Jim Crow traditions in the deep South, and the political and civil rights actions that came before and after the case. When it came to writing the book, I had to decide how much historical context was necessary and how to translate that information to my readers. Similar to what Taylor had done in *Roll of Thunder*, I created a naïve narrator, Hiram Hillburn, who arrives in Mississippi shortly before Till is kidnapped and who becomes the lens through which my readers experience the story. The novel, though, is not about the Emmett Till case; it's about a white boy who is changed by his summer in Mississippi, only a part of which is related to the murder of Till and the trial of his killers. Early drafts taught me that I had to carefully sift the historical record to eliminate details that, though interesting, ultimately weren't relevant to Hiram's path to maturity. My goal was similar to that of Wiles and Taylor: to create a story and characters that bring readers up close and personal to history.

Years ago, I heard the children's science writer Seymour Simon say that if we really wanted to learn about a scientific principle, the best place to start would be a children's book because children's books get to the heart of the matter faster and more clearly than adult books do. I've found this to be true, but I believe that it also applies to historical fiction and nonfiction for children. The translation or mediation—or whatever we choose to call it—that history written for young readers undergoes renders it a more compact, more refined, more interesting product than some adult books. Of course, because the stories have been translated, these historical narratives may lack the depth, the density and calories of adult "meat," but as historical milk, they can nourish young readers well enough to get them on their way to meatier histories more suitable for when the time has come for them to "put away childish things." The historical translation involved in excellent children's historical fiction and nonfiction allows young readers to see history through a glass lightly—a less nuanced, less intricate view—but a clearer, sharper, more potent representation of the past that is informative and appropriate for its young audience.

Note

1. Devery S. Anderson's manuscript would become *Emmett Till: The Murder That Shocked the World and Propelled The Civil Rights Movement* (UP of Mississippi, 2015).

Works Cited

Aronson, Marc. *Beyond the Pale*. Scarecrow, 2003.

Atwood, Margaret. "In Search of *Alias Grace*: On Writing Canadian Historical Fiction." *American Historical Review*, vol. 103, no. 5, 1998, pp.1503-16.

The Bible. Authorized King James Version. Zondervan, 2010.

Bradbury, Ray. *Zen in the Art of Writing*. Joshua Odell, 1994.

Brown, Joanne, and Nancy St. Clair. *The Distant Mirror: Reflections on Young Adult Historical Fiction*. Scarecrow, 2006.

Crowe, Chris. *Death Coming Up the Hill*. Houghton Mifflin, 2015.

_____. *Getting Away with Murder: The True Story of the Emmett Till Case*. Dial/Phyllis Fogelman, 2003.

_____. *Mississippi Trial, 1955*. Dial/Phyllis Fogelman, 2002.

Dickinson, Emily. "Tell all the truth but tell it slant," Poetry Foundation. www.poetryfoundation.org/poems/56824/tell-all-the-truth-but-tell-it-slant-1263. Accessed 10 Apr. 2012.

Haviland, Virginia, ed. *Children and Literature: Views and Reviews*. Scott Foresman, 1973.

Kennedy, David M. "The Art of the Tale: Story-telling and History Teaching." *Reviews in American History,* vol. 26, no. 2, 1998, pp. 462-73.

Lewis, C. S. *Of Other Worlds: Essays and Stories.* Harvest, 2002.

MacLeod, Anne Scott. "Writing Backward: Modern Models in Historical Fiction," *The Horn Book.* vol. 74, no. 1, 1998, pp. 26-33.

Martin, Rhona. *Writing Historical Fiction.* 2nd ed., Black, 1995.

Paterson, Katherine. *A Sense of Wonder: On Reading and Writing Books for Children.* Plume, 1995.

Speare, Elizabeth George. "Newbery Award Acceptance." *Horn Book,* vol. 35, Aug. 1959, pp. 265-70.

Taylor, Mildred D. *Roll of Thunder, Hear My Cry.* Dial, 1976.

Thom, James Alexander. *The Art and Craft of Writing Historical Fiction.* Writer's Digest, 2010.

Thompson, Raymond H. "Interview with Rosemary Sutcliff," *Taliesin's Successors: Interviews with Authors of Modern Arthurian Literature,* 1999.d.lib.rochester.edu/camelot/text/interview-with-rosemary-sutcliff. Accessed July 17, 2012.

Townsend, John Rowe. *A Sense of Story: Essays on Contemporary Writers for Children.*Trinity, 1971.

Volmer, Mary. "The Tourist, The Expat, and the Native: A Traveler's Approach to Crafting Historical Fiction." *Fiction Writers Review,* 25 Apr. 2016. www.fictionwritersreview.com/essay/the-tourist-the-expat-and-the-native-a-travelers-approach-to-crafting-historical-fiction/. Accessed May 1, 2017.

Walsh, Jill Paton. "History Is Fiction," *The Horn Book,* vol. 50, Feb. 1972, pp. 17-23.

_____. "The Lords of Time," *Quarterly Journal of the Library of Congress,* vol. 36, no. 2, 1979, pp. 96-113.

Wiles, Deborah. *Freedom Summer.* 2001, Atheneum, 2014.

finding common ground with his white brethren, while Hawkeye retains the privilege of traversing Euro-American and American Indian lines. One side of the friendship opens possibilities while the other closes them.

That Natives must lose themselves in their friendships with Euro-Americans is a common belief in America's most famous historical contact narratives. Published only a year after *The Last of the Mohicans*, Sedgwick's *Hope Leslie* ends in a similar fashion. Set during the aftermath of the Pequot War when English colonists fought Native peoples for terrain, Pequot Princess Magawisca becomes enmeshed in a love triangle between herself and two Puritans, Everell Fletcher and Hope Leslie. While Everell and Hope are well-intentioned in their caring for the Native princess, they are unable, or perhaps unwilling, to direct explicit change that accepts her story or culture into their society in any substantial way. At the end of the novel, Magawisca seems to understand this lack of full commitment on their parts. Whereas Hawkeye took Chingachgook's hand, she joins Everell's and Hope's together, seeming to bless this union that excludes her from its symbolic future of a racially pure nation. "The Indian and the white man can no more mingle, and become one, than day and night," she states, lamenting that while "we must part—and for ever . . . my spirit will joy in the thought . . . that you are dwelling in love and happiness together" (349-50). Magawisca is depicted as selfless: she acquiesces to a fate predetermined in the narrative, that of the "Vanishing Indian." In nineteenth-century discourse, depicting Natives as the last of their race like Chingachgook or as one of the few remaining like Magawisca became common practice. Sedgwick takes this concept a step further, though, suggesting that Magawisca believes the separation of Natives and non-Natives is an inevitable outcome of their relationship. In other words, Magawisca "vanishes" because she believes it is the best way to enact cross-cultural friendship. She sacrifices herself to reduce conflict with those whom she loves. Even though Everell and Hope "breathe silent prayers for her," they take no definitive action after Magawisca reveals her plans to leave them, and "in a few brief moments [Magawisca] disappeared for ever from their sight" (354). If Euro-Americans imagined a history in which Natives peacefully acknowledged white superiority by tacitly bequeathing their land, as Magawisca does, then they did not necessarily have to feel guilt for their imperialist aims. Sympathetic narratives like Sedgwick's and Cooper's invite white audiences to consider the responsibility they may bear for their actions toward American Indians, but they ultimately absolve these actions, suggesting Natives exhibited understanding and thereby a sense of complicity that their lands and culture were fated to be seized.

For contemporary readers, the question begged is how historical fiction depicts narratives of first contact today. During the Jacksonian era, these depictions questioned the prevailing political and cultural assumptions that Natives were rightfully being ousted from their land (Mielke 1-2). While the most popular narratives like those cited above ended in Natives succumbing to seceding their land almost benignly, it is still noteworthy that the American populace yearned to understand the cultural differences between the races and clamored for historical fiction that discussed such scenes of first contact. Arguably, historical fiction opens the possibility for change: perhaps Euro-American readers could be so compelled by these stories that they could decide to try for a new, more equal future. Readers usually see themselves in contrast to the past, and they assume that their culture has progressed beyond what is depicted in a specific narrative. This assumption is supported by psychologist Daniel L. Schacter's hypothesis of change bias, or the belief that most people exaggerate the changes they see in themselves from one point in their lives to another because "we believe that we have, or should have changed over time" (141). The past, then, unavoidably becomes situated as a place of opposition, one readers interpret as trailing behind more refined, present viewpoints. Today, issues such as the lack of federal recognition for self-governance, the use of Indian mascots in sports, and treaties that have yet to be upheld dating back to the time of first contact are a mere few that still plague Native tribes and remain embedded in social and political discourse. Interestingly, historical fiction about first contact is also still popular, especially in young adult fiction, and it provides an inroad to understanding how current problems in Euro-American and American Indian relations might be discussed and confronted.

In one recent study about American Indian themes in recent young adult historical fiction, Paulette F. Molin states that these "narrative are primarily about Euro-Americans figures and their perceptions of Indians, not about Indian people themselves (or Indian perceptions of themselves)" (77). That is, these stories mirror Sedgwick's and Cooper's plotlines in many respects. However, to tease out the distinctions that contemporary contact narratives have when compared to their past counterparts remains important and beneficial. What messages do these novels send to their readers, and what can readers extrapolate about the ramifications of these messages on current Euro-American and American Indian relationships and understandings of each other? How might current readers see themselves as different, or changed from the past, and in what ways might they be inspired to enact change in their present circumstances?

Seeing the Light: Mary Pope Osborne's Reimagining of Cross-Cultural Friendship

Standing in the Light: The Captive Diary of Catharine Carey Logan by Mary Pope Osborne is a title from Scholastic's Dear America series. The novel centers on Catharine, a young Euro-American girl who is captured and forced to live with the Lenape tribe in the months following the French and Indian War. The Lenape changed allegiance throughout the course of the war to support Great Britain when promised the settlers would protect their interests. This did not prove the case; even after the war, British settlers continued to kill Natives in droves, and historian Amy Schutt relays that more Lenape lives were lost in the months following the war than during it (118). As such, *Standing in the Light* takes place during a pivotal time in America's historical relationship with its Native inhabitants, and readers are faced with the truth that, while Catharine's story is harrowing, her Euro-American community is to be blamed for much of her experience.

In essence, Osborne's novel revamps Cooper's and Sedgwick's past contact narratives for a modern audience, one not necessarily out of sync with their original reading demographic. While today Cooper and Sedgwick are usually identified as practitioners of adult fiction, their readers encompassed a variety of ages. Acclaimed historical fiction critic George Dekker confirms that stories like Cooper's "survived chiefly as classics of children's literature—books whose virtues, if any, were not those of the 'grown-up' realist novel" (26). In this genre, then, sympathetic responses were often deemed romantic: the imagined worlds where Euro-Americans and American Indians could bond over friendship to overcome obstacles seemed to have no place in the day-to-day, real-life adult activities of war and violence. However, these novels provided spaces that optimistic youth were presumed to revel in and perhaps even helped influence their future perspectives.

The Dear America series targets middle to early high school female students, though a quick Internet search will reveal its appeal to adult fans, too, suggesting a broad audience that mimics its historical fiction predecessors. In 2014, one of the series' avid readers explained in a "Love Letter to the Dear America Series" that the books have "a great adult quality" that makes them compelling (Lewis par 1). The series is vastly popular. As of 2017, it comprised forty-three books, and while it began in 1996, there was a relaunch in 2014 after a ten-year publishing hiatus. At this time, selected texts, including *Standing in the Light*, were republished with new marketing. In 1999, HBO created television adaptions of some of the books, and Catharine's story was the first released. Although each novel in the series is written by a different author, Mary Pope Osborne is one of its most famous contributors. Author of *The Magic Tree House* series which has sold more than 134 million books worldwide, she is currently one of America's best-known contemporary children's authors. Readers of this series would likely know her by name, and it is important to iterate that, like Cooper's and Sedgwick's novels, *Standing in the Light* has incited and will continue to incite wide-ranging discussion about Euro-American and American Indian relations. Moreover, it invites its audience to contemplate the cross-culture interactions within the novel in the context of responding to the past, an activity that also necessarily leads to responding to the present and the future.

As mentioned, Osborne's fictional diary offers a modern rendition of a captivity narrative, the most popular genre in Early America. In these stories, a woman is taken by a Native tribe and forced to learn to coexist with them. In explaining the basic constructs of the genre, Roy Harvey Pearce relays that it is "for the greater part Puritan; and their writers find in the experience of captivity, 'removal,' hardships on the march to Canada [during the French and Indian wars], adoption or torture or both . . . and eventual return (this is the classic pattern of captivity), evidences of God's inscrutable wisdom" (2). Mary Pope Osborne's tale differs slightly from this structure because the author chooses to focus on a young Quaker girl rather than on a Puritan one; as a result, the final emphasis on "God's inscrutable wisdom," as Harvey puts it, is altered to fit a Quaker rather than a Puritan paradigm. Most early American captivity narratives espoused religious propaganda that used the cross-cultural experience with Native culture to justify the superiority of Euro-American Puritanism. Catharine's diary, however, recounts a struggle between her father's more accepting ideology and her own nascent one, which is rooted in fear, a difference Osborne emphasizes.

Not surprisingly, the stark differences between Puritan and Quaker beliefs also buttress Osborne's tale. Unlike the Puritans, who were hierarchical in their approach to religion, early American Quakers believed they could enjoy a relationship with God without the mediation of clergy. They believed that all people, regardless of race or gender, had access to an inner light direct from God that could guide them morally (Taylor 86). For Quakers, American Indians were presumed to be on equal footing with their white neighbors. "If we treat the Indians fairly, they will treat us fairly," Catharine's father (Papa) advises his daughter (Osborne 14). While Catharine agrees that she is "sad for the Indians," she still confess that "I worry more about our safety right now . . . *Later* we can seek justice for the Indians" (16). Catharine's father teaches her that one-on-one contact (i.e., treating each other fairly) should help solve the misunderstandings between these two cultures. Catharine, while sympathetic, dismisses the belief that the answer is as simple as he makes it, instead relaying that she cares about herself first—that communicating with the Natives under their current, strained circumstances would prove futile. As someone who is growing in her faith, Catharine's justifications for her conflicted feelings potentially mirrors that of readers who may sympathize with Catharine's practical mindset over her father's. With her decision to explore Quakerism over Puritanism, Osborne thoughtfully resituates the narrative to a perspective most readers would not necessarily know about, allowing them an additional outside lens to help establish objectivity.

Moreover, because Quakerism as a belief system was one of the few in early America that, in its best form, attempted to treat all races equally, an attempt is made to portray the feelings and circumstances of both sides during this tumultuous period. Catharine's father aptly describes the basis of the open-minded, Quaker philosophy during a meeting when he admonishes his community members for their lack of action to help the local tribe after "backwoodsmen" attacked them without warning. "Why can the governor not to do more to protect the innocent?" he inquires passionately: "It is *truth* we must strive for . . . not *victory*" (Osborne 34). Catharine's father reminds his friends that their religion promotes truth, or moral righteousness, at all costs and that they should forgo personal interest for the good of all those they encounter, especially those whom they have contributed to hurting. Here, it is worth noting that though Puritan governor John Winthrop in *Hope Leslie* is depicted as worried about the "dangerous perplexity" of Hope and Everell's relationship with Magawisca, he does not entirely condemn the cross-cultural friendship, which suggests that he is more fair-minded than the majority of his community. However, he does identify Everell's covert actions to help Magawisca when she is imprisoned for her affiliation with her tribe as both "unlawful and indecorous," suggesting that unlike Catharine's Papa, Winthrop is most concerned with keeping his society peaceful, not necessarily morally perfect. In extending this logic, he also appears to want homogeneity in thought as well as in the type of people who make up Puritan America (362). For Catharine's father, this type of moral waffling for the cause of peace sets back rather than moves forward God's will.

At its core, Catharine's story becomes one of redemption, of how best to act morally when faced with diverse sentiments and peoples. In discussion about fairness toward the Natives between Catharine and her father, they are debating more broadly about whether or not to leave their colony to go to the city of Philadelphia where it is safer. Catharine's father wishes to stay because he believes they must "prove to the Indians that we trust them" (Osborne 20). William Penn's descendants were not as egalitarian as the Quaker colony's founder: they cheated the Lenape out of land west of the Delaware River. Years earlier, Penn had purchased land from the Lenape the approximate distance a man could walk in a day and a half (about thirty miles). Penn's descendants hired a professional runner and forged an easier path for themselves when the treaty was enacted, doubling the agreed-upon territory (Spero 95). Papa cites the breakdown of trust that resulted from this Walking Treaty as the primary reason he wants to stay in the countryside (Taylor 129). Catharine reveals that her "Papa sounded so peaceful" in a decision she finds baffling, and she divulges that "I wish *he* would be my inner voice and speak wisely to me forever . . . I despair that I shall never find my own way to stand in the light, or find my own still, small voice" (Osborne 17). Importantly, readers perceive at the tale's outset that Catharine's moral compass is in flux, that she does not follow her inner light but seeks it out in others. Captivity, rather than tainting her because of its contact with American Indians, contains the potential to redeem her. That Catharine views the Natives with fear rather than sympathy is intricately tied to her inability to trust in the Quaker inner light. If Papa is the one she most looks up to, then it is expected that Catharine will evolve to be more like him.

Both in the traditional Puritan captivity narrative and in Catharine's, "capture by the Indians was no military or secular accident," yet there is an optimism that undergirds Catharine's tale that is lost in the Puritan ones (Vaughan and Clark 1). As Alden T.

Vaughan and Edward W. Clark point out, for the Puritans, "Captivity was God's punishment; redemption was His Mercy, and New England must heed the lesson or suffer anew" (1). Stated simply, Puritans believed that the trauma of captivity was foisted upon them because they were not living up to God's expectations. Their narratives, the most famous of which was Mary Rowlandson's *Sovereignty and Goodness of God*, symbolized not only personal redemption but also communal redemption. After all, the Puritan project in America was to fulfill God's will in the New World. Captivity from "the bloody heathens" and "wretches" as Rowlandson called the Narragansetts who attacked her village indicated that God was unhappy with their attempts to live up to his standards (33). These narratives provided a roadmap about how to achieve God's grace again, and doing so hinged upon the captive retaining and strengthening her Christian virtue even when faced with extreme hardships, including the murder of friends and family, being kidnapped and separated from those who remained alive, and being forced to travel with her captors while starving. For a captive to maintain and even strengthen spiritual doctrine during this time represented to the Puritan community at large that their troubles as a whole could be eradicated: if they were more vigilant against all of the woes that the American wilderness plagued them with, then God would save them from further turmoil, just as he did those captives like Rowlandson who turned to him when plagued with unyielding punishment.

Whereas in Puritan captivity narratives, the community was the one at risk, for young Catharine, it is her soul alone that is in peril—and that is what makes the Quaker girl's narrative unique. It is not hellfire and brimstone that threaten her and those around her; rather it is a turning away from God and the goodness she believes can be found in his presence. However, this quest to achieve inner light is not easy. When Catharine is first taken captive, she channels the angry rhetoric of Rowlandson, unable to remember her father's reminder to be fair to her experience as well as to the Lenape's. Once captured, Catharine is adopted by a Lenape family, a common occurrence historically because American Indian tribes often used Euro-American children to replace the children who had been killed in war. Catharine's adopted family renames her Chilili, and she writes in her diary, "They try to befriend me . . . and smile, but I do not answer. Their tender treatment will not soften me . . . I will not ever be kind. I despise [them]" (Osborne 48-49). She later shares that upon tripping and being offered help from a tribe member, she "pushed him away." "I should die if any of them touch me," she states bitterly, "They are more animal to me than the bloody game I help carry" (50). Her heart is hardened, yet the Lenape are kind to her, so much so that they nurse her to wellness when she is sick and allow her to see her brother even though they worry it will hinder the siblings' ability to embrace their new identities. Eventually, Catharine begins to open herself up to the American Indians, a transition that would have constituted a symbolic loss of soul to the Puritans. Indeed, Eric J. Sundquist notes that in Puritan narratives, "[t]he captive's greatest risk was not death but rather the temptation to identify with the alien way of life and become a savage" (219). Catharine's slow softening of mind and heart toward the Natives, achieved through friendship and cross-cultural sympathy, is what is ultimately heralded as the epitome of moral goodness in the story— not a detraction from it.

Specifically, Catharine befriends Snow Hunter, who she assumes is full Lenape but later discovers was captured from a Euro-American home as a child. After he tells her about the Lenape Creation story and the distinctive methods the tribe uses to administer medicine to those who were sick like herself, Catharine arrives at an epiphany in her journal: "I have never believed that plants and trees have spirits, or that one should stir medicine in the direction the sun travels. I consider all these customs now. I know they are not the truth as *we* know it, Papa. But here is another truth: When thee lives close to a different people, it is hard not to dream what they dream" (Osborne 103). This revelation is a pivotal one in the trajectory of the book and in Catharine's development. Catharine does what no historical Puritan captive ever approached according to Sundquist because of the spiritual message it could send to the larger community: she "becomes a savage." Likewise, unlike Hawkeye or Everell and Hope, she does not accept that her culture and the Native culture cannot mix; rather, she finally intermeshes totally with them, expressing that "sometimes I feel [they] are my new family" (125). Catharine's captivity narrative concludes with her return to her Quaker community, but the last pages mirror the beginning of the book. Rather than being excited about the possibility of returning home, Catharine begins to fear being taken captive by Euro-American soldiers. "We do not have enough provisions," she writes in her diary, now including herself fully as part of the Lenape tribe, and she admits that she is "worn out with fear" that this new family she has joined will be harmed (135; 134). Indeed they are: White Owl, whom Catharine has become betrothed to, presumably dies in battle, along with her adopted family, all while she and Thomas are taken back to their parents, weeping about the fate of their new friends.

In the concluding pages of the narrative, Catharine shares her diary with her Papa, the arbiter of morality whom readers met at the beginning of the story and who Catharine fears will judge her time with the Lenape harshly. "He may want nothing to do with me, for now he knows that I was willing to forsake my old life and live forever with the Lenape," she worries. After waiting for days to talk with her, most likely because he is so affected by her narrative, her father finally reveals to her that "her diary taught him that [she] stood in the light. But this is all he said!" (Osborne 150). While Catharine is overjoyed that her father is not resentful of her, she realizes that he, nor anyone else, will ever fully comprehend her journey, and she is saddened to realize that her life now will be one of "loneliness" because no one will ever grasp "the truths [she] has learned" (151). Her father requests that she not share her story with the community because he fears it will ostracize her even more than she is already. For Catharine, then, the title edict of Standing in the Light gives her moral freedom, but it separates her from her Quaker friends who are presumptively not following their religion as faithfully. Even Catharine's mother who is rarely mentioned in the text seems put off by her embracing of Lenape culture. In the book's epilogue, Osborne reveals that Catharine never marries, apparently never moving beyond her romantic promises to White Owl. She becomes a teacher in Philadelphia as well as a reformer for abolitionism and American Indian rights, especially within the Quaker community. Her brother similarly becomes an advocate for Native rights with the American government.

Conclusion

So, what can Osborne's recent historical contact narrative teach its readers about contemporary relationships between Natives and non-Natives? Most significantly, it presents an invitation for activism. If, because of change bias, readers believe they have progressed further than Catharine in their cross-cultural relationships, then one can assume that they will want to build on her gains at the novel's conclusion. This call to action is perhaps the most important part of the narrative. Catharine does not stand by and watch her Native friends "vanish"; rather, she separates from her community and fights for justice for both of her "families," a heartening contrast between this account and its famous nineteenth-century counterparts. In fact, Catharine is the one who refuses to marry, suggesting that Quakerism as it stands is not worthy of replicating. For her, only a union between White Owl and herself creates a future worth raising children in—a future in which both races are equal and both cultures accepted.

That is not to say that Osborne's modern-version narrative is perfect: certainly, it still centers on a white, young woman's perspective, as Paulette F. Molin points out, and it is a story that could easily be reversed because Natives were often taken captive by Euro-Americans. Further, White Owl is not Native born, so while he culturally identifies with the Lenape tribe, it is unclear whether Catharine would have loved him had his ancestry differed. Admittedly, their union is made easier because of their ability to communicate and his background can be attributed to a plot device to further their relationship. This dilemma, though, remains unresolved. Finally, the Natives in this narrative still "vanish." Osborne reveals in the epilogue that "For many years, Thomas inquired after the small Lenape band . . . [but] No one seemed to know the[ir] fate" (Osborne 158). These sentences are undoubtedly reminiscent of Cooper's and

Sedgwick's descriptions of ill-fated tribes who harbored no hope for future vitalization. Optimism perseveres, though, in that Catharine and her brother do continue that search for their friends: they do not sit idly by and bemoan what they cannot change or accept that providentially their superiority is preordained. Instead, they fight for a better future through both political and social realms, and this empowering ending communicates to the book's readers that they, too, might find their own ways "to stand in the light." They only need open themselves to the possibility of transformation through cross-cultural friendship and exchange, no matter the obstacles that may lie in their paths.

Works Cited

Cooper, James Fenimore. *The Last of the Mohicans: A Narrative of 1757.* Edited by Susan L. Rattiner. Dover, 2003.

Dekker, George. "Cooper and American Romance Tradition." *James Fenimore Cooper: New Historical and Literary Contexts.* 1826. Edited by W. M. Verhoeven, Rodopi. 1993.

Lewis, Jessi. "A Love Letter to the Dear America Series." *Book Riot,* 7 Nov. 2014, www.bookriot.com/2014/11/07/love-letter-dear-america-series. Accessed 5 July 2017.

Mielke, Laura L. *Moving Encounters: Sympathy and the Indian Question in Antebellum Literature.* U of Massachusetts P, 2008.

Molin, Paulette F. *American Indian Themes in Young Adult Literature.* Scarecrow, 2005.

Osborne, Mary Pope. *Standing in the Light: The Captive Diary of Catharine Carey Logan.* 1763. Scholastic, 1998.

Pearce, Roy Harvey. "The Significance of the Captivity Narrative." *American Literature*, vol. 19, Mar. 1949, pp. 1-20.

Rowlandson, Mary. *The Sovereignty and Goodness of God. Puritans Among the Indians: Accounts of Captivity and Redemption, 1676-1724.* 1682. Edited by Edward Clark and Alden Vaughan. Harvard UP, 1981, pp. 29-76.

Schacter, Daniel L. *The Seven Sins of Memory: How the Mind Forgets and Remembers.* Houghton Mifflin , 2001.

Schutt, Amy. *Peoples of the River Valleys: The Odyssey of the Delaware Indians*. U of Pennsylvania P, 2007.

Sedgwick, Catharine Maria. *Hope Leslie: Or, Early Times in Massachusetts*. 1827. Edited by Carolyn L. Karcher. Penguin, 1998.

Spero, Patrick. *Frontier Country: The Politics of War in Early Pennsylvania*. U of Pennsylvania P, 2016.

Sundquist, Erik J. "The Frontier and American Indians." *The Cambridge History of American Literature*. Edited by Sacvan Bercovitch, vol. 2. Cambridge UP, 1995.

Taylor, Alan. *Writing Early American History*. U of Pennsylvania P, 2005.

Vaughan, Alden T. and Edward W. Clark. "Cups of Common Calamity: Puritan Captivity Narratives as Literature and History." *Puritans Among the Indians: Accounts of Captivity and Redemption, 1676-1724*. Edited by Alden T. Vaughan and Edward W. Clark. Harvard UP, 1981, pp. 1-28.

"We Must Have Some Sport": The Afflicted Girls of Salem in Fiction for Young Adults_____

Marta María Gutiérrez-Rodríguez

> It began in obscurity, with cautious experiments in fortune telling.
>
> (Boyer and Nissenbaum 1)

In the year 1692, the most famous witch hunt in colonial America occurred in Salem Village, the present-day Danvers, Massachusetts. Among the many aspects of the event examined by historians, the motivations that prompted a group of adolescent and teenage girls known as "the afflicted girls" to accuse and send community members to the gallows remain a mystery. The true medical triggers of the "fits," or seizures, suffered by members of this group have not been established. Consequently, despite centuries of research, attempts to supply a definitive explanation have proven less than satisfactory, although many theories have been proposed (Demos 189-215).

Fiction authors have shared the interest of historians to establish a final explanation, and their works have contemplated various fictional solutions to this historic conundrum. Since the publication of the anonymous "Salem Witchcraft: An Eastern Tale" (1820), the first literary work centered on this historical event, works of historical fiction have offered diverse versions. While they base their narratives on established historical theories, authors frequently take advantage of the freedom offered by fiction to present their own theories in the hope of shining light on history's darkness (McHale 87) where the true motives of the afflicted girls wait to be revealed. While any record that confirms the precise accuser motivations may never be discovered, young adult (YA) readers may still learn from the novels a common theme: one's personal choices may result in very public consequences.

Because most of the accusers were teenagers, their selection as the protagonists of young adult novels offers a natural appeal.

Despite the considerable number of novels written about the Salem accusers, especially since the 1980s (Gutiérrez Rodríguez 93), scholarly investigation has yet to analyze the representation of this historical event in YA fiction. This chapter addresses that neglect by analyzing three contemporary YA novels that adopt the Salem Witchcraft Trials as their main topic and focus attention on the role played by the young accusers.

This chapter divides discussion into two main sections. The first section includes an overview of traditional explanations offered by historians of actions by the "afflicted girls" and their roles in the development of the accusations and subsequent deadly consequences. The second section analyzes three representative contemporary young adult novels with focus on the Salem Witchcraft trials. They include Suzy Witten's *The Afflicted Girls: A Novel of Salem*, Suzanne Weyn's *Invisible World*, and Katherine Howe's *Conversion*. Each adopts a different narrative approach. Witten produces what can be labeled a canonical historical novel, closely adhering to historical facts. Weyn includes fictional characters and the fantasy aspect of magic in her historically based novel. Howe's novel establishes a connection between what happened in 1692 and the present day through parallel narratives. By analyzing these three narrative approaches, readers may better understand the possible approaches to creating YA historical fiction in general, and more specifically as pertains to the topic of the Salem Witchcraft Trials.

The analysis section devotes attention to four elements that provide the research framework. The elements include first, the number, identity, and assumed group role of the members of the afflicted group; second, the origin of their symptoms; third, how the accusations begin; and fourth, the influence exerted by adults, with the third and fourth elements considered together. The four elements limit analysis to elements directly associated with the afflicted girls.

Overview of Traditional Explanations

Much of the debate focused on the role of the "afflicted girls" has revolved around the hypothesis of their dabbling in fortune-telling and magic tricks to foretell their future. Supporters of this theory suggest that the consequent fear of being discovered practicing the black arts (Starkey 35) by their strict Puritan families provided the starting point for a chain of events resulting in the hanging of nineteen people and the imprisonment of several hundreds. John Hale, a Puritan minister with experience in treating cases of possession wrote in *A Modest Enquiry into the Nature of Witchcraft* about the topic of experiments with the occult. He also outlined the consequences of such experimentation as the cause of the behavior of the accusing girls. In 1867, Charles W. Upham, whose work *Salem Witchcraft* had been considered for more than a century the "first significant story of the Salem witchcraft trials" (Le Beau viii), bestowed academic authority on Hale's interpretation. Therefore, the attempts of the girls to contact the invisible world through "palmistry and other arts of fortune-telling" was established as the main explanation for what happened (Upham 320). Whether Tituba, a slave from Barbados working in the village parsonage, was associated with this practice remains a matter of disagreement among historians. Maryse Condé's 2009 historical fiction, *I, Tituba, Black Witch of Salem*, creates a childhood for the slave, who was imprisoned for two years and then released under an order of general amnesty for all except six of the convicted witches (Noble). Because Condé's novel does not focus on those "afflicted," it falls outside of this analysis.

Nothing available in historical records, however, supports this interpretation. Primary sources provide little more than the names and the number of accused, as well as the content of the accusation. Official documents record that the afflicted girls began showing symptoms like those of people allegedly possessed (Sebald 67, 69-70; Levack 17-18). In fact, this was the diagnosis of the Salem village doctor, Dr. Griggs, when he was unable to find a medical explanation for their illness (Upham 321).

The lack of information has led a great number of authors to present other explanations. Rosenthal (*Salem Story* 32-50) and Baker (98-124) emphasize the unlikeliness of the practice of magic tricks, and they consider fraud and malice as the leading forces behind accusations of witchcraft. They argue that adults with a personal interest in eliminating those the girls accused prompted their claims. Both sources support the idea that the girls enjoyed the fame and power that followed their accusations and could not see the risks and the consequences of what they called "some sport" (Rosenthal, *Records* 537).

Marion L. Starkey (47) and ChadwickHansen (x) are among the first to consider a medical explanation for the behavior of the girls. They agree that the girls likely suffered hysteria, which probably originated in fear of being discovered playing magic, of the strict Puritan environment in which they lived, and of the damnation pulpit discourse preached every Sunday. Additionally, Linnda R. Caporael (23-25) and Mary K. Matossian (356) mention ergot poisoning as causing the behavior. Though this theory was strongly rejected by Nicholas P. Spanos and Jack Gottlieb (1391-92), intoxication of some kind remains one of the most plausible explanations for the symptoms. Mary Beth Norton (4, 11-12) proposed posttraumatic stress following family losses in Indian confrontations as an explanation. Other conditions considered include Lyme disease (Drymon), and encephalitis (Carlson 124).

Despite the variety of interpretations, almost all historians agree that the group of girls was responsible for the executions and imprisonments that history records, attributing different degrees of responsibility. Attribution of blame seems to have increased over time. Thus, Thomas Brattle's first reference to the afflicted as "blind, nonsensical girls" (Burr 188) who should have been themselves accused of witchcraft has evolved into progressively more negative references such as "wretches" (Burke 158), "malignant and fiendlike accusers" (Upham 83-84), "profligate accusers" and "miserable prosecutors" (Godwin 455), or "a pack of 'bobby-soxers'" (Starkey 14).

Having explored the major traditional theories explaining the role of the "afflicted girls," the remainder of this chapter will focus on the analysis of the above-mentioned novels. Each of the four identified elements will be applied.

Analysis of Three Representative Contemporary Young Adult Novels

The number, identity, and assumed group role of the members of the afflicted group

In Suzy Witten's *The Afflicted Girls*, the group of accusers includes a reduced number of members from those historically involved: Abigail Williams, Mercy Lewis, Susannah Walcott, Lucy Putnam, Betty Parris, and John Doritch. The first two are the main characters. Abigail represents the leader; she persuades the others to practice fortune-telling and uses the witchcraft paraphernalia about which she learned in witchcraft books to incriminate others and encourage more accusations. She also most enjoys the attention received by friends and adults, and, consequently, is most interested in perpetuating the witch hunt.

The novel opens with Abigail and Mercy arriving to Salem after a long journey; both are orphans who must work as servants, having lost their families during Indian attacks. Consequently, Mary Beth Norton's theory about the importance of trauma suffered by victims of the Indians conflict plays a prominent role. However, this is the only element that the two girls share, as Mercy's outstanding characteristic is "her kindness" (11) whereas Abigail "unlike her friend, . . . was neither prayerful, nor fearful... only furious" (14). Both girls are literate, uncommon for that era. Mercy is especially well-read as she had read everything in her employer's house; he is a Methodist minister. Susannah Walcott and Lucy Putnam are cousins; Susannah enjoys gossiping and Lucy is "unusually sensitive" (67). Lucy must care for her younger sisters because their mother suffers mental illness following the loss of several boy infants. Betty Parris is the youngest character and suffers loss of attention from her father, the Reverend Parris, after the arrival of her cousin Abigail. Finally, Witten includes one "afflicted boy" (249), John Doritch, who joins the girls in the woods. He will become a main accuser.

Equally reduced is the number of girls among the afflicted in Weyn's *Invisible World*. Her group of characters includes Abigail and Betty Parris as well as Ann Putnam and a girl named Elizabeth whose surname is not provided; however, the two latter girls are introduced only to show that more girls joined the fortune-telling practices begun by Abigail. Nonetheless, this novel includes an important new element: the main character, Elsabeth, is fictional and presented as a "real" witch. She descends from an ancient dynasty of Scottish witches who arrive in Salem Village after a shipwreck and a stay of several months on Wandalaw Island. On the island, Elsabeth learns how to manage her ability to hear the thoughts of others and to master the use of herbs. She also meets the Parris family, who take her in as their servant, and she encounters Abigail, who will become the ringleader of the afflicted. When these two girls meet on the ship transporting them to Salem Village, Abigail is playing with an "odd deck of cards" (Weyn 145) and Elsabeth soon feels "something in her that makes her think that she [Abigail] was not to be trusted" (147-48). Although Elsabeth only uses her powers for good, she later considers herself responsible for "the hideous, demonic creature that I have let loose on Salem Village" (1). She blames herself because when she tries to return her dead governess to life during the journey, a malignant spirit enters the woman's body and travels with them to Salem Village.

Katherine Howe's *Conversion* revolves around the general challenges shared by all teenage girls regardless of the era in which they live. In order to demonstrate that some teen experiences are universal, Howe creates two sets of "afflicted girls." The first group lives in 1692 where their strict Puritan environment and the trying conditions under which servant girls survive motivate their accusations of witchcraft against others. They feel called to rebel against a life that offers them no future and makes them nearly invisible to adults. One character pointedly asks, "Do you know what it's like… not to be listened to?" (Howe 169). The girls in this group include Ann Putnam. Ann later decides to publicly repent in 1706 for the role she played in the events. She confesses the story of what happened in 1692 to Reverend Green. Thus, this novel offers a first-person account from one of the afflicted, which is based on fact; she is the sole accuser to do so publicly. The other members are Abigail and Betty Parris, whose characterization is similar to that in the additional novels: the former is ruthless and enjoys running riot.

Abigail, however, is exploited by the Parris family, which demands too much work for a girl of her age, so her reaction is not surprising. Abigail continuously plots to shirk her assigned chores and most benefits from the accusations that do result in liberation from her duties. Abigail especially directs her rage against her cousin Betty, who is assigned fewer duties. Finally, Betty Hubbard and Mary Warren also join the accusers.

Howe's second group of "afflicted" girls live in 2012, and contemporary readers may better identify with their problems. They study at an elite school in Danvers, Massachusetts (former Salem Village) and are finishing high school. They seem to react against pressures due to all the issues proper to their age, namely, age-appropriate complex relationships with friends, boys, and their families, as well as stress brought on through university applications. As is true in the original Salem, one group leader exists, and her cohort soon follows her lead in their display of symptoms.

As readers discover, almost all of the novels offer characters that share rather similar roles and are based in historical reality. However, fictional characters are also included in *Invisible World*, the work that presents the most unreal version of events. That is due to the introduction of magic as a believable, practical and useful element.

The origin of symptoms

The Afflicted Girls hints at the origin of the symptoms and aligns with some traditional historical explanations. The girls' behavior triggers may be categorized as three main elements: the (mis)use and consumption of herbs, the visits to the specific location of Bishop's tavern, and the practice of fortune-telling in the woods. All activities are forbidden and lead to severe punishment. In addition, the girls' craving for attention from adults or boys contribute to the behavior.

Many herbs remain available in the parsonage kitchen, as the Reverend is fond of them, and his slave, Tituba, takes charge of herb collection and preservation. Abigail discovers a bunch of "red Patty-cakes" (Witten 15) cooked by Tituba, which she hides in her apron. She also follows Tituba to the woods and observes her collecting "prickly pods" (156) that the slave labels "journeying weed" (158). However, Abigail does not see that Tituba only chews—but does not swallow—the plant, and she misunderstands how to cook it: "[…] *her* [Tituba's] cake brought visions quicker, and then the vilest headache she'd ever suffered, with the foggiest vision in her memory and the sharpest-cramped gut ever felt" (226). The mandrake plant proves crucial to the love charm that Bridget Bishop teaches Mercy to make for use on Joseph Putnam: "Carve the mandrake into your lover's shape. Bury it in his father's grave with one part milk, three parts water, and as many drops of your own blood as the years you wish to keep him" (167).

When the five adolescents go to the woods to learn their future by reading the shape of an egg and using the "sieve and scissors and shears. Then with the Psalter and Key" (214), they also eat the red cakes that Abigail has been collecting. Only Mercy avoids them and, thus, suffers no reaction. Mercy also uses herbs to make the Putnam family sleep. That allows her to slip away to Bishop's tavern to learn more charms and to see Joseph Putnam. Thus, the use of herbs, the visits to the tavern, and the practice of fortune-telling are intimately connected, as Mercy requested the charm when she realized that boys at the tavern did not pay any attention to the girls.

After discovering what Mercy has learned, the other girls also want to attempt the practice of magic. While enjoying a rarely permitted picnic in the woods, they try out what should be harmless little magic tricks. Shortly after this experience, all except Mercy experience "fits" or seizures. Their condition improves, but worsens as soon as they eat more cakes. Mercy Lewis finally establishes the connection between the cakes and her friends' physical reactions. Although she tries to get an antidote from Bridget Bishop, news about the girls' condition has spread, and the search for witches begins. Epilepsy, a brain lesion, and scarlet fever are among the diagnoses that the girls receive, until the village doctor establishes that "the evil hand is upon her [Betty]. The Devil has visited [the Parris] house" (231).

Lastly, *The Afflicted Girls* suggests age-related issues suffered by the main characters, specifically first love, first romantic rejections, and their first experience with sexual intercourse. To accommodate these topics, Witten alters the historically accurate age of some of the characters. For example, historically Abigail was age 11, but in this novel she is 16. In addition, Witten introduces conflicts derived from such teen issues as competition for attention. Abigail cannot bear the attention Mercy receives from Joseph Putnam; Betty Parris cannot admit that her father takes Abigail into more consideration than her; and John Doritch hates that the girls only have eyes for other boys. Thus, tensions inside the group of accusers also contribute to the creation of the accusations. This can be clearly seen when one member of the group receives attention and the others imitate that individual's behavior hoping for the same.

Readers will recognize similarities in the causes of seizures the girls suffer in *Invisible World*. In this novel two main causes activate the events: the presence and practice of real magic and the eating of what the girls themselves label "dream cakes" (Weyn 172). As noted above, the "good witch" Elsabeth calls an evil spirit while attempting to bring her governess back to life. Three malignant hags accompany the spirit and impersonate Tituba, Sarah Good, and Sarah Osborne. They are the first three women accused of witchcraft in the novel as well as in historical reality. Consequently, when the girls make accusations, they are in fact telling the truth: "I knew Abigail wasn't lying and neither was Betty. They *had* seen Tituba in the woods, as well as the two Sarahs. The girls were telling the truth as best they understood it" (180). Therefore, the fortune-telling practices of Abigail and the other girls are overshadowed by the presence of real witchcraft. However, Elsabeth also suspects the accusations because she "can't believe [the women are] bewitched at every second" (184). It is then that Elsabeth suspects the dream cakes as important to the accusations. She notices something strange in the baking rye: "Only then I noticed the black specks scattered through the remaining kernels of tan rye on the floor" (173). When she tries one of those specks she "felt a powerful fatigue and drifted to sleep" (185). At that moment, she sees the evil spirit and the hags who tell her "You have eaten the ergot rye... You can't get away from us" (186). Thus, visions caused by the consumption of ergot provide the gateway through which malignant forces from the invisible world enter the minds of the afflicted and cause their symptoms.

Conversion does not explain why Betty falls ill. What is clear is that Abigail follows, because she saw it was the only way to liberate herself from her chores: "If Betty's too sick to fetch and carry, why can't I be, too? Perhaps she's given me her vile distemper. Anyway, I'm much tireder than she is all the time" (Howe 121). After this confession, Ann Putnam learns how Abigail makes marks on her arm by biting herself and Abigail also bites Ann. Thus, the two servant girls bear the marks of the supposed witch attacks. Without knowing how, the young Putnam girl also joins the two Parris girls. As she tells the story in retrospect, she explains that, even though she wanted to tell the truth, when the moment came, she was unable to do it: "Instead, I feel powerful" (218).

In the case of the 2012 girls included in *Conversion*, they are all concerned about university interviews. The pressure they endure causes some of them to experience strange symptoms, such as sudden hair loss or the inability to speak or walk. The "ailing girls" (Howe 90), as they are called, receive a lot of attention, and the moment national television shows an interest, the girls seem to improve and begin to behave as if they are celebrities. Their complex diagnosis is appropriately updated from that of their predecessors, ranging from a reaction to the vaccine to prevent human papillomavirus to environmental intoxication provoked by toxins buried under their school building. Finally, the real cause behind their "fits" is established to be a mental condition known as "conversion disorder" (331-32) that implies that "the body does not know how to handle a lot of stress and converts it into physical symptoms" (332).

How the accusations begin and adult influence

The third and the fourth elements involved in the accusations are intimately connected, and are therefore best discussed together. *The Afflicted Girls* emphasizes connections between the individuals named as witches and the enemies of Reverend Parris and the adults in the Putnam family. Adult influence is clear, as the girls hear their parents complain about unfair treatment in terms of inheritances the families never received. They also overhear the adults plotting against their enemies. The moment the village doctor diagnoses the girls with possession, the Reverend Parris blames his slave Tituba for bringing magic into his house. When Bridget Bishop tries to tell the Reverend Parris that his niece Abigail has baked and eaten cakes that are responsible for the seizures, he then considers Abigail "the witch who'd sent affliction into the village!" (Witten 280). Ruth Osborne and Sarah Good are next accused, emphasizing the chain of accusations derived from historical reality.

In *Invisible World*, the accusations start after the consumption of the dream cakes and the visions of the malignant forces that accompanied Elsabeth to Salem Village. However, nothing in this novel makes readers think that the adults influenced the girls. Instead, it emphasizes the true causes of the accusations as malignant forces and witches in the village.

Finally, in *Conversion*, young Betty Parris first accuses others of witchcraft. She cannot tolerate the pressure put upon her by adults to name the witches, and she finally accuses the person who seems to best fit the witch stereotype. In part because Tituba is a slave, Betty singles her out and remains confident that village adults will believe her. The other girls are intoxicated with fame and attention. As Ann Putnam herself explains, for the first time they are not invisible; the adults who previously marginalized them are now allowing them a voice. They are overwhelmed by the attention that suddenly empowers them. Liberated from work duties, an important goal for each, Abigail and the other maids find their social status improves markedly, simply because they have the power to identify witches. As in *The Afflicted Girls*, the conflicts among the village adults strongly influence the girls' accusations. Ann Putnam states that her parents have "their own theories about which families might be harboring the sin" (Howe 135). It comes as no surprise that those accused are considered enemies by the Putnam family.

Within the modernized 2012 group of afflicted girls, although no accusations of witchcraft arise, some characters suffer the consequences of the afflicted girls' condition. For example, the school nurse overemphasized the vaccine as the cause of their symptoms.

She then suffers the brunt of negative public opinion after that explanation is debunked. The afflicted girls and their parents turn on the nurse, and she loses her status as an educated, professional woman. Howe demonstrates that more than 300 years after the Salem Witch Trials, the tendency of humans to seek a scapegoat for what may be their own failings, or simply based on prejudice and irrational fear, remains a bulwark of society. In addition, the possible consequences of such actions are too often not considered.

Conclusion

Several conclusions about the use of history in young adult fiction may be drawn based on the analysis of Suzy Witten's *The Afflicted Girls: A Novel of Salem*, Suzanne Weyn's *Invisible World*, and Katherine Howe's *Conversion*. Regarding the members of the group of afflicted and the roles they fulfill, the three novels all feature fewer members than historical accounts reveal. The reduction in characters allows greater focus and character development, hallmarks of quality fiction. To that end, they each project the historical character of Abigail Williams as the leader of the accusing girls. In all three novels, Abigail's character is that of a liar, conspirator, and manipulator who utilizes her rhetorical skills to involve others in an accusation scheme that benefits her. In *The Afflicted Girls* and *Invisible World*, the causes of the "fits" or seizures are linked to the consumption of herbs or to ergot poisoning, thus establishing connections with some of the most important theories established by historians. Similarly, in both novels the practice of fortune-telling is presented as the activity most strongly supporting the accusers' strange behavior. Moreover, all three novels establish a connection between some of the behavior of the girls and the trauma provoked by historically validated Indian attacks. That connection particularly reinforces Mary Beth Norton's plausible explanation of posttraumatic stress disorder (PTSD) as one possible motivation for the accusers' actions. Similarly, all three novels highlight the lying and malice framing the witchcraft accusations. Young readers may be able to identify with the motivation, if not the result, as they can with the accusers' attention craving. The girls so enjoy their promotion to celebrity status based on self-proclaimed abilities to see witches that they simply disregard possible complications. As those complications escalate into accusations with deadly results via execution for some members of their community, and imprisonment for others, the accusers simply cannot acknowledge their own fabrication. So fearful are they of the possible consequences of such a confession that they choose silence rather than save human lives.

The identity of those accused as witches complies with historical fact in each novel, as does the pattern of the accusations. The personal motives that result in adult influence on the girls' actions are clearly presented in the first and third novels. In those narratives, the existing village rivalries are emphasized even before accusations begin. The introduction of real magic into *Invisible World* has clear objectives: first, to show that its use for good ends is acceptable, and second, that nothing in the behavior of those accused connect them to its practice. Therefore, the injustice of the accusations becomes a stronger theme in Weyn's novel, because those practicing magic, specifically Elsabeth, use their powers to save lives, destroying evil forces that are harming the village. The incorporation of "real" magic in this fantasy version removes it further from historical source matter. Elsabeth's choice may still resonate with young adult readers. They may be encouraged to resist prejudicial fear and make wise choices that relate to the greater good. However, Elsabeth's fantasy existence exempts *Invisible World* from novels that more strongly focus on the fatal consequences of the accusers' actions.

Through novels based on the historical reality known as the Salem Witch Trials, young readers learn a variety of scholarly and scientific interpretations of the true events. Simultaneously, they enjoy reading about characters with whom they may realize a personal connection. The connection established with the present day in *Conversion* may especially appeal to twenty-first-century readers. That connection helps them recognize certain shared concerns and aspirations to those experienced by girls living in the United States at the end of the seventeenth century. Whatever the reader interpretation, all three novels discussed here make abundantly clear that actions have consequences, that fame and attention can blur realities of everyday life, and that an irrational desire for attention may prove costly to others.

Works Cited

Baker, Emerson W. *A Storm of Witchcraft. The Salem Trials and the American Experience.* Oxford UP, 2015.

Boyer, Paul, and Stephen Nissenbaum. *Salem Possessed. The Social Origins of Witchcraft.* 1974. Harvard UP, 2001.

Burke, Edmund. *An Account of the European Settlements in America. In Six Parts.* Vol. II. 1757. Dodsley, 1770.

Burr, George L. *Narratives of the New England Witchcraft Cases.* 1914. Dover, 2002.

Caporael, Linnda R. "Ergotism: The Satan Loosed in Salem." *Science,* vol. 192, no. 4234, 1976, pp. 21-26.

Carlson, Laurie W. *A Fever in Salem. A New Interpretation of the New England Witch Trials.* Ivan R. Dee, 1999.

Demos, John. *The Enemy Within. 2,000 Years of Witch-Hunting in the Western World.* Viking, 2008.

Drymon, M. M. *Disguised as the Devil. How Lyme Disease Created Witches and Changed History.* Wythe Avenue, 2008.

Godwin, William. *Lives of the Necromancers: Or, An Account of the Most Eminent Persons in Successive Ages, who have Claimed for Themselves, or to whom has been Imputed by Others, the Exercise of Magical Power.* Mason, 1834.

Gutiérrez Rodríguez, Marta María. "The Afflicted Girls of Salem Village: Victims or Victimizers?" *Periphery and Centre II.* Edited by Rubén Jarazo Álvarez. Asociación de Estudiantes de Filoloxía Inglesa AFI, Universidade da Coruña, 2006, 89-97.

Hale, John. *A Modest Enquiry into the Nature of Witchcraft.* Printed by B. Green and J. Allen for Benjamin Elliot under the Town House, 1702.

Hansen, Chadwick. *Witchcraft at Salem.* 1969. Braziller, 1985.

Howe, Katherine. *Conversion.* Penguin, 2014.

Le Beau, Bryan L. *The Story of the Salem Witch Trials: "We Walked in Clouds and Could Not See Our Way."* Prentice Hall, 1998.

Levack, Brian P. *The Devil Within. Possession and Exorcism in the Christian West.* Yale UP, 2013.

Matossian, Mary K. "Ergot and the Salem Witchcraft Affair." *The American Scientist*, vol. 70, no. 4, 1982, pp. 355-57.

McHale, Brian. *Postmodernist Fiction*. Routledge, 1987.

Noble, Christopher. "US Clears Salem 'witches' after 300 years." *IOL News*, 1 November 2001. Accessed 14 August 2017. https://www.iol.co.za/news/world/us-clears-salem-witches-after-300-years-76212.

Norton, Mary Beth. *In the Devil's Snare: The Salem Witchcraft Crisis of 1692*. 2002. Vintage, 2003.

Rosenthal, Bernard. *Salem Story. Reading the Witch Trials of 1692*. 1993. Cambridge UP, 1999.

_____, editor. *Records of the Salem Witch-Hunt*. Cambridge UP, 2009.

Sebald, Hans. *Witch Children: From Salem Witch-Hunts to Modern Courtrooms*. Prometheus , 1995.

Spanos, Nicholas P., and Jack Gottlieb. "Ergotism and the Salem Witch Trials." *Science,* vol. 194, no. 4272, 1976, pp. 1390-94.

Starkey, Marion L. *The Devil in Massachusetts. A Modern Enquiry into the Salem Witch Trials*. 1949. Anchor, 1989.

Upham, Charles W. *Salem Witchcraft*. 1867. Dover, 2000.

Weyn, Suzanne. *Invisible World. A Novel of the Salem Witch Trials*. Scholastic, 2012.

Witten, Suzy. *The Afflicted Girls. A Novel of Salem*. Dreamwand, 2009.

Historical Crossover in Chinese and Chinese-American Fiction: The Outlaws, Plus One Cross-dresser

by Sheng-mei Ma

Like an alloy, made stronger because of the melding of two objects foreign to each other, historical fiction as a literary genre gains resilience from its fusion of historical facts and human fancy. Historical fiction becomes malleable through the imagining of what *might have* been on the basis of what *had* been. Such crossing of fact and fiction suggests a venturing beyond one's self and one's history. One's reading of objective facts of a bygone era shapes subjective emotions, fulfilling psychological needs of this reader here and now. In our global village, students of Anglo-American historical fiction further strengthen themselves by going beyond their cultural confines, by engaging the "foreign body" of Chinese historical fiction. Such fiction has already crossed national, cultural, generic, and linguistic divides, to the extent that it mutates into Chinese-American fiction. Such engagement may draw disparate cultures closer through mutual understanding and empathy, motivating readers to resist pushing "us"—however defined—away.

Three of the four classical Chinese novels are historical fictions. The fourteenth-century *Romance of the Three Kingdoms* by Luo Guanzhong (Chinese last names come first) recounts a third-century civil war, which brought down the Han Dynasty. Wu Cheng'en's sixteenth-century *Journey to the West* (*Monkey*) imaginatively chronicles the seventh-century Buddhist pilgrimage undertaken by Xuanzang or Tripitaka. Shi Nai'an's fourteenth-century *The Outlaws of the Marsh* harks back to twelfth-century outlaws, a book subsequently edited and possibly expanded from seventy-one to a hundred chapters by Luo Guanzhong. All references in this chapter are to Shapiro's translation of the 100-chapter version. At least two other translations also exist: *The Water Margin* (1937) by J. H. Jackson and *All Men Are Brothers* (1933) by Pearl S. Buck.

All three novels are crossovers between history and fantasy. The human world and actual events are populated by deities and monsters alike. Wu's *Journey* particularly stands out in its anthropomorphizing and humanizing of both heaven and hell. Likewise, all one hundred and eight bandits in *The Outlaws* are reincarnations of Taoist spirits or celestial stars, inadvertently released and wreaking havoc in the earthly Song dynasty. *The Outlaws* stresses the rebels' physical prowess and heroic camaraderie. They are forced by corruption and injustice to cross into lawlessness of the underworld, only to return to serve the Song dynasty. Collectively, the renegades join the Song military to crush civilian revolts and foreign invasions. In the highly structured imperial dynastic China, *The Outlaws* functions as a release valve for people's fantasy of rebelliousness, while upholding law and order of the status quo in the end.

The Outlaws also resembles the other classical historical fictions in the patriarchal male-centrism, polarizing femininity as either maternal figures or demons, with vulnerable mortal women in between. Few heroines exist among the bandits. However, Chinese masculinist historical fictions countenance their premodern female doppelganger, a yin-yang symbiosis much like the paradoxical impulses of subversiveness and stability. The historical legend of Hua Mulan provides an example of this shadow female presence, having first emerged in the sixth-century "Ballad of Mulan" (See Kwa and Idema) and then being retold in various forms throughout Chinese history. In service of family and country, the historical Hua cross-dresses to substitute for her aging father in military campaigns against northern invaders. After twelve years on the battlefield, she resumes her feminine costume and self, settling into marriage and patriarchy. In the twentieth century, Hua manages to cross the ocean to legitimize Maxine Hong Kingston's ethnic struggle in *The Woman Warrior: Memoirs of a Girlhood among Ghosts* (1976) and to animate Walt Disney's *Mulan* (1998). To embody women of color's ethnic strife, Kingston adapts Mulan's *wuxia* (swordplay and kung fu) training and male impersonation, but forgoes the happy ending characteristic of Chinese historical fictions.

This chapter will focus on a number of representative crossover characters, suspended between history and fiction, heroism and banditry, traditional masculinity and iconoclastic femininity. Tattooed Monk Lu Zhisheng (Sagacious Lu) drinks his way through Chapters 3 to 7 in *The Outlaws*, violating every conceivable rule of priesthood and, as legend has it, pulling up a willow tree single-handedly. Panther Head Lin Chong in chapters 8 to 11 suffers injustice and is forced to enter the historical brigand stockade on Liangshan (Mount Liang) near Shandong's marsh region, the equivalent to Robin Hood's Sherwood Forest. Having slain a tiger in Chapters 23 to 31, Pilgrim Wu Song then avenges his brother, murdering the adulterous sister-in-law and her lover, and then fleeing to Liangshan. Chapters 38 to 43 feature Timely Rain Song Jiang, who receives Three Heavenly Books from the Mystic Queen of Ninth Heaven and guides the Liangshan fugitives back to righteousness. Indeed, characters recur throughout this episodic, picaresque novel. These are the excerpts in which some main heroes occupy center stage and can be discussed in manageable chunks of weekly reading assignments.

Compared to these heroes with their resounding nicknames, Hua Mulan is only given her "honorary" title of The Woman Warrior when she crosses over to the West. A traditional tale in support of filial piety and patriotism in "The Ballad of Mulan" is subverted by Kingston as a symbol of minority women's travail and liberation. More broadly, all these historical figures have been transformed through popular imagination into part of an unending, serial dream across China (*The Outlaws*), Chinese America (Kingston), and America (Disney's *Mulan*) in humanity's collective unconscious.

The Outlaws is inspired by the historical Song dynasty rebellion led by Song Jiang and his thirty-six comrades from the Shandong province. *The History of Song* and other historical documents have varying records of Song's revolt. Inherent in its own name, *zhongguo* ("Middle Kingdom" for China), the Chinese inclines toward balance and the golden mean rather than destabilizing extremes. This cultural trait informs the story of outlawry. The title *Shui Hu Zhuan* (Story of the Water Margin) readily juxtaposes water and land, as water's edge always meets land's end, a body of water adjacent to a land mass. Such spatial confluence finds its way into the brigands' stronghold of *Liangshanpo*, the marsh at Mount Liang. Yet *po* puns on both marshy areas and *anchor* or *perch*, the latter connotation being a sanctuary by the water. The contrast of mountain and water may in fact be a convergence. The very name of the protagonist Song Jiang circles back to this Chinese psychic preference for oneness, or symbiosis of opposites, thus deconstructing the surface story of lawlessness. The surname Song allies him with the Song dynasty, despite the hero's rebellion. His given name Jiang (river) not only denotes the marine hideout but implies that he is one with the Song orthodoxy, a tributary flowing eventually back to the source.

From the protagonist's name to the chapter titles, the Chinese proclivity for harmony and symmetry persists. All chapter titles are in the couplet form. Each consists of a couplet of two lines in perfect parallelism, a distinct feature of the monosyllabic Chinese language of one word with only one sound (syllable). For instance, Chapter 3 is titled in an eight-word couplet: "Master Shi Leaves Huayin County at Night / Major Lu Pummels the Lord of the West" (Shapiro 27). The Chinese title closely follows *duizhang*, syntactic and tonal parallelism. The first three ideograms are the two characters' names, or Shapiro's "Master Shi" and "Major Lu." The two words in the middle of the first and second line are the verbs of, literally, "night flee" (fleeing at night) and "fist pummel." The last three ideograms conclude with the objects, or Shapiro's "Huayin County" and "the Lord of the West" (to transliterate the three Chinese words: Zheng/Vanquish Gate West). This title suggests the organic flow of the chapter from one character to the next, one episode to the next. Likewise, Chapter 7 moves from Lu, now a monk, to Lin Chong.

Yet this best-case scenario of structural equilibrium does not apply to all chapters. Maintenance of rhetorical balance in each title, as well as consistency throughout, trumps content. This results in some couplets that are lopsided, a balance in name only between the two-part chapter titles. The second half of Chapter 4's title "Squire Zhao Repairs Wenshu Monastery," for instance, refers to one short paragraph where Major Lu's patron compensates the monastery for

Lu's destruction (59). This is something taken for granted in poetry, where end rhymes, alliterations, and, in the four-toned Mandarin, tonal counterpoints necessitate word choice based on sound rather than sense, or on auditory association rather than cognitive meaning. By corollary, the Chinese predisposition for the poetic overtakes logical reasoning on occasion, a parallel to the imaginary use of history in historical fiction.

The first hero Shi Jin nicknamed Nine Dragons embodies, literally, the quality of heroic, dragonlike camaraderie of *xia* (knight-errant à la James J. Y. Liu) at the core of this magnum opus of Chinese martial arts tradition. Cornered by local forces in pursuit of his sworn brothers, Shi leads the breakout from the siege. But when invited to join the bandits, Shi demurs: "My reputation is spotless. How can I sully the body my parents have given me?" (28). In the verbose translation of Nobel Laureate Pearl S. Buck, Shi's objection becomes "I am a man who is clear of all stain; how can I insult my parents by dishonoring the body they gave me?" Neither "spotless" nor "clear of all stain" does justice to Shi Nan'an's four-character maxim, *qingbaihaohan* ("clean white good fellow"). The first two words *qingbai* point to Shi Jin and more than a hundred more heroes' self-image of high-minded nobility, their eventual refuge in outlawry not withstanding; the last two words *haohan* praise masculinity in simple language. Both self-worth and manhood stem from the fundamental Confucian virtue of filial piety, as the second sentences in the preceding quotes make clear. Shi Jin is adamant in not "sullying" or "dishonoring" this gift of a body from his parents.

Herein lies the historical paradox of the Chinese body, a subtlety that seems to have fallen through the crack of critical lens over the centuries. On the one hand, Shi Jin is reluctant to join up, thus preserving the purity of the body in accordance with Confucian ideology: "From one's parents come the body, hair, and skin, which one dare not damage. This is the source of filial piety." On the other, Shi Jin has nine dragons tattooed on his body. This scarification of "arms and chest" (19) countermands the idea of maintaining the body, particularly the skin, in its pristine, natural state. Such behavior so infuriated his mother that she died. She dies from rage and resentment (*yiqi sile*, "one fury, then die," literally). Shapiro's "worry" comes as much too mild for the original (19). His father could only let him have his way; Shi Jin does not exactly personify filial piety. His actions may prove to boost that historic ideal among readers through its very dismantling.

This conundrum of Shi Jin's allegedly Confucian body inscribed with most un-Confucian wounds opens a novel of myriad crossovers or self-deconstructive hybridities. Shi Jin's story segues into the next hero Major Lu Da, a military officer endowed with superhuman strength, who beats to death a thug of a butcher. Lu then eludes the authorities by, ironically, entering the order of Buddhist priesthood. As picaresque narratives are wont to do, chance encounters, evident in Lu's flight, thread together the dramatis personae of several hundreds. Such meetings formulaically take place in the public space of teahouses, taverns, and streets, leading to the consumption of an inordinate amount of drinks and meat. These "red-blooded" heroes favor red meat and not vegetables, except Dai Zong the Marvelous Traveler. Superintendent Dai's Taoist magic enables him to travel hundreds of *li* (one third of a mile) each day, but only if he practices a strict Taoist diet sans meat.

Nomadic, ever-moving characters contribute to the sense of mobility, although this implies a downward spiral, a straying away from orthodoxy. To illustrate, Major Lu is on the run after accidentally killing the butcher Zheng and bumps into, at a teahouse, Shi Jin also on the run. Symbolically, the two "drifters" take to each other so much that they relocate from a place serving comparatively thin tea to a tavern serving strong, thick wine, culminating in their pledge to blood brotherhood, thicker yet than water and wine. Their instant bonding is contrasted with another chance encounter: in transit from the teahouse to the tavern, they come across Li Zhong, Shi's former kung fu master and now a "medicine pedlar" (35), "busking," as it were, by putting on a martial arts show. Li Zhong's miserly behavior silhouettes the two heroes' generosity and mutual devotion. This foreshadows Lu's ultimate break with Li Zhong in Chapter 5, where Lu has taken the disguise of a monk and makes off with treasures from Li's "lair," thus robbing the robbers. Despairing over stolen treasures, Li, a thief himself, curses that there is "no use locking the door after the thief is gone" (66). In a narrative equivalent to today's action thrillers, it in fact delves into human psychology. Lu despises Li and his second-in-command as "tight-wads" (60), who prefer robbing travelers who happen by for spoil as a farewell gift to Lu instead of sharing their den's accumulated wealth. Lu's perspicuity and inner thought prompt his action. If even a fierce, illiterate brute like Lu sees into the human mind and hidden motives, the other pivotal characters evince similar psychological depth.

Happenstance as they may be, these get-togethers in public spaces turn into destiny, as Lu, Shi, and many more willingly sacrifice themselves for one another after the oath of brotherhood. Lu, for one, trails Lin Chong in exile, framed for assassination of Marshall Gao, commander of the imperial guards, because Gao's adopted son lusted after Lin's wife. Just as Lin is about to be dispatched by the guards, Lu flies to his rescue. Likewise, Lu defends two damsels in distress whom he chances upon: Jin Jade Lotus, coerced into marriage and abandoned by Zheng the butcher; and Grandpa Liu's daughter at Peach Blossom Village forced to wed a bandit. Without such wrongs to right in the ascetic environment of a monastery, Lu's pent-up energy erupts twice into drunken brawls. Lu's violence-prone righteousness is misplaced in the monastery, where desires, even that for justice, are to be extinguished. Quick-tempered and ferocious, Lu has no patience and is accustomed to taking the law into his own hands. As for Dharma, laws of the Buddha, Lu is simply unable to refrain from most of the five precepts of "do not kill, steal, fornicate, drink, or lie" (42), except the third. As taking the order is merely a ruse to dodge the authorities, Lu is bound to violate these taboos. Moreover, his nickname also gives him away. Lu "the Flowery Monk" is closer to the original than Shapiro's "Tattooed Monk." The Chinese nickname does use the word "flower" (*hua*), a pun on the floral tattoo on his back and on his unrestrained, wanton behavior pattern. The latter derives from the cascade of colors and fragrances, the rush of the life force, inherent in any blossom. In terms of the precept on fornication, heroes, to a man, refrain from sex, implicitly as part of the folk belief in preserving male essence in the face of female seduction. Such patriarchal ideology leads to great problems in the private space of the bedroom and in marital relationships, a reflection of the historical power dynamics between the sexes emphasized through historical fiction.

Even in these select chapters, females cause the downfalls of three heroes. First, the adopted son of Lin Chong's superior covets his virtuous wife. Contrary to the notion of crime and punishment, Lin commits no crime, yet is so severely punished that he is marked for extermination. Even by the standards of guilty until "proven innocent" and the "legal use of torture . . . for extracting confession" that Derk Bodde and Clarence Morris describe (28), Lin is subject to unequivocally harsh and unjust treatment. Second, Wu Song the tiger slayer avenges his half-brother by killing the adulterous sister-in-law. Wu is the slayer of beast and of women. The latter is plural because, in Chapter 31, Wu slaughters his three foes and an entire household of a dozen family members and servants, plus four more from Chapter 30, a bona fide mass murderer, women and children included. Finally, Song Jiang slits his wife's throat not so much because he has been been cuckolded but rather to silence her because she has threatened to expose Song's bandit friends. Song's brotherly camaraderie supersedes family attachment; Wu's vengeance entails an indiscriminate bloodbath.

Whereas Chinese cosmology entails the harmony of yin and yang, female and male principle, the stronghold Mount Liang Marsh, judging by its name, seems precariously perched between mountain rocks and water flow. To associate yin with liquids vis-à-vis yang's solid matter, heroes displace the female principle from water-like women to the watery substance of alcohol, which Lu and Wu Song quaff down to turbocharge themselves prior to taking on bandits and the tiger. The more wine they imbibe, the more their strength grows, akin to biblical Samson's long hair. In denial of women, heroes transform yin into wine that fuels rather than ruins masculinity. This is most evident in Wu Song. The famed tiger destroyer accomplishes his feat only after the formulaic ritual of demanding endless rounds of wine and meat at the tavern, oblivious to the warning of drunkenness and the marauding beast afoot. His indulgence in wine

---

is flipped when the lecherous sister-in-law seduces him by serving wine, from which he abstains completely. The wine of his choosing, partaken amongst men, perhaps even the male tiger, elevates Wu's performance, opposite to the "poisoned cup," figuratively speaking, offered by a temptress in line with classical misogynist thinking.

In yet another case of Freudian transference of psychic complexes involving masculinity, wine, womanhood, and tigers, Li Kui in Chapter 43 is warned off wine in the rescue mission of his aging mother in the faraway hometown. Abstinence is blamed for Li's lackluster travel speed, "He [Song Jiang] told me not to drink any wine. That's why I couldn't walk very fast." Once he downs "a bowl or two," Li not only subdues a robber disguised as none other than himself but also slaughters four tigers that have devoured his mother (429). The false Li Kui, like his pale shadow without wine and symbolically castrated, asks for mercy with the excuse of having had to support a "ninety-year-old mother." The fake Li Kui with what turns out to be a fake nonagenarian mother are the doppelgangers to the real one on a filial pious mission. Discovering he has been duped, Li Kui kills his fake self and eats "two pieces of flesh" from his leg (437), no different from man-eating tigers he will dispose of. Fake identities continue. Li Kui's older brother, a hired hand in his hometown, had warded off guilt by association on the grounds that the Li Kui at Liangshan Marsh must have been an imposter. Once Li kills the tigers and is hailed as a hero, he pretends to be Zhang the Brave, only to be exposed by the robber's wife. Wine replaces women as both the life force and the path to death. Li drinks himself into a stupor and is arrested; Li is then rescued when his executioners unwittingly partake in drugged wine and meat.

A further twist to this psychic transference implicates Song Jiang and his most loyal follower Li Kui, the nicknames of both involving "black"—"Black Third" and "Black Whirlwind." Song Jiang is the dark shadow to the Song dynasty; Li is the shadow to Song the shadow man. Li is so devoted to Song that in the 100-chapter version, Song shares with him the poisoned wine, supposedly a gift from the emperor, for fear that Li would avenge his death by leading an insurrection. Li is content to serve him in death as "a minor ghost," Song's trusted apparition in life and in afterlife (989).

Liangshan Marsh offers a cross section of the Song society, illiterate ex-military man Lu as well as well-educated Song Jiang and Lin Chong. The latter two, plus Wu Song, stand apart as "Heroes of the Mark." The Mark alludes to Tolkienian high distinction in the vein of Rohan or Riders of the Mark as well as to Song dynasty practice of face-branding criminals bound for frontier military outposts. These three bear the mark of cruel and unusual punishment by modern standards. The novel is indeed historical in reflecting Song laws: "The prefect directed the tattooer to place the mark of a criminal on Lin Chong's cheek" (83). This leads to a fleeting moment when the fourteenth-century Ming dynasty author(s) registers the passage of time in a textual gloss. Lin's official escorts in exile to the frontier are instructed to kill him en route and "bring back the golden print on Lin Chong's face as proof. . . In Song times, prisoners to be exiled were always tattooed on the face. To make it sound better, the mark was called 'the golden print'" (86). Euphemistic indeed in gilding an inhuman penalty of the past, this footnote, nonetheless, registers the elapse of time. History is illuminated via a backward glance that constitutes the narrative perspective at the heart of any fiction.

In Wu Song's case, he takes on the guise of a *xingzhe*, "a pilgrim monk" with "long bangs . . . cover[ing] the tattoos" (313). On the way to avenge his benefactor Shi En, Wu Song "covered with a plaster the tattoo of the criminal on his cheek" (293). Although Wu Song resembles Lu in their destructive sprees, their tattoos and Buddhist disguises mark them as very different. Lu chose to don the flower tattoo, but Wu suffered face-branding twice for two alleged crimes. In their respective flights, Lu assumes a monk's identity because of generations of donations to a temple by his patron's family (45); Wu inherits the hair-binding metal hoop, robe, rosary, knives, and sundry items from a mendicant monk who had been cannibalized for "dumplings" stuffing (312, *mantou xian* or steamed bun stuffing). Lu's hair and beard are shaved; Wu lets the bangs down to conceal, since a *xingzhe* traditionally sports long hair.

Wordplay like "the golden print," on the face or on paper, run through the novel, first manifested in the overall rhetorical harmony in chapter titles of parallel couplets, even though occasionally stretched. Language goes to the root of the rebel leader Song Jiang's trajectory to Liangshan. If the leader joins up as a result of official misinterpretation of his words, Liangshan's heroism tries to rewrite itself, a crosscurrent against official history. Down and out, Song Jiang is so inebriated at a tavern that he writes a poem on the wall, a common calligraphic pastime for Chinese literati. The long poem includes "A criminal's tattoo upon my cheek, / An unwilling exile in far Jiangzhou, / I shall have my revenge some day, / And dye red with blood the Xunyang's flow" (391-92). This "circumstantial" evidence of a so-called rebellious poem purportedly reveals the author's subversive intent. Song's "writing on the wall" is coupled with a children's rhyme on the street: *The destroyer of our country is home and tree; water and work are armed soldiery; stretched in a line are thirty-six; Shandong will put us in a terrible fix*" (394, italics in the original). Yoking the children's rhyme with Song Jiang's poem, the official splits words (splits hairs, rather) in that "Put the top of the character for 'home' over the character for 'tree' and you've got the character 'Song' . . . Place the 'water' radical next to the character for 'work' and you've got 'Jiang, the man who will raise armed soldiers" (394). The paranoiac official attributes social unrest to Song Jiang by "decoding" a child's play and a drunkard's doodles.

Yet words carry mystical power to condemn as well as to uplift. When Song is entrusted in a dreamscape with "Three Heavenly Books" that supposedly detail the heroes' past lives and future, "The Mystic Queen of Ninth Heaven" cautions, "Familiarize yourself thoroughly with these three books. You may show them to the Occult Star [Wu Yong, one of the one hundred and eight celestial stars demoted to the earth], but to no other. After you have completed your mission, burn them. They are not to be left on earth" (428). Instead of ashes, the Chinese are left with revisions by numerous hands called *Shui Hu Zhuan* and a brood of prequels, sequels, and filmic remakes.

Crossing the ocean of languages and cultures, *The Outlaws of the Marsh* is not alone. Their female counterpart is Hua Mulan, also a historical figure become legend. The Chinese-American novelist Maxine Hong Kingston borrows Hua as the protagonist in *The Woman Warrior.* Historical elements are sprinkled throughout, if somewhat cavalierly and always fused with Orientalist fantasy and feminist politics. This is the three-legged stool on which Kingston's reputation rests: Chineseness, orientalism, and feminism. To empower female characters against Chinese patriarchy as well as against a racist, male-dominated America, Kingston resorts to legendary Chinese heroines and orientalist stereotypes.

In terms of Chinese history, Kingston confuses certain details, such as the Six Kingdoms having purportedly risen up to annihilate the Qin dynasty. It happened the other way around; that is, the First Emperor of Qin defeated all Six Kingdoms and united China for the first time in history (Kingston 78). Kingston's historical error is tantamount to saying that the South won the American Civil War (1861-1865). Likewise, Kingston has Hua's parents tattoo on her back what is associated with Song dynasty general Yue Fei. General Yue's parents allegedly carved on his back four characters to spur him on. Kingston transfers the four characters to a plethora of words on Hua's bare back. "[My father] began cutting; to make fine lines and points he used thin blades, for the stems, large blades," narrates Kingston's Hua. "My mother caught the blood and wiped the cuts with a cold towel soaked in wine. It hurt terribly—the cuts sharp; the air burning; the alcohol cold, then hot" (41). Such imaginary mixing aims to suggest the depth of agony in ethnic struggles. The "gift" comes from the parents, who pass down one's ethnicity as though it were doomed to be self-inflicted pain, inherited bane, in a white-majority society. Paradoxically, that bloodline also enables the woman warrior by means of multiple role models, not only Hua Mulan but also Maxine's mother character, Brave Orchid, who used to be a healer, a "barefoot doctor," in China, who has since deteriorated into a headstrong, foolhardy laundress in the United States.

In terms of orientalism, Kingston practices a benign splitting of immigrant characters, who provide the raison d'être for ethnicity. Brave Orchid the strong in Canton jars with Brave Orchid the fool in California. Brave Orchid the fool further jars with her sister, or Maxine's aunt, Moon Orchid the crazed. It appears that the duress of a New World either calcifies an immigrant or drives her mad; the Promised Land turns the new arrival either into an inflexible, ridiculous automaton at the Chinatown laundry or into a broken thing. This is, of course, the oldest formula for the oriental other. The unknown East is polarized into the aesthetic, the mystical as opposed to the abhorrent, the abject. China's woman warriors run aground on the shores of America, while the West anchors itself securely in the middle of reason and humanity, launching its white gaze at the unknowable nonwhites. Born and raised in California, writing in English with all its resources and "white man's burden," Kingston unwittingly reprises this orientalist legacy for the explicit purpose of feminist empowerment.

When Kingston's "Fa Mu Lan" character becomes pregnant during her campaign, she has her "armor altered so that I looked like a powerful, big man. . . . Now when I was naked, I was a strange human being indeed—words carved on my back and the baby large in front" (47). Although masquerading as a man, she in fact traverses both genders, as pregnancy epitomizes femininity, and martial endeavors crystallize masculinity. Kingston's mythical China, along with all the misinformation of an exotic land from a Chinese-American perspective, is designed to carve out an ethnic feminist identity in the sliver of space between two cultural forces, China and the United States. Seemingly belonging to both and to neither, Kingston writes a memoir among ghosts as if she were the sole human being, the soul of humanity. Kingston's classic has founded an Asian American literary tradition of taking "immigrant license," a forging of Asian-American self by way of forgery of Asian (immigrant) other.

Walt Disney's *Mulan* (1998) mainstreams Kingston's story in the multicultural teenage market, spicing it up with politically correct identity politics and the same old, same old of orientalism. The latter can be gleaned from the dramatis personae. The stereotypical Chinese dragon morphs into the Eddie Murphy-dubbed, dragon-lizard Mushu, after Mu Shu Pork. Murphy's black English provides comic relief and an anachronistic sense of multiculturalism in ancient China. The splitting of the word "cricket" creates the monosyllabic, Chinese-sounding "Cri-Kee." Mulan's steed is "Khan," after Genghis Khan. Her masculine disguise is called Ping, after one of the three imperial court mandarin-clowns in Puccini's opera *Turandot* (1926). As such, the overwhelming majority of characters have names that are at once exotic and familiar. The yoking of strangeness and banality in orientalist representations succeeds in accommodating and domesticating the unknown. Perhaps even more disturbing is Disney's Mulan-Mushu pairing in the manner of ethnic stereotypes of yellow kung fu and black jokes (Ma).

Despite its profit-driven adaptation, Disney's cross-dressing Mulan has inspired China's own revisiting of the Chinese legend, specifically in the 2009 film *Mulan: Rise of a Warrior*. This Chinese retelling advances the image of strong women as well as strong nationalism, manifested in the lead Zhao Wei's line selected as the favorite by Chinese film viewers: "I, Hua Mulan, will never betray my country." The *us* versus *them* dichotomy rallies national sentiments for China in its rise in what has been called *China's Century*. But the *us* sentiment in part reacts against *them* from Walt Disney. Ideally, in this global village of the new millennium, crossing over to our neighbors on the other side results in sharing, as in a block party, but Hua's cross-dressing demonstrates how fraught it is. Hua crosses the gender divide in order to, ironically, erect the wall between China and its so-called northern barbarians. Hua then crosses the ocean to empower Asian Americans via strong Chinese woman warriors, who are silhouetted against caricatures of their former selves in the United States. Self-enhancing is posited on self-belittling!

While one hopes for a crossing over by many cultures via historical fiction, that crossing can be fraught with challenges. Stories that open history to the culture in which it occurred may require corrective commentary to guarantee they produce the correct effect. Grappling with such conundrums, historical fictions become conceptual alloy tools for discriminating readers to pry open past history imaginatively, or their own imagination historically.

Works Cited

Bodde, Derk, and Clarence Morris. *Law in Imperial China.* U of Pennsylvania P, 1967.

Hsia, Chih-tsing. *The Classic Chinese Novel: A Critical Introduction.* Indiana UP, 1980.

Kingston, Maxine Hong. *The Woman Warrior: Memoirs of a Girlhood among Ghosts.* Knopf, 1976.

Kwa, Shiamin, and Wilt L. Idema. *Mulan: Five Versions of a Classic Chinese Legend with Related Texts.* Hackett, 2010.

Liu, James J. Y. *The Chinese Knight-Errantry.* Routledge, 1967.

Ma, Sheng-mei. "Yellow Kung Fu and Black Jokes." *Television and New Media,* vol. 1, no. 2, May 2000, pp. 239-44.

Mulan. Directed by Tony Bancroft and Barry Cook, performances by Ming-Na Wen, Eddie Murphy, and B. D. Wong. Disney, 1998.

Mulan: Rise of a Warrior. Directed by Jingle Ma and Wei Dong, performances by Wei Zhao, Jaycee Chan, andJiao Xu. Starlight International, 2009.

Shi Nai'an and Luo Guanzhong. *All Men Are Brothers.* Trans. Pearl S. Buck. John Day, 1933.

_____. *The Outlaws of the Marsh.* Trans. Sidney Shapiro. Indiana UP, 1981. /uploads/pdf/20130423230739the_outlaws_of_ the_marsh_pdf. Accessed 3 June 2017.

_____. *The Water Margin.* Trans. J. H. Jackson. Tuttle, 1937.

Wu Cheng'en. *Journey to the West.* (Hsi-yu chi.) Trans. Anthony C. Yu. Chicago: U of Chicago P, 1980.

Representation of the American Civil War in Contemporary Historical Fiction for Young Adults: Why We Read about the Civil War_____

Amy Cummins

The cataclysmic national event that we know as the United States Civil War serves as a major historical focus for contemporary literature. Frequently appearing in secondary school readings, young adult (YA) Civil War fiction can bring history to life in ways distinct from nonfiction and textbooks by transforming the general to the particular through memorable characters, plots, and themes. This essay explores how young adult historical novels about the Civil War portray four topics: the sacrifices of soldiers on the battlefield, reasons for fighting, dissent about the war, and African-American resistance to enslavement and injustice. Textual analysis focuses on five novels: *Bull Run* by Paul Fleischman, *With Every Drop of Blood: A Novel of the Civil War* by James Lincoln Collier and Christopher Collier, *Soldier's Heart* by Gary Paulsen, *Riot* by Walter Dean Myers, and *A Soldier's Secret: The Incredible True Story of Sarah Edmonds, a Civil War Hero* by Marissa Moss.

Offering diverse structures and set at different moments of the war, each novel appeals to young readers. *With Every Drop of Blood* by the Collier brothers is narrated by a teen from a Confederate family who develops friendship with a black Union soldier in 1865. Set in July 1863, Myers's *Riot* adopts a screenplay format, while Fleischman's *Bull Run*, set in 1861, is narrated in vignette form; they adapt particularly well to readers' theater, speeches, or debates. Spanning multiple years, Paulsen's *Soldier's Heart* and Moss's *A Soldier's Secret* depict lives of historically real Union soldiers Charley Goddard and Sarah Emma Edmonds, Edmonds adopting the pseudonym Frank Thompson. The authors engage in scholarly research, basing their fiction on substantial historical research and include timelines, maps, prefaces, epilogues, period photographs, or other educational materials.

As scholarly attention to the Civil War boomed in the late 1980s, a decade later, YA historical fiction grew in popularity. Joanne Brown and Nancy St. Clair discuss the importance and appeal of historical novels, but warn that readers must be alert to fiction that "promote[s] stereotypes that reinforce the hegemony of the dominant culture while negating the experiences of historically marginalized groups" (24). Readers should conscientiously question *any* book's claims and conduct their own research to verify accuracy. Historical fiction may, however, best challenge and reinforce prejudices and stereotypes about complex times such as the Civil War. While readers learn through historical fiction, "the genre also tells us much about the period in which the fiction was written, revealing writers' concerns about and attitudes toward the cultural tensions of their own times" (Brown and St. Clair 14).

Twenty-first century readers will benefit in particular from attention paid to the narrative portrayal of African Americans in US history and seek correction of traditional misperceptions. As it naturally prompts rewarding conversations about values, language choices, and the daily reality of previous eras, historical fiction is particularly suited to the classroom. However, readers and educators should be aware that Civil War fiction portrayals of African-American enslavement and human violence may prove difficult for young readers. Authors remain sensitive to such issues, often adding valuable explanations, for instance of offensive terminology related to racial issues.

The Sacrifices of Soldiers on the Battlefields

More than 620,000 soldiers died in the American Civil War from 1861 to 1865, in addition to 50,000 civilians (Faust xi-xii). Civil War fiction should acknowledge the toll of human lives at a level that shocks many readers: "More than two percent of the nation's inhabitants were dead as a direct result of the war" (Faust 266). As Abraham Lincoln expressed in his Gettysburg Address on November 19, 1863, "we here resolve that these dead shall not have died in vain" (Collier and Collier 235). The physical threats and necessity to kill faced by soldiers, many completely unprepared for the violence, constitute a prominent theme in Civil War historical novels.

Soldier's Heart by Gary Paulsen focuses on the experiences of Charley Goddard, a historically real soldier from Minnesota who enlisted at the age of fifteen. During his first major battle, the Battle of First Manassas, or Bull Run (July 21, 1861), Goddard is shocked by learn that in war, "death was everywhere" (Paulsen 21). He struggles to find a familiar comparison for the line of Rebels firing at his group, likening it to "a blade cutting grain." Paulsen effectively applies additional sensory imagery, adding that Goddard "heard the bullets hitting the men—little *thunk-slaps*—and saw the men falling. Some of them screamed as they fell. Many were silent. Many were dead before they hit the ground. Many were torn apart" (22). He prays, "I am not supposed to see this, God. No person is supposed to see this. How can You let this happen?" (25). Goddard must walk over corpses on the battlefield, realizing, "they were all Minnesota men, but the dead all looked alike. Broken. Like broken toys or dolls" (37).

The dehumanizing aspect of the war takes an emotional toll, and in Goddard's second battle, hatred and a desire to kill overwhelms him, to "stick and jab and shoot them and murder them and kill them all, each and every Rebel's son of them" (Paulsen 51). Alienated from nationalism by his third major battle, Goddard loses his faith: "He felt alone now. Always alone. He existed in a world that he believed—no, *knew*—would end for him soon" (71). Constantly expecting to die as he survives multiple skirmishes, Goddard anticipates death as release. When he is finally shot, "he saw the red veil come down over his eyes and knew that at last he was right, at last he was done, at last he was dead" (96). However, Goddard survived his full three years of enlistment, one of only forty-seven men who lived from the one thousand original soldiers of the First Minnesota Volunteers (104). The title *Soldier's Heart* is one term for what is now identified as posttraumatic stress disorder (PTSD).

Paul Fleishman formats *Bull Run* as a series of sixty vignettes, short chapters spoken by eight Southern characters and eight Northern characters. All experience the battle that became known as the First Battle of Bull Run. Union soldier Dietrich Herz, a German American, describes his experience as his division wades across the stream, charges, and is met by "a volley of rifle fire, then artillery shells" (Fleischman 61). Herz sees grievously injured men and only fires once before he is wounded. He later regains consciousness long enough to perceive looters rifling the pockets of the wounded and the dead—doing nothing to help the wounded (90). Another character's vignette reveals that Herz survives after amputation of both legs.

A Southern doctor in Fleischman's novel, William Rye, likewise witnesses the horror war inflicts as he amputates limbs of the injured: "We probed and sawed and stitched without stop and were soon as blood-covered as they were" (Fleischman 94). He realizes that although the Confederacy pushed back the Union in this battle, it was not a triumphant event for humanity: "A victory? Indeed it was, for Death upon his pale horse" (94). One young Confederate, Toby Boyce, who enlisted to kill Yankees, finds himself confronted with a dying man with "no body to speak of below his waist" who begs him, "Shoot me," but Boyce runs away, unable to do so (96). The novels dramatize how Bull Run proved the war would not end quickly as predicted.

In the Colliers' *With Every Drop of Blood*, protagonist Johnny is a fourteen-year-old Confederate civilian captured by a black soldier and his regiment. Observing battle, Johnny realizes about the soldiers, "One minute they were alive and the next minute they weren't; and now they were all being heaved into a pit.... And the whole thing was a waste, for the attack hadn't got them anything" (167). Few individuals could emotionally prepare for the cycle of killing and dying that characterizes war.

Most readers do not realize that more than four hundred women disguised as men fought in the Civil War (Moss 366). One woman soldier, Sarah Emma Edmonds emigrated to the United States from Canada. She then lived as Frank Thompson, working as a traveling bookseller before enlisting in the Union Army. Marissa Moss novelizes Edmonds's service in *A Soldier's Secret: The Incredible True Story of Sarah Edmonds, a Civil War Hero*. At the Battle of Williamsburg, Edmonds works on burials and sees the "dead and wounded lie piled together in ravines and rifle pits, covered with mud and gore" (129). Another example of her experience comes during the Battle of Fair Oaks: "The scene on the battlefield is grisly. Thousands of men are strewn in the mud, dead and wounded, while around, among, and beside them the fight rages on. I can't believe I ever considered war noble. All I see now is brutality, as men step over their fallen comrades to shoot at other men. At least we're winning. That is, I think we're winning" (165). And Edmonds thinks, "I don't feel part of a great historical moment. Instead, I'm stuck in an ugly nightmare, and it seems like dawn will never come" (Moss 207). Even before the worst of the battle, she reflects, "It's pure chance who survives and who doesn't. And the chances aren't good. For every man who dies in battle, two die from disease" (44). That ratio matches current research indicating that twice as many soldiers died from disease as from battle wounds (Faust 4).

In *Riot*, Myers portrays soldiers after the Battle of Gettysburg in Madison Square Park, sent to quell civilian riots against the Union draft in July 1863. A soldier explains his war experience, describing the rebel yells and the feeling of fear: "It wasn't the dying that scared me. It was the wounded laying out in the field calling out for their mamas. That's a bad sound" (Myers 75). Soldiers' conversations reveal the chaos of war: "He said he clean forgot what this war was about. Except for the killing, of course" (121).

Reasons for Fighting

In *Soldier's Heart*, Goddard enlists naïvely, wanting to fight in "a shooting war" and because he has heard about secession and knows "the Union was right" (Paulsen 2). Voicing a prominent question of the day, Goddard "wondered what would happen after the war when the Union had whipped the Rebels. Would they be allowed to keep their slaves? The war wasn't initially about slavery; the troops were going to stop the 'lawbreakers and wrong thinkers' that were trying to 'bust up the Union'" (15). Ironically, he encounters a black person for the first time when an enslaved woman at a train stop thanks him for serving in the Union army (16). Paulsen later features blacks who serve, as do the two novels discussed below, in order to elucidate the added peril of discrimination in war.

With Every Drop of Blood features multiple perspectives and motivations to fight. The Colliers go beyond the fact of conscription to focus on the plight of blacks who willingly served. They first introduce Johnny, whose gravely wounded father makes his son promise not to enlist, because he has already fulfilled their family obligation to Virginia. Johnny's father says that he served because:

> "The U.S. Constitution says each state is equal, and if Virginians let the Federals take away our slaves or say we can't take them into the new territories out west, there's no telling where they'll stop. Next thing you know the Federal government will try to tell us what to grow or who we can sell our cotton and tobacco to. No, Johnny, this here war isn't about slaves at all—It's about a state's right to govern itself." (Collier and Collier 29)

Johnny constantly puzzles over the importance of slavery to the conflict. His father insists that the disagreement is not about keeping slaves but rather "about who decides—the states or the Federals" (31). Johnny reflects that "Everybody seemed to have a different idea of it—states' rights, honor of the South, slavery. Why were these fellas in it?" (62), adding "It seemed like a lot of people were fighting the Yanks just because they were here" (64). He is later captured by the Union in a failed attempt to earn money for his family by driving his mule team on a supply run to Confederate troops. Johnny begins to understand the part slavery plays in the war as he talks with a black soldier: "'My pa says the war isn't over slavery, it's over states' rights.' The darky soldier laughed. 'You tell that to a black man and see how far it takes you.' I could see that" (137).

Johnny's transition from a practice of racism to awareness of his complicity as supporter of slavery has a powerful impact on readers. That impact is in part because the first-person narrative forces readers to see the dispute through a Confederate viewpoint. A Union captain later tells Johnny to "read the Constitution," because it begins with "'We the people of the United States,' not

'We the states.' You can't have every state that disagrees with the laws thumbing its nose at the national government and going off by itself" (Collier and Collier 150).

The heart of the novel resides in Johnny's developing relationship with black Union soldier, Private Cush Turner, allowing the novel to emphasize war service by blacks, and how it differs from that of whites. At the outset, Johnny does not question his own racist views because he is isolated from blacks, enslaved or free. During his capture by a black Union soldier, he is "shock[ed] to hear a darky called by a last name" (Collier and Collier 81). He gets to know Cush, who arranges for Johnny to receive food if he will teach Cush to read. Johnny knows teaching slaves to read is illegal, because they might think that "it put them on a level with white folks, and it wasn't right for a white person to help in that" (99).

Johnny eventually learns that he and Cush have much in common. He also comes to understand why slavery must be abolished, after learning the daily reality of those enslaved. He realizes that he has not given "much thought one way or another" to black people, "but now I'd got to know a darky, and I could see it wasn't simple" (Collier and Collier 145). In addition, the individual sympathy he extends to Cush should apply to all slaves: "And if it wasn't right for Cush to be whipped regular, why was it right for any of them to get whipped?" (184). When Cush is injured and captured, Johnny rescues him and knows that he cannot leave Cush to die because "We'd got to be friends by mistake" (176). The sentiment he attributes to Cush is actually his own: "He couldn't think of me as the enemy anymore" (183). The novel's setting at war's end proves crucial to the survival of Cush and Johnny, for they are in Appomattox, Virginia, on April 9, 1865, the day General Robert E. Lee surrenders to Lieutenant General Ulysses S. Grant.

The novel that most strongly features blacks in service is Fleischman's *Bull Run* in which the most active narrator is a light-skinned black man named Gideon Adams. In his home of Cincinnati, Adams and his friends try to organize "a company of Home Guards," so black men could protect the city, but white citizens protest, "You'll do no damn parading about with guns!" (8). Then they are rejected as soldiers because blacks are only assigned roles as ditchdiggers, cooks, or teamsters. Adams vows, "I would stand at the front of the fray, not the rear, and would hold a rifle in my hand" (15). Adams cuts his hair, dons a hat, and passes as white, enlisting as an infantry soldier under the name of Able. Despite his pride in being black, he passes because he wants to fight for justice for black Americans. Adams observes racist behavior among the soldiers, who say they are "fighting against secession, not against slavery" (39). Disappointed after the defeat at Bull Run and the attitudes of men who will not reenlist after their ninety days expire, Adams vows he would "join a three-year regiment, and that I wouldn't return to Ohio until the Rebels had been beaten" (95). Fleischman accurately represents the historical record regarding blacks serving during the Civil War.

While men of African descent could not enlist in the Union army when the war began, in 1862, the expanded Military Act made free black men and emancipated slaves eligible to serve. By the end of the war, "nearly 10 percent of federal forces" were black soldiers (Faust 44). In total more than 180,000 black men enlisted, despite "inequalities in pay and opportunity," representing a substantial contribution to the Union effort (Faust 44).

Various war-related legal actions supported abolition and provide necessary context for the fictional representation of slavery. They also illuminate the mounting tensions featured in Civil War historical fiction. Historian Paul Finkelman writes that "the Lincoln administration had become part of the process of ending slavery while professing not to be doing so" (24). The Union's First Confiscation Act (on August 6, 1861) allowed for the seizure and freeing of slaves used by the Confederate military and thus showed that "the national government had the power to free slaves as a military necessity" (Finkelman 24). In March 1862, the Act Prohibiting the Return of Slaves fully overturned previous fugitive slave laws and forbade returning runaway slaves to Confederate owners or military. The "contraband" policy originated when Major General Benjamin Butler at Fort Monroe chose in May 1863 not to return fugitive slaves to Virginian owners, which "was not applied everywhere at once" but became "the beginning of a new policy for the United States" (Finkelman 22).

In *A Soldier's Secret*, Moss shows this moment's personal importance to Edmonds, serving as Frank Thompson. Edmonds meets contrabands who have escaped from building Confederate river fortifications. As she provides medical attention to a wounded black man, she realizes he "is like all of us. He's just the same" (89). The effect on Edmonds is clear, as she thinks, "For me, the war has been about saving the Union. Now it's also about something else, something that claws in the pit of my stomach—it's about freeing a whole class of people condemned to being treated like animals. It's about justice" (90). She articulates her sense of purpose, saying "I enlisted in the war to preserve the Union, but now I have another reason to fight: to save people from the tyranny of other people" (90). Edmonds identifies with the plight of enslaved Americans, wondering, "Why should they be slaves simply because of their skin color? It's the same with women—why should we have such limited lives? Are we really lesser people?" (90). Her sense of purpose strengthens as she spies on Confederates in the guise of a free African American. When an officer roars, "As long as there's a Confederate army, y'all belong to SOMEONE!" (112), Edmonds feels even more determined. She thinks, "All the slaves will be free, so long as *my* heart beats strong!" (113). Later in the war, she speaks about the Emancipation Proclamation and affirms that "getting rid of slavery is an excellent reason to fight" (281).

Readers of these novels will gain a better understanding of the motivations that moved both factions to engage in the Civil War. Some characters change their points of view, but others do not, as history records. Still others found an already existing resolve strengthened through interaction with those from both sides.

Dissent about the War

Many white Southerners dissented, supporting neither the Confederacy nor secession. As Williams writes, Southern attitudes about the Confederacy were characterized by "internal domestic hostility" and disaffection (13). Nevertheless, state conventions, "dominated by slaveholders, ignored majority will and took their states out of the union" (14). While early Southern enlistment was strong because of the threat of invasion, it declined immediately, and at least 300,000 Southern whites served Union forces (22). Thus, the Confederate Army instituted a draft well before the Union. Southern conscription laws in 1862 did allow wealthy men to "avoid the draft by hiring a substitute or paying an exemption fee." Congress also "exempted one white male of draft age for every twenty slaves owned" (14), creating an economic disparity that gave rise to the expression "rich man's war, poor man's fight" (Williams 15; Strausbaugh 262). Some dissenters joined antiwar organizations, formed armed gangs, or defended communities as dramatized in the movie *Free State of Jones* (Ross).

Opposition to conscription laws appeared in the South and in the North. Myers's novel, *Riot*, traces the tensions that led to the three-day riot that began on July 13, 1863, in New York City. It alludes to Southern dissent when a soldier says ironically, "I heard the rebs had to kill a bunch of people to get them to report for duty" (68). Transferring recruitment responsibility from states to the federal government, Congress passed the Enrollment Act, which made men between the ages of 20 and 45 liable for military service. "The law was worded vaguely enough to make black men as well as white men eligible," which angered people who opposed abolition or emancipation (Strausbaugh 262). And "then came the staggering lists of the twenty-three thousand Union casualties at Gettysburg," a reminder of the possible consequences of military service (Strausbaugh 274). The demand that certain segments of the American population enlist to defend slaves ignited the smoldering anger in a city where Irish Americans especially suffered poverty, discrimination, and overcrowding. At least 119 people died in the outburst, most of them rioters, and 400 more were injured (Strausbaugh 289). More than eleven black men were lynched, and the Colored Orphan Asylum was burned to the ground. Thankfully, the asylum's 200 occupants escaped.

The rapid pace of *Riot*, formatted as a screenplay, conveys the tense atmosphere. African Americans could not safely walk the streets, gangs took advantage of the situation, as did political forces to meet personal agendas, and violence was exacerbated by stolen alcohol (Strausbaugh 279). Maeve, a sixteen-year-old Irish-American character, views the reasons for the rioting as "How the Irish are the ones being pushed around. And how the swells are looking to send us off to fight for the Coloreds" (31). John Andrews, a lawyer and prominent Southern sympathizer (277), incites Maeve's fiancé, Liam, who is later killed, Liam provokes the crowd to action by shouting, "Lincoln said that he was fighting to preserve the Union, but we all know the real reason—to free the darkies so they can come and take what little chance we have to feed our own" (Myers 46). In an author's note, Myers states plainly, "The causes of the New York City Draft Riots began in 1619, when the first Africans were brought across the Atlantic as slaves" (161). As Myers makes clear, any analysis of the American Civil War requires consideration of African-American history, which historical fiction uses to its advantage.

The memory of the New York City Draft Riots resonates in *With Every Drop of Blood*, set two years later in Virginia. A black soldier refers to the incident, which he blames on "immigrant crackers" (138). Johnny, having read about the riots, thinks: "When Lincoln started up the draft, the Irish and I guess lots others said they weren't going to get themselves killed for the colored. They tore up New York and hung a bunch of darkies from lampposts" (138). The infamous incident casts a long shadow in history and shows the centrality of race and economic class to the war.

Finally, dissent manifests itself in doubts about military and political leadership. In *A Soldier's Secret*, Edmonds often notes problems caused by flawed leaders and their ill-informed decisions. For example, after the Battle of Fredericksburg, December 1862, in which Union casualties exceeded 12,000 soldiers, Edmonds thinks: "The stupidity of the sacrifice galls me" (Moss 262). Her anger with General Burnside causes her to wonder, "How can I stay in an army led by such an arrogant, ignorant, pompous ass? What is my true duty? Is it to him or to the Union cause? … What is a loyal soldier supposed to do when obeying a superior officer means betraying the army he serves in? How can I follow orders that are obviously suicidal?" (262). Readers may identify with Edmonds's frustrations, in that such questions continue to be asked of those who serve.

African-American Resistance to Enslavement and Injustice

Priscilla in Myers's *Riot* learns about slave resistance from her Great-Aunt Esther, whose father moved the family North to freedom. Priscilla and Claire, the protagonist, discuss "how the slaves make quilts in the South that are really like maps. They have a star and paths that lead to the star" (Myers 7). Priscilla's Great-Aunt Esther and the next generations of the family had been able to live free only because her father fled slavery. When Priscilla and Claire check on Great-Aunt Esther, they discover she has passed away, and they must take shelter from the riots in a black church where the congregation has gathered for safety and support. Claire wrestles with the meaning of her black and Irish biracial identity as she is victimized by blatant prejudice. She expresses a universal desire: "I just wanted to be a human being" (129). Claire's father, John, bravely opposes the antiblack violence by shepherding the children from the Colored Orphan Asylum to a boat and escaping to Blackwell's Island after the orphanage is burned. Priscilla's family will leave New York at the end of the book, their move representing the fact that the city's black population decreased by twenty percent after the riots (Strausbaugh 280).

From the outset of the Civil War, enslaved African Americans resisted injustice by fleeing to Union lines. By the middle of 1864, nearly 400,000 slaves had reached Union lines, constituting "about ten percent of the entire slave population of the South" (Hahn 110). In *Bull Run*, Fleischman portrays such resistance through a Southern character, Carlotta King, enslaved by a Confederate officer. Before the battle, King looks at the hills and hopes for a Union victory. After the Confederacy wins that battle, she decides, "I couldn't sit and wait for the Northerners to whip the South" (89). She seizes the chance for freedom, crossing the creek and heading north. Historian Steven Hahn asserts that "the Civil War involved two rebellions: a rebellion of slaveholders against the authority of the federal government (secession and the formation of the Confederacy); followed by a rebellion of slaves against the authority of their masters" (112). From this point of view, slave resistance proved partly responsible for an end of slavery "by a combination of military action, executive order, and constitutional amendment" (Hahn 114).

The novels feature and/or reference real historic characters as well as events. For example, Frederick Douglass is referenced in *With Every Drop of Blood*. When Johnny expresses surprises at Cush's insistence on learning to read, Cush explains that many African Americans can read and write and that Frederick Douglass "wrote a wheelbarrow full of books" about his important ideas (Collier and Collier 109). Johnny expresses white superiority when he remarks, "Most likely this here Douglass must of overheard some white man say it first" (109). Cush engages in additional resistance taking his surname from insurrectionist Nat Turner, leader of a bloody rebellion of slaves in 1831. Assumption of a last name allowed Cush to join the Union army (121).

The words and principles of Lincoln's Gettysburg Address track throughout the novel and demonstrate Johnny's change of heart. Cush, who already knows the alphabet, insists on learning to read his treasured copy of Lincoln's "Gettysburg Address." As Johnny explains the speech to Cush, word by word, he too better understands it—as does the reader. Cush is enraged when Johnny confesses he had taught him wrong information: "You was determined to keep me from finding out the real meaning of it—about all men being created equal—about what Lincoln promised, what the Declaration promised" (Collier and Collier 192). In addition to allowing readers connection to the characters, inclusion of the Gettysburg Address as an epilogue allows readers to review the words themselves with, perhaps, new insight.

Enslaved persons resisting bondage before the Civil War are portrayed in many additional novels such as *Nightjohn* (1993) and *Sarny* (1997) by Gary Paulsen; *To Be a Slave* (1968) and *Day of Tears* (2005) by Julius Lester; and *Copper Sun* (2006) by Sharon Draper. The genre of the *neo-slave narrative*, which includes books

---

"written by contemporary authors who retell or re-envision the slave experience in America," emphasizes "the humanity, resilience, and guile of enslaved men, women, and children" (Hinton 50-51). While an analysis of additional such novels is beyond the scope of this chapter, readers may easily access them and also turn to true neo-slave and antebellum narratives to better contextualize the Civil War.

Looking Back and Looking Ahead

The novels *With Every Drop of Blood*, *Bull Run*, *Soldier's Heart*, *Riot*, and *A Soldier's Secret* demonstrate important Civil War themes contextualized by an era that proved a turning point in US history. They offer readers an understanding of soldiers' battlefield experiences, their reasons for fighting, dissent about the war, and African-American resistance to enslavement and injustice. Meriting analysis for literary and historical reasons, the novels, like all quality historical fiction, stand ready to shed light on cultural and social issues central to understanding nineteenth-century America.

Works Cited

Brown, Joanne, and Nancy St. Clair. *The Distant Mirror: Reflections on Young Adult Historical Fiction.* Scarecrow, 2006.

Collier, James Lincoln, and Christopher Collier. *With Every Drop of Blood: A Novel of the Civil War*. 1994. Dell, 1996.

Draper, Sharon. *Copper Sun*. Atheneum, 2006.

Faust, Drew Gilpin. *This Republic of Suffering: Death and the American Civil War*. Knopf, 2008.

Finkelman, Paul. "Lincoln and the Preconditions for Emancipation: The Moral Grandeur of a Bill of Lading." *Lincoln's Proclamation: Emancipation Reconsidered.* Edited by William Blair and Karen Fisher Younger. U of North Carolina P, 2009, pp. 13-44.

Fleischman, Paul. *Bull Run*. Harper, 1993.

Hahn, Steven. "But What Did the Slaves Think of Lincoln?" *Lincoln's Proclamation: Emancipation Reconsidered.* Edited by William Blair and Karen Fisher Younger. U of North Carolina P, 2009, pp. 102-19.

Hinton, KaaVonia. "Following Tradition: Young Adult Literature as Neo-slave Narrative." *Embracing, Evaluating, and Examining African*

American Children's and Young Adult Literature. Edited by Wanda Brooks and Jonda McNair, Scarecrow, 2008, pp. 50-65.

Moss, Marissa. *A Soldier's Secret: The Incredible True Story of Sarah Edmonds, a Civil War Hero*. Abrams, 2012.

Myers, Walter Dean. *Riot*. Egmont, 2009.

Paulsen, Gary. *Soldier's Heart: Being the Story of the Enlistment and Due Service of the Boy Charley Goddard in the First Minnesota Volunteers*. Random House, 1998.

Ross, Gary, director. *Free State of Jones*. STX Entertainment, 2016.

Strausbaugh, John. *City of Sedition: The History of New York City During the Civil War*. Hachette, 2016.

Williams, David. "Southern Dissent." *Civil War America: A Social and Cultural History*. Edited by Maggi Morehouse and Zoe Trodd. Routledge, 2013, pp. 13-23.

"Sixty Million and More": Family and Sacrifice in the African-American Historical Novel_____

Jericho Williams

Beyond the popularity of modern hip-hop lyrics, the most common forms of African-American literature include documented oral tales, nineteenth-century slave narratives, protest novels such as Richard Wright's *Native Son* (1940) or Ralph Ellison's *Invisible Man* (1950), nonfiction writings from major figures such as W. E. B. Dubois, James Baldwin, and Martin Luther King Jr. associated with cultural and political movements such as the Harlem Renaissance and the Civil Rights Era, and the poetry of Phillis Wheatley, Maya Angelou, and Nikki Giovanni. Regardless of the form, these examples emerge from the need to address social injustices inherited from prior generations, and they often speak directly to their present era. This chapter seeks to broaden appreciation of a less-acknowledged form with an emphasis on a more distant past, so it investigates African-American historical fiction, an equally valuable subfield that enables greater reflective opportunities within a rich cultural history. The essay spotlights Mildred Taylor and Toni Morrison, two authors who exhume and reimagine forgotten eras associated with the lingering struggles of race and oppression in America. Within the past half-century, their collective works have elevated historical fiction to becoming a central literary mode in understanding African-American life. Each author's oeuvre captures how this fiction offers insight into American history, and they present compelling visions that offer nuance and complexity instead of "blame and victimization" (Smith 277). Their novels portray vital, alternative histories of people who were excluded from the machinations of political power in America yet were nonetheless integral to the country's evolution. Moreover, in their approach to historical fiction, Taylor and Morrison clarify the value of stories about African Americans that undo stereotypes. They offer portrayals beyond their traditionally historicized roles as members of slave revolts or civil rights leaders.

In Mildred D. Taylor's *Roll of Thunder, Hear My Cry* and Toni Morrison's *Beloved* and *A Mercy*, family and sacrifice frame the celebration of African-American contributions to American history. In lieu of emphases on political dynasties or prominent historical figures or key events, Taylor and Morrison focus on American norms that fostered fear and undermined fundamental relationships within African-American families. In their explications of the difficult lives of disenfranchised African Americans, Taylor and Morrison suggest that the deeper people immerse themselves into the underpinnings of American history, the blurrier relationships based upon race and ethnicity become. Their novels complicate a sometimes too black-and-white history by presenting untrammelled shades of gray within stories that extend our understandings of African-American experiences beyond the inevitable simplifications found in textbooks or compressed public histories such as modern plantation tours (Adams 64-65). They also pose progressively difficult reading challenges, as if to critique clear, linear trajectories of American history and help readers embody the enforced unconventionalities of African-American life during the past two centuries. Altogether, the authors reveal how African Americans responded to trying situations associated with race.

In *Roll of Thunder, Hear My Cry*, Mildred D. Taylor depicts one family's attempt to unite through land ownership during the Great Depression. Her novel culminates in a great gamble that the family makes to combat racism and to organize a divided community. Her contemporary Toni Morrison probes further into the past and emphasizes earlier assaults on the African-American family. In *Beloved*, she unveils slavery's misdeeds and traces the haunting repercussions of one woman's great sacrifice. In the bleaker novel *A Mercy*, she employs the perspective of a relinquished child to reveal the limitations of divided families amidst the early and tumultuous settling of America.

Mildred D. Taylor: *Roll of Thunder, Hear My Cry*
In *Roll of Thunder, Hear My Cry*, Mildred D. Taylor recounts a story of family hardship through the eyes of a nine-year-old girl named

---

Cassie. Set in rural Mississippi in 1933 during the Great Depression, the novel depicts the trials that a land-owning African-American family faces while defending themselves and other disadvantaged people in their community (Bader 672). The family includes Big Ma (Cassie's grandmother), David and Mary Logan (Cassie's parents), her siblings Stacey, Christopher-John, and Little Man. L. T. Morrison, a man who works on the farm while Cassie's father is away, and Uncle Hammer, her father's brother, are also central to Logans' lives. In close proximity to resentful whites nearby, Cassie and her family rely on each other while remaining close to the land they own and farm, which provides them income, respectability, and independence, as well as a safe refuge from the unpredictable moments of ridicule from whites in their community. However, when the Logans take a stand against the Wallace brothers, a violent trio associated with lynching and the Ku Klux Klan, they risk losing their property. In an effort to thwart potential violence against African Americans in the community, David sacrifices their family's stability for the possibility of peace by setting their fields ablaze, thereby forcing the entire community to band together to respond to the fire and dissolving a dangerous mob set upon lynching an African-American man.

A firm reliance upon family is a dominant theme throughout Taylor's novel, which she develops through the context of land ownership. After the Civil War, many dispersed slaves sought a way to foster their own communities; property offered one possibility (Bethel 194). When the novel begins, the Logans occupy four hundred acres that Big Ma's late husband purchased during the half-century following the Civil War. To provide a sense of its importance, Taylor shares the land's history at the beginning of the novel before revealing much information about its inhabitants. She writes, "In 1887, Grandpa had bought two hundred acres ... and in 1918, after the first two hundred acres had been paid off, he had bought another two hundred" (3). The land, which still requires a mortgage payment for the latter purchase, in addition to annual taxes, requires great commitment, time, and labor. Although it is very isolated and they struggle to eke out a profit from it, the land empowers the Logans

---

and serves as a great source of family pride. As Rudine Sims Bishop notes, it also grants them "a degree of independence," shields the Logan children from "some of the most blatant[ly racist] actions of their neighbors," and helps them resist exploitation and violence (266). The Logans' home also strengthens a sense of family that was formerly denied to African-American adults and children. Taylor unveils a panoramic view of the Logans' lives that details the multiple functions of the land and home. It is where Big Ma shares accumulated stories from the past, where Cassie and her siblings play and learn, and where their parents regroup in the face of danger and prepare to react to coming threats. The land also harbors those in need, such as L. T. Morrison, an older man potentially at risk from white authorities. Altogether, Taylor affirms the possibility of land ownership as integral to understanding the evolution of African-American experience from the post-Civil War Reconstruction Era through the early twentieth century. Taylor shows how this new possibility is beneficial—from uniting family members to undermining racial barriers that facilitated violence and exclusion (237).

The Logans' layered, protective family unit acts as a buffer against the social pressures of their day. They struggle with "institutionalized power structures," which disproportionately benefit whites, who resist and seek to undermine change (Barker 132). In a sparsely populated community where a few white members amass wealth and exert great influence, the Logans challenge the status quo. Their foremost nemesis is Harlan Granger, a plantation owner desperate to reacquire their land since it once belonged to his ancestors. Granger is a descendant of a family forced to sell two thousand acres of land as a result of their financial decline after the Civil War. Livid that African Americans can own a portion of his family's former property, Harlan repeatedly pressures Big Ma to sell the Logans' farm with requests and then direct and indirect threats. In Big Ma's resistance, Taylor positions the Logans as leaders of an emerging strand of African-American society. However, partly because of the rural setting and poverty throughout Mississippi, they exist as outliers and outsiders within a community that associates large land holdings with whites. Taylor exposes how Harlan uses every means possible to obtain the Logans' property as part of his attempt to reestablish a segregated past. When Cassie asks Big Ma why Harlan continually harasses her, Big Ma replies that he already "has more land than he know what to do with" (67). Motivated by control instead of need, Harlan symbolizes a potential deterrent to the family's progress. However, Big Ma and the adults intuit what is at stake. By retaining their land, they deepen their family ties and challenge prior historical norms.

Land ownership also unites the Logans as community leaders and curators of local history, an idea that Taylor reinforces as she details the educational injustices that Cassie and her siblings endure in their segregated grade school. When the year begins, a teacher provides the students with their first set of textbooks. Cassie notes, "Everyone gasped, for most of the students had never handled a book at all besides the family Bible" (14). Yet, almost immediately, Cassie's little brother Little Man becomes irate when he realizes that the books are castoffs from the community's more privileged school for white children. As Cassie attempts to come to his defense, Taylor unpacks the brave actions that they take within an educational system orchestrated to hamper their progress. She depicts the Logan children as knowledgeable of the inequity and determined to take a stand against receiving inferior textbooks. Taylor notes that the disparity between white and African-American schools also extends beyond the schoolhouse to include transportation. Until the Logans and their friends organize a stunt that sabotages the county's school bus for white children, the bus driver repeatedly runs them off the road as they walk to school each day.

The Logans' insistence on historical truth also exposes the family to threats to their land and lifestyle. When the novel begins, David often works away from home to help support the family and Mary teaches at the children's school. During one of his visits, the family gathers and shares stories. Taylor notes that the children take delight as "Papa and Uncle Hammer and Big Ma and Mr. Morrison and Mama lent us their memories" (111). However, as the evening passes, the tales progress from an emphasis on family remembrance to darker, terror-filled encounters with the Ku Klux Klan. Mary initially objects to the children hearing these stories, but she relents when her husband explains, "These are things they need to hear, baby. It's their history" (112). Here, Taylor asserts that acknowledging and making sense of the past's violence against African Americans is central to American history. Otherwise, the Logan children remain ignorant of the relationship between previous atrocities and present-day inequities. By listening to their older relatives, they become privy to a history that exists beyond textbook accounts designed by a white culture that suppresses African-American lives (McDowell 215). Taylor calls attention to the ways that African-American families passed down personal histories absent from dominant American narratives. Later, she also shows how surfacing these truths within a school setting can prompt grave consequences. When Harlan and members of the school board visit Mary's class during a lesson about slavery, they become irate when she teaches information not included in the established textbook; subsequently, they dismiss her when she defends her decision. The loss of her job is difficult for Mary, as it provided an important source of income. However, Taylor implies that the absence of historical truth about slavery for the next generation of African-American children is a far more insidious loss because it denies them access to knowing how their histories factor into larger historical paradigms. This tension between the Logans and Harlan continues to simmer until the story's pivotal conflict.

The culminating moment of racial strife in *Roll of Thunder, Hear My Cry* reveals the greatest sacrifice that the Logans make to improve community relations. When T. J. Avery, one of Stacey's African-American friends, commits a robbery alongside two white boys, local whites form a mob with the intention of lynching him. Faced with the oncoming violence, David Logan feels called to protect T. J., which he explains to his wife: "If I don't [stand up for the boy], they'll hang T. J. This thing's been coming a long time, baby, and T. J. just happened to be the one foolish enough to trigger it" (198). David disappears into the night to guard T. J., but soon after his departure, he sets the Logans' cotton field on fire. By morning, in a scene that conveys that novel's most memorable instance of unity, both whites and African Americans work together to put out the fire. Each of the adults in the family plus Harlan Granger and others work silently to prevent the spread of what might otherwise result in a major agricultural disaster. Although their motives are mixed and there is no guarantee of further reconciliation, opposing groups unite in a collective effort, sparked by the fire. Yet it is not without loss, and in the novel's concluding sentences, Cassie bemoans the situation: "I cried for T. J. For T. J. and the land" (210). Here, Taylor hints that even if the fire furnishes the possibility of improved race relations, its occurrence represents ongoing risk for the entire family. Consequently, the conclusion is neither fully comfortable nor overly pessimistic, but it reinforces the necessity of sacrifice among African-American families long after the abolition of slavery.

Toni Morrison: *Beloved* and *A Mercy*

Roll of Thunder, Hear My Cry occasionally alludes to prior atrocities that Toni Morrison confronts directly in two of her novels, *Beloved* and *A Mercy*. Throughout her career, Morrison has created stories from previous generations as a means to examine the harsh realities of African-American life. Of her eleven novels, eight are set during various times in the twentieth century long before their publication date; only one, Morrison's most recent *God Help the Child* (2015), is set in the present. *Beloved* and *A Mercy*, the remaining two works, are Morrison's only novels set before the twentieth century; each story focuses on the hellish circumstances related to slavery. *Beloved* concerns Sethe, a free woman who lives in isolation in a haunted house in Ohio with her daughter Denver in 1873. Their lives change when Paul D, a former slave at Sweet Home plantation where Sethe lived in captivity before her escape, appears and encounters Sethe for the first time in eighteen years. When he last saw her in 1855, a pregnant Sethe had escaped to follow her two sons Buglar and Howard and her daughter Beloved to her mother-in-law Baby Suggs's house in Ohio. After plans went awry, Sethe gave birth to Denver along the way. Later, when her master and slave catchers found her at Baby Suggs's house, Sethe murdered her older daughter and was temporarily placed in prison. Upon her release, she returned to live with Baby Suggs (who passed), Buglar and Howard (who left), and Denver (who remains at home when Paul D appears). Before he arrives, Sethe and Denver exist at a distance from their community with a ghost that occupies their home, called 124. Not long after Paul D agrees to stay with them, a mysterious woman named Beloved appears. Immediately, Sethe accepts and cares for her, but obsession slowly overcomes her in response to her guilt of murdering her daughter, also named Beloved. As her guilt increases and begins to terrorize Sethe, Denver, and Paul D, the tension increases until she cannot function. Members of her community have to step in to offer help.

Beloved teems with observations about African-American life just before the abolition of slavery through the early years of the Reconstruction. As Juda Bennett notes, the novel is "less important as a fictional document of a single and specific experience" than as a critique of the limitations of the way that stories—and histories— are told (38). *Beloved* presents a tangled story from an alternative angle, one separate from accounts of slavery explained in purely quantitative terms or generalized as an element within Civil War. Describing one of her goals as a writer, Morrison pushes against an American literature canon that inevitably silences the lives of former slaves. She proclaims that "the contemplation of [a] black presence [in American history] is central to understanding our national literature," and that to come to terms with slavery and its legacy remains an important mission (*Playing* 5). Historical fiction offers Morrison a means to shed light on the possible lives of the voiceless buried in history's forgotten heap and to imagine their lives as a way to improve understandings of slavery as well as to broaden American literature.

Like Taylor in *Roll of Thunder, Hear My Cry*, Morrison emphasizes homes in *Beloved*. However, in contrast to the Logans' family property, Morrison offers two unstable environments; in the process, she demonstrates the failure of the traditional house as a protective shelter for African Americans. The novel's opening sentences drop readers into the chaotic, haunted atmosphere of

Sethe's house: "124 was spiteful. Full of baby's venom. The women in the house knew it and so did the children" (5). Morrison uses a third-person omniscient narrator and relies heavily on flashbacks to share varying perspectives within a haunted home. When the story begins, 124, the house that once housed six members representing three generations of a tight-knit family, now shelters an isolated woman, her daughter, and an inimical spirit. After losing her mother-in-law, who passed, and her two sons, who abruptly vanished, Sethe now seeks to pacify the ghost of the daughter, Beloved, whom she murdered to free from slavery. Moving from the present to just before the Civil War, Morrison links Sethe's ongoing struggles to Sweet Home Plantation, where she once lived in Kentucky. Originally owned and operated by Mr. and Mrs. Garner, Sweet Home largely shielded Sethe from the horrors of slavery until the passing of Mr. Garner and the coming of schoolteacher, the new slave master who manages the plantation as Mrs. Garner's health progressively declines. The new horrors of Sweet Home, which include violence, murder, and sexual assault, drive Sethe to escape and to later commit infanticide.

Morrison explores the potential dissolution of a family at risk while coping with slavery's aftermath. She exposes the ramifications of the troubling division between African Americans and white Americans, whose lives intertwined through the rise of "capitalism, industrialization, and democracy" (Gilroy 54). At Sweet Home, Sethe experiences bearable discomfort before schoolteacher arrives. Yet, prior to the shift, Sethe retains little power to make decisions for her family. Morrison reminds readers that throughout Sethe's lifetime, "men and women were moved around like checkers ... [and] those who hadn't run off or been hanged, got rented out, loaned out, bought up, brought back, stored up, mortgaged, won, stolen, or seized ... [and part of] the nastiness of life was the shock ... [of] learning that nobody stopped playing checkers just because the pieces included her children" (22). She suggests that schoolteacher's demeanor, the cycle of violence, Sethe's escape, and her subsequent murder of her daughter Beloved exists not solely in a nightmarish, isolated instance, but rather as an indictment of a system of economic exploitation that fostered racial injustice throughout U.S. history. To this degree, Sethe's and her family's story is not simply about race. Instead, *Beloved* suggests that an entire segment of society lived among fragmented and dangerous circumstances that ultimately propped up a rapidly evolving nation. As a result, the novel reaffirms John Ernest's notion that race is not a "presence in literature" so much as a social order "to which writers respond ... [and] develop an approach to the art of what can be said against the force of the unspeakable" (5). By unpacking the injustices that exert influence and threaten Sethe's family's future, Morrison conveys how slavery's damage continued far beyond its historical end date.

Beloved also describes the reformation of a fractured family. Morrison's story begins with an isolated mother and daughter haunted by their past and separated from other family members. She employs a nonlinear narrative, and introduces and then repeatedly returns to the idea of Sethe's "rememory":

> I used to think it was my rememory. You know. Some things you forget. Other things you never do. But it's not. Places, places are still there. If a house burns down, it's gone, but the place—the picture of it—stays, and not just in my rememory, but out there, in the world. What I remember is a picture floating around out there outside my head, I mean, even if I don't think it, even if I die, the picture of what I did, or knew, or saw is still out there. Right in the place where it happened. (34)

Sethe suggests that the horrors of slavery still exist, and she relives them through both self-initiated and unexpected rememories. Evelyn Jaffe Schreiber notes that this form of intergenerational trauma associated with the concept of rememory later manifests into the physical form of Beloved, "whose return [in a real life] challenges the community to learn how to live with the trauma of slavery" (32). Sethe commits infanticide, a crime that was widely publicized to reinforce the notion held by many whites in the nineteenth century that free African-American women were unfit mothers. Felicity Turner notes that presentations of infanticide throughout the southern states (e.g., Amy Whitted, Nancy Trimble, and Sooky Bishop) were disproportionately slanted against African-American women (359). In imagining the fictional aftermath of this situation, Morrison builds upon many of these highly publicized situations of infanticide. When an older Beloved appears at 124, Sethe, Denver, and Paul D have grown closer than when Paul D first arrived. His presence has helped alleviate 124's uncomfortable and quietly oppressive atmosphere, and Morrison highlights their potential as family when the trio attends a carnival. On the way, Morrison writes, "They were not holding hands, but their shadows were," (44) an image she returns to in the chapter's final sentence: "And on the way home, although leading them now, the shadows of three people still held hands" (46). However, the coming of Beloved results in Sethe's increased isolation and creates a rift that causes Paul D to leave, shattering the possibility of family until the end of the novel. After nearly twenty years of seclusion, Sethe finally finds support from a long-absent community that previously rejected and ostracized her with the steadfast help of Paul D, who encourages her to relinquish her guilt. Morrison concludes the novel with the hope that family may be restored, but she also suggests that the process will not be easy given all that Sethe has lost. Emphasizing a mother's great sacrifice, she condemns the demands that a young nation placed upon African-Americans, who bore the lasting injustices of slavery through rememories and lasting social injustices. Yet from within African-American culture, Morrison also celebrates the potential for healing with the reestablishment of community ties that slavery undermined.

Twenty years after *Beloved*, Toni Morrison ventured deeper into the past and reimagined the repercussions of another mother's sacrifice in *A Mercy*, a novel set in the late 1600s. In the novel's exploration of slavery, indentured servitude, and abandonment in early America, Morrison shows how debt, hardscrabble poverty, and disease unite a multicultural collection of outcasts. Converging on one farm during a "period before racism was inextricably related to slavery," a group lives together amidst a relatively unpopulated, unforgiving landscape, while each character privately struggles to come to terms with loneliness and preconceived allegiances (Brophy-Warren). The novel's main character is Florens, a young African-American woman torn from her mother when their plantation owner (Senhor D'Ortega) barters Florens to cover a portion of a debt he owes Jacob Vaark, a free man who has immigrated to America from England. Loosely plotted and character-driven, *A Mercy* focuses largely on Florens as she comes to terms with her mother's absence while she ventures away from the Vaark's farm to seek medical treatment for Jacob's wife Rebekka.

A Mercy notably lacks the detailed portrait of home as found in either *Roll of Thunder* or *Beloved*. Instead, Morrison portrays the perilous, ever-changing lives of the downtrodden in colonial America by emphasizing a disparate set of voices during the course of the novel's twelve chapters. Grounding the story is Florens's first-person narration, which comprises each of the odd chapters. The even chapters alternate through each of the other characters' perspectives, including that of Jacob (Chapter 2), a young Native American woman named Lina (4), Rebekka (6), a young woman named Sorrow who washes ashore from the Atlantic Ocean (8), two indentured servants named Willard and Scully (10), and Florens's mother, named a minha mãe (Portguese for *my mother*) (12). Fused together, their voices convey the various perils and difficulties of existing alongside very different others. Yet, despite the intensity of some their relationships, Morrison implies that greater dangers may lurk beyond the Vaarks. For example, as Florens travels to locate the blacksmith, she reflects, "With the letter [provided by Rebekka] I belong and am lawful. Without it I am a weak calf abandoned by the herd, a turtle without a shell, a minion with no telltale signs but a darkness I am born with" (115). Like the other women in the story, she experiences few options aside from a subservient role in early America.

In its attempt to reconcile the painful separation between mother and daughter, *A Mercy* imagines African-American women's unrecorded sacrifices during early American history. Florens's unsatisfied longing for a minha mãe comprises the final lines in her narrative: "I will keep one sadness. That all this time I cannot know what my mother is telling me. Nor can she know what I am wanting to tell her" (161). The novel does not provide a direct resolution, as mother and daughter remain apart at the story's end. Here, Morrison suggests that the power of the "vanished living" may be equally, if not more, troubling as the "terribly perished" central to *Beloved* (Christiansë 55). The best that Florens and her mother can express are hope and the desire for mercy. In the closing chapter, Morrison presents a minha mãe's point of view. She says, "To be female in this place is to be an open wound that cannot heal. Even if scars form, the festering is ever below" (163). A minha mãe challenges the evils that accompany enslavement and explains that she orchestrated her daughter's trade to best protect her. When she notices that Jacob Vaark looks at her daughter "as a human child" rather than as a dark-skinned being worth a certain value in coins, a minha mãe realizes that he may represent Florens's best chance at avoiding some of the horrors of slavery (166). In its final pages, *A Mercy* distinguishes the difficulties of one mother's choice to separate from her daughter. In a novel where "no character is wholly evil," with the possible exception of Senhor D'Ortega, Morrison reminds readers that amidst difficult economic circumstances, African-American women often bore the brunt of violence, sexual abuse, and separation from their children (Gates). Though Florens locates a partial family at the Vaarks' farm, she continually longs for a relationship with her mother, who remains lost to history and a silent member in captivity. Probing at their shared losses, Morrison advances a small window of understanding into the great, unspoken pain and sacrifice underpinning African-American history.

Mildred D. Taylor and Toni Morrison proclaim African-American history as central to fuller understandings of American history. *Roll of Thunder, Beloved,* and *A Mercy* reveal people striving to overcome arduous circumstances amidst instances of pointed, race-based hostility. They also expose what surveys of history inevitably ignore—the personal costs of racism and how its consequences transmit pain and prompt struggle through subsequent generations. Moreover, in reconsidering African-American families and their sacrifices, Taylor and Morrison champion historical fiction as a means to breathe life into prior eras that sometimes appear abstractly distant. Each author demonstrates that family stories allow readers to understand not only the lives of their American ancestors, but also encourage them to better respond to generational trauma and to strive to build more inclusive relationships. If each of their works shows that peering into the faraway past may not always be pleasant, each also informs readers about the trials that African Americans endured and reacted against. Collectively, Taylor and Morrison educate readers that a cultural legacy from the prior centuries remains vital, as it continues into the present day.

Works Cited

Adams, Jessica. *The Wounds of Returning: Race, Memory, and Property on the Postslavery Plantation*. U of North Carolina P, 2012.

Bader, Barbara. "How the Little House Gave Ground: The Beginnings of Multiculturalism in New, Black Children's Literature." *Horn Book Magazine*, vol. 78, no. 6, Nov./Dec. 2002, pp. 657-73.

Barker, Jani L. "Racial Identification and Audience in *Roll of Thunder, Hear My Cry* and *The Watsons Go to Birmingham—1963*." *Children's Literature in Education*, vol. 41, no. 2, June 2010, pp. 118-45.

Bennett, Juda. *Toni Morrison and the Queer Pleasure of Ghosts*. State of NY, 2014.

Bethel, Elizabeth Raul. *The Roots of African-American Identity: Memory and History in Antebellum Free Communities*. St. Martin's, 1997.

Bishop, Rudine Sims. *Free within Ourselves: The Development of African-American Children's Literature*. Heinemann, 2007.

Brophy-Warren, Jamin. "A Writer's Voice." *Wall Street Journal*, 7 Nov. 2008, p. W5.

Christiansë, Yvette. *Toni Morrison: An Ethical Poetics*. Fordham UP, 2012.

Ernest, John. *Chaotic Justice: Rethinking African American Literary History*. U of NC P, 2009.

Gates, David. "Original Sins." *New York Times Book Review*. 30 Nov. 2008. Accessed 15 Aug. 2017. http://www.nytimes.com/2008/11/30/books/review/Gates-t.html.

Gilroy, Paul. *Against Race: Imagining a Political Culture beyond the Color Line*. Harvard UP, 2000.

Hardstaff, Sara. "'Papa Said One Day I Would Understand': Examining Child Agency and Character Development in *Roll of Thunder, Hear My Cry* Using Critical Corpus Linguistics." *Children's Literature in Education,* vol. 46, no. 3, 2015, pp. 226-41.

McDowell, Kelly. "*Roll of Thunder, Hear My Cry*: A Culturally Specific, Subversive Concept of Child Agency." *Children's Literature in Education*, vol. 33, no. 3, 2002, pp. 213-25.

Morrison, Toni. *Beloved*. 1987. Penguin, 2000.

_____. *A Mercy*. 2008. Vintage, 2009.

_____. *Playing in the Dark: Whiteness and the Literary Imagination*. Harvard UP, 1992.

Schreiber, Evelyn Jaffe. *Race, Trauma, and Home in the Novels of Toni Morrison*. LSU P, 2010.

Smith, Valerie. "Toni Morrison." *Cambridge Companion to American Novelists*. Edited by Timothy Parrish, Cambridge UP, pp. 270-79.

Taylor, Mildred D. *Roll of Thunder, Hear My Cry*. Scholastic, 1976.

Turner, Felicity. "Rights and the Ambiguities of Law: Infanticide in the Nineteenth-Century U.S. South." *The Journal of the Civil War Era*, vol. 4, no. 3, 2014, pp. 350-72.

New Voices of History: The Depression Era and Historical Fiction in America_____

Sara Rutkowski

Depression Era: History Now!

In 1936, as the Great Depression gripped the nation, three historical novels were published months apart: Arna Bontemps's *Black Thunder,* William Faulkner's *Absalom, Absalom!* and Margaret Mitchell's *Gone with the Wind.* The latter became an instant hit, while the former two enjoyed critical praise but a small readership. All three novels powerfully confront the painful history of the American South, but in dramatically different ways. Together they tell a complex story about the past, but also about the 1930s culture— one perhaps uniquely welcoming to the genre of historical fiction.

That these novels emerged when they did is not surprising. The 1929 onslaught of the American Depression effectively ended a way of life. Millions unemployed—nearly half the country at its peak— and families uprooted and often pulled apart; desperation, poverty, and food shortages became a part of daily existence. Perhaps just as significantly, the Depression ended an *idea* of life. A generation of Americans awakened to the reality that the progress they believed to be inevitable was an illusion; America was not on an unstoppable upward trajectory, and was vulnerable to the wrath unleashed by the collapse of free-market capitalism. The concept of history therefore assumed new meaning as Americans wondered what caused such a calamity. How had the promise of Abraham Lincoln, of equality, of modernity and progress, been shattered?

The 1930s are well known for producing an extensive body of writing that expressed a social purpose: confronting the reality of the Depression head on. John Steinbeck's *Grapes of Wrath* (1939) chronicling the plight of Oklahoma sharecroppers during the 1930s has become shorthand for the kind of literature that flourished in this era. Simultaneously, the 1930s witnessed a surge in books and films recounting America's past. Tapping into a nostalgia for both simpler and seemingly grander times, historical fiction offered Depression victims escape from the present reality and an opportunity to immerse themselves in a distant, often romanticized, past. However, escapism only partially motivated Americans to turn to this genre. The national appetite for the new body of historical work cannot be reduced to a desire for diversion. A more complex cause prompted such hunger.

Historical fiction authors have a singular role to play in addressing problems of the past. Unlike traditional historians, they populate their books with characters in whose minds they imaginatively travel; they can *interpret* the actual past through the lens of fictitious individuals to whom readers can relate. This gives them extraordinary power to shape our collective sense of history.

In the 1930s, an urgent need developed for such historical interpretation. The Depression caused a crisis of national identity, which itself precipitated a crisis of narrative. Both crises coalesced around two questions: What can the past tell us about the present? Who gets to tell this story? In this cultural climate *Gone With the Wind*, *Black Thunder*, and *Absalom, Absalom!* each offered a competing, if overlapping, narrative of American history. Each addresses the subject of race from a divergent perspective, a unique point of departure that captures the nation's struggle to reconcile its values with—or denial of—the plight of its black citizens. More generally, each novel describes the national character vividly, employing three distinctive and dissimilar literary styles. But together these novels reveal a somewhat paradoxical truth: historical fiction provides not an escape from the present, but an immersion into it.

Gone with the Wind: History as Solace

Few novels gain the popularity that *Gone with the Wind* enjoyed when it burst onto the scene—all 1,037 pages—with lightning force in August, 1936. Within the first year, 1.7 million copies sold, and the novel remained the nation's number one best seller for two consecutive years. Within three years, its popularity was reinforced by its stunning film adaptation, starring Vivien Leigh and Clark Gable. *Gone with the Wind* was a literary sensation. Margaret

Mitchell had told *the* Southern story, an epic romance about the Civil War and the pain of Reconstruction. The novel offered rich material with which 1930s Americans could identify: a way of life lost, a sense of utter disorientation, and extensive human suffering. The 1860s South was *all* of America in the 1930s, and this tumultuous past mollified readers because it was over and the nation had survived. As Blanche Gelfant writes, *Gone with the Wind* "immersed contemporary readers in poverty, struggle, dispossession, and loss, problems immediate to the thirties but displaced to an historical past in which they had already been resolved" (6).

The novel portrayed not only the struggle of the South in the Civil War's wake, but also something fierce and persevering in the American character. Scarlett O'Hara's journey from entitled, self-serving Southern belle and Georgian plantation owner's daughter to devastated war victim who fights to rebuild her life provided Depression-era readers with a powerful narrative of survival and fortitude. Hers is ultimately a story not of lost innocence, but of rebirth. Scarlett discovers a passionate courage and ferocious drive to expel and overcome the degradation, captured most succinctly in her proclamation: "I'm going to live through this, and when it's over, I'm never going to be hungry again. No, nor any of my folks. If I have to steal or kill—as God is my witness, I'm never going to be hungry again" (593).

Hers is also a love story; Rhett Butler serves as Scarlett's psychic counterpart, a seasoned and calculating misanthrope who shares her will and wit to rise from the rubble. Together they champion the "gumption"—the word Mitchell assigns her characters—that fuels the American spirit. A longing for the Old South does not compel these heroes to fight back. Scarlett is unlike other fallen Southern belles, who, as Alyssa Rosenberg writes, "define themselves by their longing for the past and their fury about having been forced into the future." Instead, she devotes herself to work, to scheming, and to hard labor. Her sharp eye toward the future propels her forward. She finds potential in loss and rejects "the bitter-eyed women who looked backward, to dead times, to dead men, evoking memories that hurt and were futile, bearing poverty with bitter pride because they had those memories" (593). As Carolyn Porter argues, "the deep conviction that determination, intelligence, and a heavy dose of savvy would pull the nation out of the Depression was renewed as the true story of the South" (708).

But if Scarlett willingly charged forward into a new South, she was still—or Mitchell was—reluctant to surrender the racism upholding the slavery system. Neither she nor any other character rejects the Confederacy's racist views. On the contrary, Scarlett muses how the Yankees "did not know that negroes had to be handled gently, as though they were children, directed, praised, petted, scolded" (940). Mitchell's narrator describes Atlanta under Reconstruction and laments that "the negroes were living in leisure while their former masters struggled and starved" (915). The shadowy black characters are two-dimensional figures whose only salient features are submissiveness and allegiance to their white masters, most notably the character of Mammy, Scarlett's dutiful nanny. The implicit message: blacks did not possess the rugged individualism that could save Americans from destruction.

Although racism provides both a steady stream of racial slurs and bigoted portrayals, the plot never directly confronts issues of race. None of the characters think or speak about racism, whether decrying or defending it, even as they fight to protect a system based on it. "Their blindness," Rosenberg writes, "is a testament to the persistence with which Confederate apologists would deny that their beliefs have anything to do with race—and to the idea that you don't have to walk around fulminating about the inferiority of African-Americans to participate in keeping them in bondage" (n.p.).

Gone with the Wind's significance to 1930s culture was thus twofold. It provided a compelling hero who triumphed over adversity *and* it permitted white Americans to look away from the structures of racial oppression. Its mythology of American individualism and perseverance consciously excluded blacks, despite their integral role in the society that the novel portrays.

But the decade teemed with historical romances that delivered similar messages. Stark Young's Civil War saga *So Red the Rose* was a bestseller. Set in 1860s Natchez, Mississippi, the novel traces the plight of two slave-owning aristocratic families, weaving in historical figures like General William Sherman and Jefferson Davis. Like *Gone with the Wind*, *So Red the Rose* portrays devastation of the Southern way of life, the violence and humiliation that antebellum families suffered from Union forces who plundered their homes into ruin. Even the slaves reject the Yankees; upon hearing of imminent freedom, a group of field hands flee only to return after being rounded up and placed in Union stockades. Like Mitchell, Young portrays blacks as simpleminded and self-serving, accessories to white superiors, whose struggles alone invite readers' sympathies.

Other popular novels of the period mined different historical accounts, while conveying the same theme. Hervey Allen's *Anthony Adverse* exhaustively details the life of the eponymous protagonist, a world traveler assuming the roles of African slave trader and Louisiana plantation owner. Walter Dumaux Edmonds's *Drums Along the Mohawk* presents a fictional retelling of the Mohawk Valley settlers during the American Revolutionary War. In *Northwest Passage* Kenneth Roberts follows a colonial force fighting the British during the Seven Years' War between 1756 and 1763.

These popular historical novels (and their film adaptations) present portraits of individuals fighting change and rebuilding their lives, while affirming a determination at the core of white American identity. Blacks and Indians are denied any individuality, much less heroism. Within the character of white Americans lay the pioneers' stamina and the promise that calamities can be overcome. In these stories, one message rings clearly: it was not the collective energies of many that would win the day, but the gumption of the individual.

The New Voices of History

If *Gone with the Wind* and historical novels like it re-entrenched traditional tenets of American identity—offering a measure of justification for racial segregation and reassurance that individual grit would help the nation rise from economic mayhem—then another body of historical work offered a radically different vision, one marked by diversity, collective action, and struggle for social change.

For many, the Depression had weakened faith in the grand narratives and soaring heroes of the past, partly because they had lost relevance and their ability to accurately capture the nation's identity. Among the cultural legacies of the Depression era was a commitment to broaden the parameters of what it means to be an American. No longer could the singular voices of white mainstream America speak for everyone. Responding to the economic crisis, intellectuals, artists, historians, filmmakers, and social scientists began to focus on individuals and groups who had long been on the margins of mainstream notions of Americanism, those of immigrant backgrounds, African Americans, the poor, and the working classes. In the literary arena, writers like James Agee, Zora Neale Hurston, John Steinbeck, and others rose to prominence in part for their insistence that America's poor and disenfranchised had a story to tell that was just as "American" as any other.

Indeed, the federal government was itself deeply involved in the new documentary spirit of the decade, forging its own bureaucratic wing devoted to documenting lives of Americans from every corner of the country. The Federal Writers' Project (FWP) was part of President Franklin Delano Roosevelt's New Deal program designed to offer relief to the unemployed. But the FWP provided more than a paycheck; it gave roughly 6,000 professionals and aspiring writers the opportunity to document the nation and its history during the economic crisis. The Project trained writers in techniques of fieldwork and documentary writing and published an extensive series of guidebooks to US cities and towns, oral histories, collections of folklore, and ethnographic essays. Among its signature achievements is its collection of narratives from former slaves, the last generation of whom were still alive during the Depression.

Under the guidance of folklore editor Benjamin Botkin, a poet and noted folklorist, and Negro Affairs editor Sterling Brown, the program also insisted that writers—not trained historians or social scientists—tell that story in a way resonant with meaning for the broadest possible American audience. Because it advocated for this merger between literature and history, the FWP was uniquely welcoming to the genre of historical fiction. And because it also embraced a grassroots historiography placing special value on the historical memory of those outside of mainstream, white definitions of *American*, the project was also keenly open to a new kind of historical fiction that would chronicle the voices and experiences of those omitted from traditional narratives of American history.

Arna Bontemps joined the FWP a year after publishing his novel *Black Thunder*, a fact significant both because the novel remarkably illustrates the principles and techniques that the FWP espoused, and because the novel's poor sales prompted Bontemps to seek support via the relief program. A far cry from *Gone with the Wind*, *Black Thunder* recounts the story of a slave rebellion through the perspectives of the slaves themselves, with the courageous young Gabriel Prosser at the helm. Though critically praised, the novel sold poorly. Bontemps would later write in the introduction to the 1968 edition, "the theme of self-assertion by black men whose endurance was strained to the breaking point was not one that readers of fiction were prepared to contemplate at the time" (xxix).

But despite its lack of popular appeal, *Black Thunder* was at the time—and certainly in retrospect—a striking example of a new kind of historical writing that was shaped by the philosophy, rigor, and spirit of grassroots documentary. It was notably published only a year after W. E. B DuBois's *Black Reconstruction in America: An Essay Toward a History of the Part Which Black Folk Played in the Attempt to Reconstruct Democracy in America, 1860–1880*. In it, DuBois, by then a famous scholar of African-American history, author, editor, and one of the leaders of the Harlem Renaissance movement of the 1920s, had in effect rewritten the history of the Reconstruction era, upending the dominant historical narrative of the time that significantly downplayed—or ignored altogether—the contributions by blacks in the efforts to rebuild the South after the Civil War. *Black Thunder* goes back further than DuBois's account, to 1800 when, as Bontemps describes, eleven hundred slaves, led by the precocious young field-worker Gabriel Prosser, organize a revolt at a plantation near Richmond, Virginia. But the insurgency is ultimately halted when a massive flood overwhelms the army. Prosser is later hanged for his crimes.

In crafting his narrative, Bontemps conducted extensive historical research, examining newspaper accounts, court records, and letters. Among the most authoritative accounts from the period was Thomas Wentworth Higginson's 1862 retelling, "Gabriel's Defeat," which Bontemps relied on for important historical facts. But he also revises Higginson's version and tells the story through multiple points of view, including subjective accounts of the events, along with slave folklore and interior monologues. Bontemps distinguishes the novel by capturing the slaves' characteristic vernacular and their oral culture. Orality—verbal expression, rather than written—was central to the culture of slaves, who were largely illiterate. By highlighting orality in its myriad forms—conversations, songs, internal speech—Bontemps, as Daniel Reagan argues, "restores Gabriel's voice to the record of history, and challenges the power of writing to define reality" (72). Bontemps took control of a narrative too long determined by white, written culture, thus writing black voices into history, creating a literary rebellion resembling the one he describes. As Mary Kemp Davis writes, Bontemps "overthrows Higginson, the benevolent retriever and keeper of the Gabriel Prosser tradition, just as the slaves sought to overthrow their masters" making "the slaves actors and himself a creator of history" (21).

Bontemps's historical accuracy is apparent in the full version of his title, Black Thunder: Gabriel's Revolt: *Virginia, 1800*, which amends the common term for the rebellion, "Gabriel's Defeat" (a title that Higginson used and other accounts echo). Use of the word *revolt* instead of *defeat* challenges conception of the event as a failure, even suggesting its affinity to a larger history of American revolt not limited to slaves. Moreover, the image of *Black Thunder* merges the black race with a storm, signaling the powerful potential of collective force among a subjugated people. Thus, the novel speaks to the contemporary 1930s culture in which Gabriel's mission still resonated.

To readers in the thirties, the contemporary relevance of Bontemps's historical account was self-evident. A 1936 review in the *New York Times* notes that it would be "ridiculous to say that 'Black

Thunder' is limited in its meaning to its historic circumstance." Bontemps, the review continues, "is primarily concerned with the spectacle of human dignity as manifest in the revolutionary spirit time out of mind" (Tompkins). Later scholars noted parallels between Gabriel's plight and that of the so-called Scottsboro Nine, nine black Alabama teenagers convicted and sentenced to death for raping two white women on a train in 1931. The case proved a watershed for the American justice system, laying bare the stark unfairness of all-white juries, juvenile convictions, lynch mobs, and the reality that racism thwarts fair trials. Beyond implicit contemporary references, the novel resonates more generally with the racial segregation, violence, and tensions that marked the Depression era, along with the black radicalism that such enduring racism had inspired. As such, the novel reads as a cautionary tale about the costs of racial oppression.

Working for the FWP in Chicago alongside writers Richard Wright, Nelson Algren, Jack Conroy, Margaret Walker, and Frank Yerby, among others, Bontemps continued mining black history. His series of interviews traced individual journeys of ordinary black Americans for a planned, but never published, FWP book entitled *The Negro in Illinois*. But he and Conroy would use much of the material they gathered for a historical study of black migration entitled *They Seek a City*. Although not billed as a fictional account, this book nevertheless employs many of the strategies of historical fiction, blending facts and events with rich personal portrayals of the individual migrants.

Not surprisingly, other black writers shaped by the FWP would produce literature blending sociology and history with fiction. Indeed, the larger field of African-American history and the genre of black historical fiction were unquestionably advanced by the Writers' Project, its philosophy, and the large numbers of black writers it helped to mobilize. Notably, Margaret Walker would write *Jubilee*, a monumental historical novel published in 1966, but a product of years of exhaustive research begun in the 1930s while Walker worked for the FWP. Walker based *Jubilee* on the life and stories of her grandmother, born into slavery. *Jubilee*, a blend of folklore, historical documentary, and explorations of subjectivity, reflects Walker's work collecting "negro lore" in Chicago, which included children's games and songs, recipes, folktales, industrial lore, and religious customs. As the first novel about slavery written from the point of view of a black woman, its perspective is grounded in the emotional and domestic sphere of female experience largely omitted in other fictional accounts.

Frank Yerby would also write a series of historical romances, blockbusters throughout the postwar era, making him the first best-selling black novelist. Among the most famous was his first, *The Foxes of Harrow* (1946), adapted later for the screen. Although it and other Yerby novels follow conventions of antebellum South "costume dramas," he challenges key aspects of that genre with complex black characters and white characters that are neither heroes nor impervious to the moral quandary of slavery.

The efforts of writers like Bontemps, Walker, and Yerby, among others FWP participants, represent a profound shift in national perspective on black historical experiences exerting a lasting impact on American writing. Such writing that focused on Americans long excluded from established accounts of history would help lay groundwork for the civil rights and other social equality movements in the postwar era. In rewriting history, these writers also attempted to rewrite the future.

Historical Memory and the Problem with Truth

If Mitchell's *Gone with the Wind* and Bontemps's *Black Thunder* represent two strains of 1930s historical fiction that both attempt to reconstruct historical truth, then William Faulkner's *Absalom, Absalom!* signifies a third strain. It questions the whole notion of historical truth, suggesting that the past remains subjective, always elusive.

Like Mitchell and Bontemps, Faulkner turned his eye toward the American Southern historical crisis. In linear terms—though it is anything but linear—the novel chronicles the life of Southern plantation owner Thomas Sutpen and his children Henry and Judith. In college, Henry befriends Charles, who later becomes engaged to

Judith. Soon Sutpen realizes that Charles is his own son, the product of an earlier marriage. He deserted his first wife when he discovered she was part Negro. Sutpen reveals this truth to Henry after he and Charles had spent four years fighting in the Civil War. Out of anger, Henry murders his friend, less because of the potential incest than for the miscegenation. Years later, Sutpen is murdered by the father of a young girl who bore his child.

This is the framework of the story, but its telling is circuitous. The novel proves an exercise in historical reconstruction, with four separate narrators speaking decades after the events. Each tries to produce Sutpen's story, as his notorious rise and fall in Civil War-era Mississippi assumes different trajectories and meanings depending on the teller. Quentin Compson, the most prominent narrator, attempts to explain the South to his Harvard roommate Shreve in 1909 by interpreting and reinterpreting competing stories of his father, Mr. Compson, his grandfather, and his great-aunt, all of whom had different relationships with Sutpen. Shreve, a Northerner, further complicates the story with observations and inferences based on his friend's retelling. The resultant patchwork investigation, through which Quentin and Shreve attempt to "discover" the South, ultimately recognizes the fall of the system of white supremacy upon which it was built.

Among fifteen Faulkner novels set in Mississippi's fictional Yoknapatawpha County, *Absalom, Absalom!* has been labeled Faulkner's best, if most challenging. It amplifies the author's signature writing style, one marked by temporal fragmentation, shifting narrations, and stream of consciousness. Rejecting a continuous narrative form, Faulkner frequently switches between narrators without warning or weaves in flashbacks, juxtaposing inner speech with outward reality, forcing readers to sift through the account and find their bearing. His story-telling approach appears at odds with the 1930s, a period marked by politically charged works of stark realism. If anything, it seems more aligned with the modernist experiments of the 1920s. Indeed, because of this Faulkner has often been excluded from the literary-historical paradigm of the 1930s, or he has been treated as the outlier who rebuffed the dominant themes and styles of his contemporary culture. As Morris Dickstein points out, "Faulkner's work is so different from other main currents in the 1930s that it's tempting but misleading to push him off into a separate category of 'southern writer' or 'twenties modernist.'" But to extract him from the period in which he published most of his novels, Dickstein concludes, would be to "draw the parameters of the decade to leave out its best writer" (153).

Moreover, one could argue that Faulkner belongs to the thirties not in spite of, but at least partly *because* of his experimental narrative style. Although the influence of 1930s writers on later generations is now widely acknowledged, less appreciated is that previous decades shaped those writers. The period seemed to spontaneously produce a new body of work utterly divorced from earlier writing. Writers coming of age in the experimental 1920s continued to write into the future, carrying literary innovations into a new era. Modernist techniques offered apt expression for the disorientation felt in the thirties and the cultural longing for an oblique past. John Dos Passos famously inscribed his *U.S.A.* trilogy with the perplexity of historical memory. The three novels—*The 42nd Parallel* (1930), *1919* (1932), and *The Big Money* (1936)—offer sprawling, collagelike accounts of American industrial capitalism, incorporating popular media, snapshots of major historic political and cultural figures, and long passages of first-person stream of consciousness. Similarly Josephine Herbst, a writer and political radical, produced a trilogy of semi-autobiographical novels— *Pity is Not Enough*, *The Executioner Waits*, and *Rope of Gold*—that trace events from the Civil War to the present, weaving in familial interpretive accounts and stories. Both Dos Passos's and Herbst's use of fragmentary narration upset linear conventions of storytelling while registering the subjective nature of time and history.

Faulkner's novel can be viewed as part of this experimental body of historical fiction, though his work is typically treated as a genre unto itself. Like other thirties writers, he saw in the past—in particular the history of the South, of slavery and civil war—the roots of current distress, both the literal and metaphorical fabric of the nation's collapse. In his 1951 novel *Requiem for a Nun*, Faulkner wrote "The past is never dead; it's not even past" (73), a line that resonates throughout *Absalom Absalom!* as the narrators strain to find meaning and "truth" in the disconnected strands of stories and memories. Indeed, Faulkner also understood that truth is ultimately unknowable. As we strive to reconstruct the past, we perpetually face the obstacle of our own biases, our own narrow, modern vantage points. Faulkner's fragmentary, disorienting, nonchronological structure allows readers to grasp that the history we seek exists in composite form, filtered through the present.

Absalom, Absalom! Therefore is not only a novel but a theory of history—as Cleanth Brooks argues, "a persuasive commentary upon the thesis that much of 'history' is really a kind of imaginative construction" (311). This theory is crystallized when Mr. Compson offers his version of the past, but then digresses to mediate on the problem of historical truth that supports the entire novel:

> We have a few old mouth-to-mouth tales, we exhume from old trunks and boxes and drawers letters without salutation or signature, in which men and women who once lived and breathed are now merely initials or nicknames. . .; we see dimly… the people in whose living blood and seed we ourselves lay dormant and waiting, in this shadowy attenuation of time possessing now heroic proportions, performing their acts of simple passion and simple violence, impervious to time and inexplicable… They are there, yet… they are like a chemical formula exhumed along with the letters from that forgotten chest, carefully, the paper old and faded and falling to pieces, … almost indecipherable, yet meaningful, familiar in shape and sense, the name and presence of volatile and sentient forces; you bring them together in the proportions called for, but nothing happens; you re-read, tedious and intent, poring, making sure that you have forgotten nothing, made no miscalculation; . . and again nothing happens: just the words, the symbols, the shapes themselves, shadowy inscrutable and serene, against that turgid background of a horrible and bloody mischancing of human affairs. (100-01)

Faulkner gives voice to the cultural yearning for knowledge the past held. His handling of the unstable nature of memory and consciousness, as Morris Dickstein remarks, "connects ironically to the distressed lives of so many other ordinary families in the decade" (153). While the past seems to signal answers, it is an enduring enigma, accessible only through fragments.

Faulkner also suggests that the past filtered through the present offers potential for moral clarity. Through their efforts at historical reconstruction, Quentin and Shreve, young men of a more modern era, witness the moral crisis at the novel's heart of the system of slavery and racism that accounts for Sutpen's fall, and by extension the fall of the South. In the end of *Absalom, Absalom!* Quentin recounts returning to the Sutpen plantation with Miss Rosa Coldfield, sister of Sutpen's wife, Ellen, to find a now elderly and sickened Henry. They call an ambulance, but before it can reach the home, Clytie, Thomas Sutpen's daughter with a slave woman, sets the plantation on fire, killing herself and Henry. The blaze signifies not only the fall of this once dynastic family, but again of the South, which still cannot bear of the weight of its history.

Faulkner's novel implicitly challenges widespread nostalgia for the Old South—the narrative of lost innocence, embodied in Mitchell's novel and in other stories that over time established themselves as links to historical truth. Through a structure of composite perspectives, Faulkner reveals the mythological nature of these stories and their inability to resolve reality. Like *Gone with the Wind*, *Absalom, Absalom!* envisions the fall of one Southern family as a microcosm for the fall of the entire South. But in Faulkner, there is no emergence from that fall, no "tomorrow is another day," as Scarlett famously proclaims.

The Past Is the Future

Gone with the Wind, *Black Thunder*, and *Absalom, Absalom!* all allegorize the American South, transforming its crisis into a powerful metaphor of the Depression era. The 1930s were an acute moment of national pain, economically, socially, and politically, and works of historical fiction allowed temporal distance to bring the present into focus. Underscoring Faulkner's own premise that the past depends on the teller, the three strains of writing offered different visions of American history, competing lenses through which to confront the present. But all would have a lasting influence not only on the genre of historical fiction, but on American identity itself—who we are and where we are going.

Works Cited

Allen, Hervey. *Anthony Adverse.* Holt, 1933.

Bontemps, Arna. *Black Thunder: Gabriel's Revolt: Virginia, 1800.* 1936. Macmillan, 1968.

_____, and Jack Conroy. *They Seek a City.* Doubleday, 1945.

Brooks, Cleanth. *William Faulkner: The Yoknapatawpha Country.* Yale UP, 1963.

Davis, Mary Kemp. "Arna Bontemps' Black Thunder: The Creation of an Authoritative Text of 'Gabriel's Defeat.'" Black American Literature Forum, vol. 23, no. 1, 1989, pp. 17-36.

Dickstein, Morris. *Dancing in the Dark: A Cultural History of the Great Depression.* Norton, 2009.

Dos Passos, John. *The U.S.A. Trilogy.* Library of America, 1938.

Du Bois, W. E. B. *Black Reconstruction in America: An Essay Toward a History of the Part Which Black Folk Played in the Attempt to Reconstruct Democracy in America, 1860-1880.* 1935. Oxford UP, 2007.

Edmonds, Walter Dumaux. *Drums Along the Mohawk.* 1936. Bantam, 1992.

Faulkner, William. *Absalom, Absalom!* 1936. Vintage, 1972.

_____. *Requiem for a Nun.* 1951. Vintage, 1996.

Gelfant, Blanche. "'Gone with the Wind' and the Impossibilities of Fiction." Southern Literary Journal, vol. 13, no. 1, 1980, pp. 3-31.

Gone with the Wind. Directed by Victor Fleming, performances by Vivien Leigh, Clark Gable, Hattie McDaniel, and Olivia de Havilland. Metro-Goldwyn Mayer, 1939.

Herbst, Josephine. *The Executioner Waits.* Harcourt, 1934.

_____. *Pity Is Not Enough.* Harcourt, 1933.

_____. *Rope of Gold.* Harcourt, 1939.

Higginson, Thomas Wentworth. "Gabriel's Defeat," *Atlantic Monthly,* Sept. 1862, pp. 337-45. www.encyclopediavirginia.org/_Gabriel_s_

Defeat_by_Thomas_Wentworth_Higginson_September_1862. Accessed 6 May 2017.

Mitchell, Margaret. Gone With the Wind. 1936. Simon & Schuster, 2011.

Porter, Carolyn. "Gone With the Wind." *A New Literary History of America*. Edited by Greil Marcus and Werner Sollers, Harvard UP, 2009. www.newliteraryhistory.com/gonewiththewind.html. Accessed 3 Apr. 2017.

Reagan, Daniel. "Voices of Silence: The Representation of Orality in Arna Bontemps' *Black Thunder*." *Studies in American Fiction*, vol. 19, no. 1, 1991, pp. 71-83.

Roberts, Kenneth. *Northwest Passage*. Doubleday, 1937.

Rosenberg, Alyssa. "Why We Should Keep Reading 'Gone With the Wind.'" *Washington Post*, 1 July 2015. https://www.washingtonpost.com/news/act-four/wp/2015/07/01/why-we-should-keep-reading-gone-with-the-wind/?utm_term=.1a3b3042e1a5. Accessed 3 Apr. 2017.

Tompkins, Lucy. "Slaves' Rebellion; Black Thunder." Review of *Black Thunder: Gabriel's Revolt: Virginia, 1800*, by Arna Bontemps. *New York Times*, 2 Feb. 1936, p. BR7.

Walker, Margaret. *Jubilee*. Houghton Mifflin, 1966.

Young, Stark. *So Red the Rose*. 1934. Sanders, 1992.

Meeting the Mirabals in *In the Time of the Butterflies*: Real Figures in Historical Biographical Fiction

Christine De Vinne

> The story won't save us, but the *telling* of the story is redemptive;
> we understand; we can bear the suffering.
>
> (Alvarez, "Fixed Facts" 37)

Dominican-American writer Julia Alvarez, a leader in the Latina literary movement for the past quarter century, published her first historical novel, *In the Time of the Butterflies*, in 1994. Following the success of her poetry, essays, and semiautobiographical *How the García Girls Lost Their Accents* (1991), her painstakingly researched second novel won a finalist nomination for the National Book Critics Circle Award, became a Notable Book selection of the American Library Association, and cemented her reputation among US audiences. Passionate about the novel's protagonists, the revolutionary sisters who helped overthrow Dominican dictator Rafael Trujillo, Alvarez uses her art to turn the actual Mirabals into characters in historical fiction. In doing so, she provides a critical example of how real figures can function in a historical novel and how a biographical novel in particular stretches the interface between assembled facts and the creative impulses of fiction.

To tell the story of Patria, Dedé, Minerva, and María Teresa Mirabal, Alvarez negotiates all the hybridity of historical biographical fiction, where key figures from the past appear not just incidentally, perhaps to help establish the time period or lend realistic commentary to narration, but as centerpieces of the work. Unlike a historical novelist, whose characters may be pure fabrications, a biographer attempts to tell a subject's real life accurately and interpret it responsibly. Scott Donaldson, calling literary biography an "impossible craft," describes biographers as "artists under oath— committed to telling as much of the truth as may be ascertained," in comparison to novelists, for whom "[i]nventing is what they do" (53, 54).

Weighing the obligations of the biographer against the freedom of the novelist, even one pledged to historical authenticity, Alvarez long deliberated her approach to *In the Time of the Butterflies*. She began researching the sisters to contribute descriptions of them for a postcard project about Latina women. Fascinated by their lives, especially after meeting their families, she resolved to extend her microcomposition to full biography. What most intrigued her, however, was their development as individuals, not just the public but also the private workings of their lives. "Character, then, became my focus," she realized, "and for me, that is the province of fiction: recreating what evolves in that character, the truth according to that character" ("Fixed Facts" 28). Drawing on her talent as poet, she began by writing verses in each of their voices. However, when she finished her manuscript, the poems having dropped away, she worried that the grim story might be too painful for their family, and she was prepared to disguise names, set everything in an imaginary location, and turn it into pure fiction. Only with the consent, even the urging, of Minerva's daughter Minou on behalf of the family, did Alvarez publish the text we have today ("Fixed Facts" 28).

As a historical biographical novel, *In the Time of the Butterflies* communicates a powerful message both by its subject matter and by its aesthetic composition. In the Latin-American literary tradition, it adapts fiction's "willing suspension of disbelief" to the truth-telling of *testimonio*, a form of witness forcefully adopted by the silenced to speak back to power—in this case, women in a hyperpatriarchal society fighting the bloodiest dictator of twentieth-century Latin America. It stretches participatory readers to consider how a novelist's art expands an understanding of history, how permeable the border between fact and fiction remains, and how reading can become an ethical act that inspires insight and invites response. Alvarez's choice to present the sisters' lives, first within the text and then throughout multiple essays, interviews, and web pages where she reveals its back story, make her novel a model for the art and purpose that define the work of historical biographical fiction.

From Historical Record to *In the Time of the Butterflies*

With a story that opens in 1938, on the island that was her home for most of the first decade of her life, Alvarez introduces the Mirabal sisters, heroes of the underground known by their codename, *las Mariposas*, the Butterflies. In a tight-knit extended family, they grew up under the dictatorship of Rafael Trujillo, whose thirty-one-year rule saw the deaths of tens of thousands of people in the cities and countryside of the Dominican Republic but also, infamously, at the border with Haiti. Patria, Dedé, Minerva, and María Teresa, nicknamed Mate, came to political consciousness as young adults in the late 1940s and '50s. While Dedé hesitated, her sisters became increasingly active, assembling weapons, distributing antipropaganda pamphlets, and founding the Fourteenth of June Movement. Along with their driver Rufino de la Cruz, the three were killed by soldiers one night in the mountains, on their way back from visiting their husbands in prison. Only Dedé survived, to her abiding shame, living to see Trujillo assassinated six months later, raising their children and hers in the family home, and sustaining their celebrated legacy until her death in 2014.

With her second novel, Alvarez determines to "bring acquaintance of these famous sisters to English-speaking readers" (324). She had honed her skills in real-life character portrayal with *How the García Girls Lost Their Accents*, drawing on her own history to describe, with warmth and sensitivity, the life of Dominican immigrants in New York City. Having adapted family members to the uses of fiction, she recounts with wry amusement their reaction to the novel, their indignation at the portrayal, and their competing memories of pivotal scenes ("Note" 166). In vain, she tries to persuade them that she peopled her pages with fabricated characters, life translated into art. "[T]here was just enough truth in it to make them ask why I was lying," she confides (Rosario-Sievert 35). "They felt betrayed," she recalls, "not because I had written specifically about them, but because there were shadowy resemblances, resonances, characters who reminded them of themselves . . . . I think what upset them was the shadowy and shifting territories of lies, lives, and fiction, which they had wanted me to keep separate" ("Note" 165-66).

Among these "shifting territories," Alvarez occupies a Spanish homeland where *historia* carries the dual meaning of "history" and "story." *In the Time of the Butterflies* partakes of the rich tradition of the Latin American historical novel, which, before Alvarez, had been the exclusive province of male authors. Gender aside, it is a field that appreciates, as José de Piérola notes, the fusion of "fiction with 'facts' from the historical record," in a design that "makes it difficult, if not impossible, to differentiate which is which" (152). Decoding a historical novel, then, requires the active participation of audiences who bring what he calls "historiographical consciousness" to the hermeneutic exercise of reading (157). The resulting tension not only reminds readers of the unreliability of history, partial and not impartial, composed under pervasive systems of power, but also reveals the ethical purposes of the novelist.

Alvarez announces her own purposes in the two-page Postscript that concludes *In the Time of the Butterflies*: "I wanted to immerse my readers in an epoch of the life of the Dominican Republic that I believe can only finally be understood by fiction, only finally redeemed by the imagination. A novel is not, after all, a historical document, but a way to travel through the human heart" (324). Micha.el Lackey, who interviews Alvarez on the topic of biographical fiction, points out that novelists, historians, and biographers all borrow from the same store of rhetorical techniques to fashion their narratives (2). Agreeing, Alvarez sets out "a mongrel novel," a "genre-bending" text, a "kaleidoscope" of the verifiable and the verisimilar in her quest for "that kind of truth which is more than fact, but includes the facts" ("Fixed Facts" 28-29, 31). Committed to the enterprise of fiction, she expects readers to join her quest, not to compare her novel event for event, character for character, with official history.

In fact, Alvarez must struggle to fill substantial gaps in official record, accounts of the resistance overwritten by the rule of despotism. Chronicles of the Trujillo years, she discovers visiting the National Archives, pay no attention to the sisters, nothing but a provocation to the regime, in an era when women were marginalized in any case, their lives left largely to oral tradition. On a 1986 trip to the Dominican Republic, she complains to a cousin that the only thing she can find in print about the Mirabals is a comics-style history. To her surprise, her cousin responds by introducing her to Noris, Patria's daughter, and soon she meets Minou, Minerva's daughter, who shares stories, memories, even love letters that her mother and father had smuggled to each other in prison: "All I can do is fill myself with illusions. To be asleep in your arms, my head on your breast. ¡Vida mía!" ("Chasing" 201). On successive trips, she meets Dedé, holds Minerva's favorite books in her hands, sees Patria's blood-stained dress, fingers Mate's thick braid, cut off at death. "Everywhere we went," she writes, "it seemed we could reach out and touch history. And always there were plenty of living voices around to tell us all their individual versions of that history" ("Chasing" 207).

Amid this embarrassment of riches, says Alvarez, the Mirabals "became real to my imagination. I began to invent them" (323). As historical biographical novelist, she remains true to the contours and contexts of her main characters, their family circumstances, religious background, education, physical environment, and political activity, with the larger-than-life figure of the dictator looming over them. Their thoughts, feelings, frustrations, temperaments, and conversations, however, she must confect by absorbing truths about the Butterflies that history failed to record. She registers Mate's small secrets in a diary, even before learning that the girl actually kept one, and she delights when Dedé claims to remember scenes invented for the novel. She confesses that her "best compliment" is Dedé's declaration that she had "*captured* the spirit of her sisters," not that she had gotten every fact about them right ("Fixed Facts" 35). She produces, in her words, "not the Mirabal sisters of fact, or even the Mirabal sisters of legend," but "the Mirabals of my creation, made up but, I hope, true to the spirit of the real Mirabals" (324).

Steve Criniti, within his wider argument that Alvarez applies collective US narratives to a Dominican story, explores the latitude behind her admission: "I sometimes took liberties—by changing dates, by reconstructing events, and by collapsing characters or incidents," with the example of Sinita Perozo, Minerva's boarding school classmate (324). He identifies Sinita as an amalgam of activist Tomasina Cabral, whom she met years later at university, and the Perozo family, decimated by Trujillo's forces; the fictional Sinita stands metonymically for multiple political influences in her adolescence and, simultaneously, for countless victims of tyrannical brutality (49-50). Among other secondary characters, Virgilio Morales, modeled after revolutionary hero Pericles Franco, serves in fiction as the would-be suitor Dedé loses to Minerva, while his nickname, Lío, meaning "complication," links Minerva's menarche, which she calls her "complications," to the emergence of her adult partisanship (20). The family's elderly neighbor Don Bernardo, who defies political expediency to stand as baptismal godfather to the sisters' children, seems not identified in historical record but bears the same name as the real Bernardo Vega whom Alvarez credits with helping her write the book (325).

Emily Sutherland, describing the process of co-opting actual figures like these for historical fiction, would remind Alvarez that although she exercises creative freedom, "historians are looking over [her] shoulder." Within the bounds of a "credible scenario," Sutherland continues, the novelist has license to invite not only historical but also extrahistorical figures into her cast. Thus, Magdalena, a sympathetic young prostitute, becomes Mate's confidante in prison, and Fela cares for the Mirabal children and serves as fortune-telling *santera*, setting up candles and altar in a shed behind the home. Where María Teresa once asked for a spell to catch a beau, Minerva's daughter Minou visits her in adulthood to hold communion with her lost mother. Shara McCallum questions the advisability of these fanciful additions on the grounds that they reinforce stereotypes, the tragic mulatto and the mystic healer (112), yet, arguably, they enlarge the novel's chorus of voices by giving even marginalized women the chance to speak.

The dominant narrative voices of *In the Time of the Butterflies*, of course, belong to the sisters, who make the novel, in Lynn Chun Ink's cogent image, "[a] national epic written as a family saga" (793). In the frame story, Dedé submits reluctantly to the questions of the *gringa dominicana* whose visit prompts her reminiscences, in chapters ricocheting among the 1930s, '40s, and '50s, delivered through the personae of the four sisters and closing on November 25, 1960, the day of their assassination. Distinct voices—first-person for Patria, Minerva, and, unmistakably, Mate's diary; third-person limited for Dedé—enable them to contribute to family and national history from their unique perspectives, hinting at the ideals, whims, or flaws that motivate them. Patricia Meyer Spacks, who recognizes in Boswell's life of Johnson that "[t]he desire to worship and the desire for intimate knowledge oppose one another," would likely argue that Alvarez's rhetorical construct supports her goal of individualizing and demythologizing the Mirabals, despite the critical consensus that the novel leaves their legendary aura intact (101).

Scholars who analyze the narrators' four-part harmony admire Alvarez's feminist, postmodern appreciation for destabilized history. Ink, although not satisfied that Alvarez rises above masculinist and mythologizing discourse, affirms, "The multivocal narrative eloquently conveys how this past is constituted by many different concurrent and often contradictory stories" (792). The "*competing* truths" that result, Alvarez asserts, are "what makes literature trustworthy, rich, opposed to propaganda or what you have in a dictatorship, whether political or canonical, in which there's 'one official story,' the hegemony of one approved point of view and required allegiance to it" ("Fixed Facts" 29). Charlotte Rich, invoking Mikhail Bakhtin's notion of *heteroglossia*, the interplay of overlapping voices, reasons that the very structure of the novel mirrors its theme, resistance against the power of dictatorship (166), reinforced as the sisters, especially Minerva, pepper their chapters with sarcasm, mockery, and other forms of linguistic sabotage that subvert Trujillo's myth of power (175-79).

The subversive voices of the Butterflies, then, help right the propaganda of a tyrant and the official annals of history. In the face of David O. Stewart's warning, "We never know enough to tell a past story completely," Alvarez applies manifest invention to create of fissures and fictions a faithful accounting of their lives (64). Privileging universal truths over documented facts, she affirms historical biographical fiction for its ability not just to imitate but to inspire. "What you hope for in a story," she declares, "is that it opens up some little insights, some knowledge of character and of self that wasn't there before, that it nurtures the human spirit and gets passed on, so that we're able to make different choices and be a little more aware of each other, of the human experience" (Martínez 13).

Testimonio and the Power of Witness

If Alvarez intends the Mirabals' lives as a lesson for the world, it is a lesson her family learned firsthand. Her father, his life at risk for membership in the same underground, fled with his wife and daughters to New York City in August 1960. Alvarez counts their escape, based on her memories at age ten, "one of the most traumatic experiences of my life" ("Citizen" 21). With a deeply felt connection to the murdered Mirabals, she finds herself "compelled" to tell their story ("Julia Alvarez"). Her insistence on fiction, rather than biography, as vehicle stems from her conviction that by it she can remain true to their essence, individualize them, and safeguard them from "deification" as heroes, "wrapped in superlatives and ascended into myth" (324).

The historical biographical novel's balance between fact and fiction is critical to Alvarez's goal in exposing the barbarism of the Trujillo regime while honoring the human courage of those who resisted. She finds inspiration in the testimonial literature that emerged from Latin America in the second half of the twentieth century, related in purpose to the traumatic witness of the Holocaust, which imposes a numbing responsibility: "The story seemed to me almost impossible to write. It was too perfect, too tragic, too awful. The girls' story didn't need a story. And besides, I couldn't yet imagine how one tells a story like this. *Once upon a holocaust, there were three butterflies*" ("Chasing" 202). Studying slave narratives, records of women in the French Resistance, and the rule of other Central American dictators, she affirms, "Certainly I was influenced by literature of the Holocaust and the testimonial literature that comes out of Latin America—that whole tradition, the Mothers of the Plaza in Argentina" ("Citizen" 28).

Latin-American *testimonio*, a textual form of resistance that imparts a direct experience of survival under systemic forces of political power, becomes central to Alvarez's project. Related to such autobiographical modes as confession and diary, *testimonio* introduces a first-person narrator, speaking not for only him- or herself but for an oppressed group, in the shape of collective memory. John Beverley argues that the narrator's ability to convey sincerity and establish *testimonio*'s "truth-effect" is critical in communicating the individual's story and the "absent polyphony of other voices" whom he or she represents (27, 28). While democratic in urging solidarity with the subaltern, it typically relies on an interlocutor to redact a story told by an unlettered victim and addresses an audience more privileged than the narrator. The results emerge, then, from collaboration between the I-narrator and the editor, a collusion that risks re-silencing the witness by awarding the editor interpretive control of the story. Apt as *testimonio* is for Alvarez's subject matter, then, its ventriloquized, potentially fictionalized nature makes it equally apt for her thematic approach. Thus, she redoubles rather than minimizes her metanarrative frame, first introducing the privileged *gringa dominicana* as internal listener and then mediating the sisters' voices through Dedé's recollections. This dual frame calls attention to the witness value of the account as well as to the self-reflexivity of the narrative, prompting Nereida Segura-Rico to label it "metatestimonio" (173). Even more, Segura-Rico argues, Alvarez displaces the revolutionary purposes of *testimonio* to foreground the act of inscription; by raising questions of what gets told, by whom and for whom, in a historical novel, she challenges readers to ask similar questions about the artifices of history (175).

If the whole of *In the Time of the Butterflies* is testimonial, Alvarez approaches recognized *testimonio* most closely in the single chapter set in La Victoria Prison during Minerva and María Teresa's captivity. The last of Mate's chapters, it here partakes of the legacy of prison diaries. Confined to a cell, she reflects, "It feels good to write things down. Like there will be a record" (227). She uses a notebook sent by her mother, knowing her daughter's devotion to keeping a "little book," and smuggled in by a sympathetic guard whom the prisoners nickname Santicló, after the gift-bearing North American icon. Mate composes its entries in secret, away from cellmates and guards, often by moonlight. The intimacy and familiarity of her voice assert the truth value of her story, over against the editorial manipulation latent in *testimonio*.

In bearing witness to the outrages of the Trujillo era, the chapter is critical for providing the novel's only view of political detention, although in a depiction that Ink rightly calls "sentimentalized" (796) and Criniti, "romanticized" (57). Its opening entry on March 16, the sisters' fifty-fifth day of captivity, includes Santicló's words of encouragement, "You're safer in here than out there, bombs and what not" (Alvarez, *In the Time* 227). The ordeals of prison—sharing a bucket and less than 500 square feet of space with two dozen cellmates, the constant threat of interrogation, the sexual abuse by callous guards, the scant, inedible food—only reinforce Minerva's resolve and enfold Mate in a circle of kindhearted companions. While she admits that "[t]he fear is the worse part" and despairs of seeing her husband and daughter again, she weeps on the night before her release, telling Magdalena that "[t]his relationship has been the most meaningful experience of [her] whole life" (227, 253).

In terms of character development, the chapter completes a coming-of-age story that Alvarez conceives for the youngest Mirabal. Here, the naïve girl who in 1946 drew beribboned patent leather flats, bought while shopping for First Communion shoes, symbolically loses the gold cross that she has worn ever since, confiscated in retaliation for the "Crucifix Plot" (*In the Time* 237). Here, she not only attends Minerva's "little school," after Castro's model, but learns from her cellmates, the thieves, murderers, and prostitutes "[she] once thought were below [her]": "Magdalena has taught me more about how privileged I really am than all of Minerva's lectures about class" (233, 230, 248). Here, she experiences her first homosexual encounter and, crucially, undergoes interrogation at La Cuarenta [40], where she is shocked with electric prods in front of her husband, Leandro, to force him to reveal names of his compatriots. With it, her education is complete.

The last two and a half pages of the chapter, an account of that beating, are central to the novel as *testimonio*. Artful retrospective recounting of the event heightens its brutality. In early April, she had worried whether her missed periods were an effect of two months' incarceration or, as the reader suspects, a pregnancy. Then, after a lapse of time marked with a note, uncharacteristic for Mate, "*Not sure what day it is*," entries resume with the revelation that she has "either bled a baby or had a period" (*In the Time* 240). So traumatized that she can tell only Magdalena, at her sister's urging she writes, on April 26, "Here is my story of what happened in La 40 on Monday, April 11th." The reader, however, sees nothing but a bracketed note, "[pages torn out]" (242). In inverted dramatic irony, the audience knows less than what Mate confides to Magdalena and, later, allows Minerva to read.

After the gap, Mate's entries continue into the summer, when, on June 30, she includes a newspaper clipping, slipped to her by Patria, announcing that the Organization of American States (OAS) will investigate reports of human rights abuses. Officials, required to send one prisoner per unit for interview, select Mate. Minerva presses her to carry two written statements to convey what she dare not speak aloud, one by the Fourteenth of June collective, the second ripped out of her diary, those missing pages from April 26. Mate conceals the papers in her thick plaits, a ploy that had been set up elaborately in her June 30 entry—"We've found a great new hiding place, my hair!" (246)—and foreshadowed in the frame story, where Dedé displays Mate's braid. Her August 6 entry, however, confesses that she delivered only the first statement, not her own. Yet those pages appear, absent any editorial explanation, at the conclusion of the chapter, addressed to "*the OAS Committee investigating Human Rights Abuses*" and candidly introduced: "*This is a journal entry of what occurred at La 40 on Monday, April 11th, 1960, to me, a female political prisoner. I'd rather not put my name. Also, I have blotted out some names as I am afraid of getting innocent people in trouble*" (*In the Time* 254).

Designed for visual impact, the passage is conspicuous not just for its italic prologue but for the fifteen black blocks inking out every name. Disorienting the reader, their irregular graphic pattern imitates in print the performative disruptions of *testimonio*, with its hesitations and gaps. Dramatically, the testimony that fails to reach its primary internal audience, the OAS, fails to reveal much to its external audience, denied not only those names but also, in the intentional gap at its close, any knowledge of what Leandro confesses or what tortures result. In any case, its agonized message arrives decades too late to intervene on behalf of any of Trujillo's prisoners.

Nonetheless, the essential work of *testimonio* continues, evoking a witness-reader relationship allowing the past to erupt into the present. In Elzbieta Sklodowska's analysis, it imposes the "open-ended and endless task of rewriting human experience," lest suffering and injustice be forgotten (98). John Beverley describes *testimonio*'s effect as a complicity that engages the reader's sense of ethics (31), while James Damico and Laura Apol recognize in it "opportunities for transformative engagements with literature" (156). Reminding audiences of their own affiliation with power in the form of gender, race, or class, it denies them the comfort of consigning oppression to history. Teasing life's truths out of fiction, *In the Time of the Butterflies* urges responsive justice and begs for empathy. Alvarez hopes for it a "compassionate, sensitive, and attentive" audience, insisting, "I think the best literature exercises our souls, perhaps even helps create them" ("Fixed Facts" 39).

Never the Last Word

If historical fiction is known for its didactic nature, Alvarez in *In the Time of the Butterflies* presses historical biographical fiction also for moral purpose. The ethical stance she takes in her writer's profession converges with the *testimonio* call to transformation. She seeks to stir conviction and amend behavior, to ask "not only how history can represent the world but how it can intervene in the world" (Segura-Rico 187).

In the Time of the Butterflies insistently, persistently, intrudes on the world. Its narrative frame awards the last words to Dedé, "the one who survived to tell the story," yet the book continues, and with it Alvarez's message (312). After Dedé's first-person Epilogue come the Postscript and then a page of personal and print sources, among them not only Dedé and Minou, but also La Virgencita de Altagracia, heavenly inspiration indeed (325). The 2010 Algonquin paperback edition appends "Still the Time for Butterflies: A Note from the Author," four autobiographical pages beginning with her family's escape to New York and her father's stories of the dictatorship. On repeated visits to the Dominican Republic, Alvarez's story intersects with and overtakes Dedé's; unlike the intrusive *gringa dominicana*, she surpasses the role of interviewer to become friend, welcome the lives of the sisters' families. Her sense of belonging aligned with her sense of mission, she is driven to write; she has "a debt to pay" for the freedom her family won (330).

Alvarez makes continuous payment on that debt in the art of her writing and the generativity of her sociopolitical action. On land she and her husband own in the Dominican Republic, they direct what her website describes as "a sustainable farm-literacy center called Alta Gracia," which produces organic coffee, pays living wages, and operates a school, described in her book *A Cafecito Story*. Since 2012 she has sponsored an annual commemoration named "Border of Lights," held on the border between Haiti and the Dominican Republic to remember the victims of Trujillo's 1937 massacre. Each year she urges "Wear a Butterfly" on November 25, which the UN declared International Day for the Elimination of Violence against Women, and promises that "there are Mariposas everywhere" ("Julia Alvarez").

"[N]ovels don't answer questions, they're not solutions," Alvarez admits. Yet, as *In the Time of the Butterflies* demonstrates, historical biographical novels can personify in their characters the courage and determination that lead to solutions. They can address what Rebecca Harrison and Emily Hipchen characterize as "Alvarez's most urgent concerns," that is, "what she as a writer can do to assuage suffering, rectify wrongs, make life if not easier then richer, fuller, fairer for others" (4).

Works Cited

Alvarez, Julia. "Chasing the Butterflies." *Something to Declare*. Algonquin, 1998, pp. 197-209.

_____. "Citizen of the World: An Interview with Julia Alvarez." *Latina Self-Portraits: Interviews with Contemporary Women Writers*. Edited by Bridget Kevane and Juanita Heredia. U of New Mexico P, 2000, pp. 19-32.

_____. "Fixed Facts and Creative Freedom in the Biographical Novel." *Truthful Fictions: Conversations with American Biographical Novelists*. Edited by Michael Lackey. Bloomsbury, 2014, pp. 27-41.

_____. *In the Time of the Butterflies*. 1994. Algonquin, 2010.

_____. "Julia Alvarez." www.juliaalvarez.com.

_____. "A Note on the Loosely Autobiographical." *New England Review*, vol. 21, no.4, Fall 2000, pp. 165-66.

Beverley, John. "The Margin at the Center: On *Testimonio* (Testimonial Narrative)." *The Real Thing: Testimonial Discourse and Latin America*. Edited by Georg M. Gugelberger. Duke UP, 1996, pp. 23-41.

Criniti, Steve. "Collecting Butterflies: Julia Alvarez's Revision of North American Collective Memory." *Modern Language Studies*, vol. 36, no. 2, Winter 2007, pp. 42-63.

Damico, James, and Laura Apol. "Using Testimonial Response to Frame the Challenges and Possibilities of Risky Historical Texts." *Children's Literature in Education*, vol. 39, no. 2, 2009, pp. 141-58.

de Piérola, José. "At the Edge of History: Notes for a Theory of the Historical Novel in Latin America." *Romance Studies*, vol. 26, no. 2, Apr. 2008, pp. 151-62.

Donaldson, Scott. *The Impossible Craft: Literary Biography*. Pennsylvania State UP, 2015.

Harrison, Rebecca, and Emily Hipchen. Introduction. *Inhabiting La Patria: Identity, Agency, and Antojo in the Work of Julia Alvarez*. Edited by Rebecca Harrison and Emily Hipchen. SUNY P, 2013, pp. 1-20.

Ink, Lynn Chun. "Remaking Identity, Unmaking Nation: Historical Recovery and the Reconstruction of Community in *In the Time of the Butterflies* and *The Farming of Bones*." *Callaloo*, vol. 27, no. 3, 2004, pp. 788-807.

Lackey, Michael. "Introduction: The Rise of the American Biographical Novel." *Truthful Fictions: Conversations with American Biographical Novelists*. Edited by Michael Lackey. Bloomsbury, 2014, pp. 1-25.

Martínez, Elizabeth Coonrod. "Julia Álvarez: Progenitor of a Movement." *Américas*, vol. 59, no. 2, Mar.-Apr. 2007, pp. 6-13.

McCallum, Shara. "Reclaiming Julia Alvarez: *In the Time of the Butterflies*." *Women's Studies*, vol. 29, no. 1, Feb. 2000, pp. 93-117.

Rich, Charlotte. "Talking Back to *El Jefe*: Genre, Polyphony, and Dialogic Resistance in Julia Alvarez's *In the Time of the Butterflies*." *MELUS*, vol. 27, no. 4, Winter 2002, pp. 165-82.

Rosario-Sievert, Heather. "Conversation with Julia Alvarez." *Review: Latin American Literature and Arts*, vol. 54, Spring 1997, pp. 31-37.

Segura-Rico, Nereida. "Witnessing History: *Metatestimonio* in Literary Representations of the Trujillo Dictatorship." *Antípodas*, vol. 20, 2009, pp. 173-90.

Sklodowska, Elzbieta. "Spanish American Testimonial Novel: Some Afterthoughts." *The Real Thing: Testimonial Discourse and Latin America*. Edited by Georg M. Gugelberger. Duke UP, 1996, pp. 84-100.

Spacks, Patricia Meyer. "Biography: Moral and Physical Truth." *Gossip*, Knopf, 1985, pp. 92-120.

Stewart, David O. "Historical Fact, Historical Fiction." *Publishers Weekly*, 9 Nov. 2015, p. 64.

Sutherland, Emily. "Historical Lives in Fiction, Characters in Fiction: Are They the Same People?" *TEXT*, vol. 11, no. 1, Apr. 2007. www.textjournal.com.au/april07/sutherland.htm. Accessed 15 Aug 2017.

RESOURCES

Further Reading

This list is not intended to be exhaustive, as thousands of publications could be included. All are long-form fiction, because the theme is also a fiction genre most frequently appearing in novel form. Parameters for inclusion include popularity among various audiences, receipt of awards, longevity, discussion within this volume, and importance to development of the genre. (YA) and (C) indicate novels for young adults and children, respectively. All novels and precursors to the novel are categorized by century from the eighteenth through the twenty-first.

Eighteenth and Nineteenth Century

The Abbot (1820), Sir Walter Scott

The Antiquary (1816), Sir Walter Scott

The Bride of Lammermoor (1819), Sir Walter Scott

The Castle of Otranto: A Gothic Story (1764), Horace Walpole

The Deerslayer (1841), James Fenimore Cooper

The Fortunes of Perkin Warbeck (1830), Mary Shelley

Guy Mannering (1815), Sir Walter Scott

The Heart of Midlothian (1820), Sir Walter Scott

Hope Leslie (1827), Catharine Maria Sedgwick

The Hunchback of Notre Dame (1832), Victor Hugo

Ivanhoe (1815), Sir Walter Scott

Kenilworth (1821), Sir Walter Scott

The Last of the Mohicans (1826) James Fenimore Cooper

Les Misérables (1862), Victor Hugo

Lodore (1835), Mary Shelley

Old Mortality (1816), Sir Walter Scott

The Pathfinder: or, the Inland Sea (1844), James Fenimore Cooper

Peveril of the Peak (1823), Sir Walter Scott

The Pioneers (1823), James Fenimore Cooper

The Prairie (1827), James Fenimore Cooper

Quentin Durward (1823), Sir Walter Scott

Redgauntlet (1824), Sir Walter Scott

The Red Badge of Courage (1895), Stephen Crane

The Red Rover (1827) James Fenimore Cooper

Rob Roy (1817), Sir Walter Scott

The Spy (1821), James Fenimore Cooper

A Tale of Two Cities (1859), Charles Dickens

The Talisman (1825), Sir Walter Scott

Toilers of the Sea (1883), Victor Hugo

Valperga (1823), Mary Shelley

Woodstock (1826), Sir Walter Scott

Work: A Story of Experience (1873), Louis May Alcott

Twentieth Century

Absalom, Absalom! (1936), William Faulkner

Accordion Crimes (1996), Annie Proulx

Across Five Aprils (1964) YA, Irene Hunt

The All-True Travels and Adventures of Lidie Newton (1998), Jane
    Smiley

Anthony Adverse (1933), Hervey Allen

Beloved (1987), Toni Morrison

Black Thunder (1936), Arna Bontemps

A Break with Charity: A Story About the Salem Witch Trials (1992) YA,
    Ann Rinaldi

Bull Run (1993) YA, Paul Fleischman

A Candle in the Dark (1993), Megan Chance

Caught in the Act (1988) YA, Joan Lowery Nixon

Cold Mountain (1997), Charles Frazier

The Confessions of Nat Turner (1967), William Styron

A Dangerous Fortune (1993), Ken Follett

The Dahomean (1971), Frank Yerby

The Devil's Arithmetic (1988) YA, Jane Yolen

Dreams of Mairhe Mehan (1996) YA, Jennifer Armstrong

Drums Along the Mohawk (1936), Walter Edmonds

The Fifth of March (1993) YA, Ann Rinaldi

Forty Acres and Maybe a Mule (1998) YA, Harriette Gillem Robinet

The Foxes of Harrow (1946), Frank Yerby

The French Lieutenant's Woman (1969, John Fowles

The Girl with a Pearl Earring (1999), Tracy Chevalier

Gone with the Wind (1936), Margaret Mitchell

The Great Train Robbery (1973), Michael Crichton

If I Should Die Before I Wake (1994) YA, Han Nolan

In a Dark Wood (1998), Michael Cadnum

Incident at Hawk's Hill (1971), Allan W. Eckert

Jamaica Inn (1936), Daphne du Maurier

Jason's Gold (1999) YA, Will Hobbs

Jip, His Story (1997) YA, Katherine Paterson

Johnny Tremain (1987) YA, Esther Forbes

The Journey (1989), James Michener

Jubilee (1966), Margaret Walker

Kim (1901), Rudyard Kipling

Love Is Eternal (1954), Irving Stone

Lyddie (1991) YA, Katherine Paterson

Mamzelle: A Story of the War of 1812 (1955) YA, Gladys Malvern

Master Georgie (1998), Beryl Bainbridge

My Brother Sam Is Dead (1974) YA, James Lincoln Collier and
     Christopher Collier

The Name of the Rose (1980), Umberto Eco

Nightjohn (1993) YA, Gary Paulsen

Northwest Passage (1937), Kenneth Roberts

One Hundred Years of Solitude (1970), Gabriel García Márquez

Orphan Train Adventure Series (1987-1998) YA, Joan Lowery Nixon

     A Family Apart (1988)

     In the Face of Danger (1988)

A Place to Belong (1989)

Caught in the Act (1989)

A Dangerous Promise (1994)

Keeping Secrets (1995)

Circle of Love (1997)

Pay the Devil (1962/1999), Jack Higgins

The President's Lady: A Novel About Rachel and Andrew Jackson (1951), Irving Stone

A Ride into Morning: The Story of Tempe Wick (1991) YA, Ann Rinaldi

Rifles for Watie (1957) YA, Harold Keith

Roll of Thunder, Hear My Cry (1976) YA, Mildred D. Taylor

A Rumor of War (1977), Philip Caputo

Sarney (1993) YA, Gary Paulsen

Standing in the Light: The Captive Diary of Catharine Carey Logan (1998) YA, Mary Pope Osborne

Stealing Freedom (1998) YA, Elisa Carbone

Things Fall Apart (1958), Chinua Achebe

To Be a Slave (1968/2000) C, Julius Lester

Which Way Freedom? (1986) YA, Joyce Hansen

The Witch of Blackbird Pond (1958) YA, Elizabeth George Speare

With Every Drop of Blood: A Novel of the Civil War (1994), James Lincoln Collier and Christopher Collier

Wolf by the Ears (1991) YA, Ann Rinaldi

Twenty-first Century

A Mercy (2008), Toni Morrison

All the Light We Cannot See (2014), Anthony Doerr

Alligator Bayou (2009) YA, Donna Jo Napoli

Arthur and George (2005), Julian Barnes

The Astonishing Life of Octavian Nothing, Traitor to the Nation (2006) YA, M. T. Anderson

The Asylum (2013), John Harwood

Becoming Mary Mehan (2002) YA, Jennifer Armstrong

Between Shades of Gray (2012) YA, Ruta Sepetys

Bomb: The Race to Build and Steal the World's Most Dangerous Weapon (2012) YA, Steve Sheinkin

The Book Thief (2005) YA, Markus Zusak

The Boy in the Striped Pajamas: A Fable (2006), John Boyne

The Casebook of Victor Frankenstein (2009), Peter Ackroyd

Chains (2008) YA, Laurie Halse Anderson

Coal Black Horse (2007) YA, Robert Olmstead

Code Talkers (2005) YA, Joseph Bruchak

Code Name Verity (2012) YA, Elizabeth Wein

Copper Sun (2006) YA, Sharon Draper

Cousin's War Series/The Plantagenet and Tudor Novels, Philippa Gregory
Select Titles:

> *The Other Boleyn Girl* (2003)
>
> *White Queen, The* (2009)
>
> *Red Queen, The* (2010)
>
> *The Lady of the Rivers* (2011)
>
> *The Kingmaker's Daughter* (2012)
>
> *The White Princess* (2013)
>
> *The King's Curse* (2014)

The Crimson Petal and the White (2002), Michael Faber

Day of Tears (2005) YA, Julius Lester

Demon Camp: A Soldier's Exorcism (2014) YA, Jennifer Percy

The Ever-After Bird, (2007) YA, Ann Rinaldi

Everything Is Illuminated: A Novel (2002), Jonathan Safran Foer

Fanny (2003), Edmund White

Fever, 1793 (2000) YA, Laurie Halse Anderson

47 (2005), Walter Mosley

Girl in Blue (2001) YA, Ann Rinaldi

The Help, (2011), Kathryn Stockett

Invasion (2015) YA, Walter Dean Myers

The Invention of Wings (2014), Sue Monk Kidd

The Land (2001) YA, Mildred Taylor

The Letter Writer (2008) YA, Ann Rinaldi

A Man of Parts (2011), David Lodge

Marines of Autumn, The (2000) – James Brady

The Metropolis Case (2010), Matthew Gallaway

The Most Dangerous: Daniel Ellsberg and the Secret History of the Vietnam War (2015) YA, Steve Sheinkin

The Night in Question (2015), Laurie Graham

Out of Darkness (2016) YA , Ashley Hope Pérez

The Passion of Dolssa (2016) YA, Julie Berry

The Petticoat Men (2014), Barbara Ewing

The Port Chicago 50: Disaster, Mutiny, and the Fight for Civil Rights (2014) YA, Steve Sheinkin

Riot (2009) YA, Walter Dean Myers

The River Between Us (2003) YA, Richard Peck

Salt to the Sea: A Novel (2016) YA, Ruta Sepetys

Scandalmonger (2000), William Safire

The Shore (2015), Sara Taylor

A Soldier's Secret: The Incredible True Story of Sarah Edmonds, a Civil War Hero (2012), Marissa Moss

Trouble Don't Last (2002) YA, Shelley Pearsall

Two Girls of Gettysburg (2008) YA, Lisa Klein

The Underground Railroad (2016), Colson Whitehead

The Valley (2015), John Renehan

The Water Horse / Band of Angels (2004), Julia Gregson

When I Crossed No-Bob (2007) YA, Margaret McMullan

Worth (2004) YA, A. LaFaye

The Yellow Birds: A Novel (2012), Kevin Powers

Bibliography

American Association of University Women. *How Schools Shortchange Girls*. AAUW.org. 1992. Accessed 27 Feb. 2017. https://history.aauw.org/aauw-research/1992-how-schools-shortchange-girls.

Ames, John Edward. "Historical Fiction." *Writer*, vol. 117, no. 11, Nov. 2004, pp.34-37. *Master FILE Premier*. Accessed 11 Mar. 2017. https://www.ebsco.com/.

Baker, Jennifer S. *The Readers' Advisory Guide to Historical Fiction*. ALA Editions. 2015. *eBook Academic Collection (EBSCOhost)*. Accessed 11 Mar. 2017. https://www.ebsco.com/.

Barnes, Clive. "A View of War and Soldiering in the Carey Novels of Ronald Welch." *Children's Literature in Education*, vol. 47, no. 4, Dec. 2016, pp. 300-24. *Education Source*, doi:10.1007/s10583-015-9269-8. Accessed 7 July 2017.

Beckett, Sandra L. *Crossover Fiction: Global and Historical Perspectives*. Routledge, 2009.

Boennan-Cornell, William. "Using Historical Graphic Novels in High School History Classes: Potential for Contextualization, Sourcing, and Corroborating." *History Teacher*, vol. 48, no. 2, Feb. 2015, pp. 209-24. *Academic Search Premier*. Accessed 11 Mar. 2017. https://www.ebsco.com/.

Brown, Joanne, and Nancy St. Claire. *The Distant Mirror: Reflections on Young Adult Historical Fiction*. Scarecrow, 2006.

Brown, Lyn Mikel. *Girlfighting: Betrayal and Rejection among Girls*. New York UP, 2005.

Brumburg, Joan Jacobs. *The Body Project: An Intimate History of American Girls*.Vintage, 1998.

Burstein, Miriam Elizabeth. *Victorian Reformations: Historical Fiction and Religious Controversy, 1820-1900*. Notre Dame UP, 2014.

Carey-Webb, Allen. *Literature and Lives: A Response-Based, Cultural Studies Approach to Teaching English*. National Council of Teachers of English, 2001.

Cart, Michael. "Of Innocence and Exerience." *Booklist*, 15 Apr. 2007, p. 37.

_____. "Only a Great Man." *Booklist*, 15 Apr. 2015, p. 43.

Damico, James. S., Mark Baildon, and Daniel Greenstone, editors. "Examining How Historical Agency Works in Children's Literature." *Social Studies Research & Practice*, vol. 5, no. 1, 2010, pp.1-12. *Education Source*. Accessed 8 July 2017. https://www.ebsco.com/.

Danks, Carol, and Leatrice Rabinsky. *Teaching for a Tolerant World, Grades 9-12: Essays and Resources*. National Council of Teachers of English, 1999.

Davis, Jay Madison. "Credibility and Popularity in the Historical Mystery." *World Literature Today*, vol. 86, no. 2, Mar/Apr. 2012, pp 9-11. *MasterFILE Premier*. Accessed 11 Mar. 2017. https://www.ebsco.com/.

De Groot, Jerome. *Remaking History: The Past in Contemporary Historical Fictions*. Routledge, 2016.

Elias, Amy J. *Sublime Desire: History and Post-1960s Fiction*. Johns Hopkins UP, 2001.

Elliot, Michael A. "Strangely Interested: The Work of Historical Fantasy." *American Literature*, vol. 87, no. 1, Mar. 2013, pp.137-57.

Fink, Lisa Storm. "Historical Fiction." *Reading Teacher*, vol. 67, no. 7, Apr. 2014, pp. 561-68. *Humanities International Complete*, doi:10.1002/trtr.1245. Accessed 11 Mar. 2017.

Fisher, Jerilyn, and Ellen S. Silber, editors. *Women in Literature: Reading through the Lens of Gender*. Greenwood, 2003.

Foley, Barbara. *Telling the Truth: The Theory and Practice of Documentary Fiction*. Cornell UP, 1986.

Frank, Joan. "In Search of Heated Agreement." *Antioch Review*, vol. 67, no. 2, Spring 2009, pp. 349-55.

Gardiner, Juliet. "SIGNPOSTS Historical Novels." *History Today*, vol. 59, no. 10, Oct. 2009, pp. 54-56.

Gershowitz, Alyssa, and Martha V. Parravano. "We're With Her." *Horn Book Magazine*, vol. 92, no. 6, Nov/Dec 2016, pp.11-12. *EBSCOhost*, Accessed 31 Aug. 2017. https://www.ebsco.com/.

Harris, Katherine. "'Part of the project of that book was not to be authentic': Neo-historical authenticity and its anachronisms in contemporary historical fiction." *Rethinking History*, vol. 21, no. 2, June 2017, pp.193-212. *EBSCOhost*, Accessed 31 Aug. 2017. https://www.ebsco.com/.

Harris, Marla. "'A History Not Then Taught in History Books': (Re)writing Reconstruction in Historical Fiction for Children and Young Adults." *Lion and the Unicorn: A Critical Journal of Children's Literature*, vol. 30, no.1, Jan. 2006, pp. 94-116.

_____. "Bleak Houses and Secret Cities: Alternative Communities in Young Adult Fiction." *Children's Literature in Education*, Mar. 2002, vol. 33, no. 1, pp. 63-76.

Horton, Todd A. "'I Am Canada': Exploring Social Responsibility in Social Studies Using Young Adult Historical Fiction." *Canadian Social Studies*, vol.47, no.1, 2014, pp. 26-43. *ERIC*. Accessed 11 Mar. 2017. www.eric.ed.gov.

Howell, Jennifer. "Popularising History: The Use of Historical Fiction with Pre-Service Teachers." *Australian Journal of Teacher Education*, vol. 39, no. 12, Dec. 2014, pp 1-12. *ERIC*. Accessed 11 Mar. 2017. https://files.eric.ed.gov/fulltext/EJ1047078.pdf.

Jalalzai, Zubeda. "Historical Fiction and Maryse Condé's "I, Tituba, Black Witch of Salem.'" *African American Review*, vol. 43, no. 2/3, Summer/Fall 2009, pp. 413-25. *Education Source*. Accessed 3 Mar. 2017. https://www.ebsco.com/.

Johnson, Sara L. *Historical Fiction II: A Guide to the Genre*. ABC-Clio, 2005.

Katz, Tamar. "City Memory, City History: Urban Nostalgia, 'The Colossus of New York,' and Late-Twentieth-Century Historical Fiction." *Contemporary Literature*, vol. 51, no. 4, Winter 2010, pp. 810-51.

Kesler, Ted, Gibson Lenwood Jr., and Christine Turansky. "Bringing the Book to Life: Responding to Historical Fiction Using Digital Storytelling." *Journal of Literacy Research*, vol. 48, no. 1, Mar. 2016, pp. 39-79. *ERIC*, doi:10.1177/1086296X16654649. Accessed 12 Jul. 2017.

Klett, Rex E. "History Repeats Itself." *Library Journal,* vol. 130, no. 2, 1 Feb. 2005, p. 56.

Lamb, Sharon, and Lyn Mikel Brown. *Packaging Girlhood: Rescuing Our Girls from Marketers' Schemes*. St. Martin's, 2007.

Lucier, Makia. "Writing Historical Fiction (OR HOW RESEARCH AND CREATIVITY GO HAND IN HAND)." *Knowledge Quest*, vol. 42, no. 5, May/June 2014, pp. 78-80. *Education Source*. 11 Mar. 2017. https://www.ebsco.com/.

Lynch, Gerald. "Presenting the Past: The Tendentious Use of History in Contemporary Canadian Literature." *American Review of Canadian Studies*,vol. 43, no. 1, Mar. 2013, pp. 1-11.

Morgan, Erik J. "Imagined Histories: Biography, Fiction, and the Challenges of Historical Imagination." *Teaching History: A Journal of Methods*, vol. 41, no. 2, Fall 2016, pp. 59-72. *Education Source*. Accessed 11 Mar. 2017. https://www.ebsco.com/.

Nagy, Ladislav. "Historical Fiction as a Mixture of History and Romance: Towards the Genre Definition of the Historical Novel."*Prague Journal of English Studies* (PJES), vol. 3, no. 1, Sept. 2014, pp. 7-17.

Nilsen, Alleen Pace, et al. *Literature for Today's Young Adults*. 9th ed., Pearson, 2012.

Ott, Bill. "Historical Fiction and Me." *Booklist*, vol. 105, no. 16, 15 Apr. 2009, p. 72.

Palmer, Beth. *Neo-Victorian Fiction and Historical Narrative: The Victorians and Us*. Indiana UP, 2012.

Parlevliet, Sanne. "Is that Us? Dealing with the 'Black' Pages of History in Historical Fiction for Children (1996-2010)." *Children's Literature in Education*, vol. 47, no. 4, Dec. 2016, pp. 343-56. *EBSCOhost*, doi:10.1007/s10583-015-9270-2. Accessed 30 Aug. 2017.

Pollack, Gillian. *History and Fiction: Writers, Their Research, Worlds and Stories*. Peter Lang, 2016. *eBook Community College Collection (EBSCOhost)*. Accessed 11 Mar. 2017. https://www.ebsco.com/.

Power, Chandra L. "Challenging the Pluralism of Our Past: Presentism and the Selective Tradition in Historical Fiction Written for Young People," *Research in the Teaching of English*, vol. 37, no. 4, May 2003, pp. 425-66.

Rahn, Suzanne. "An Evolving Past: The Story of Historical Fiction and Nonfiction for Children," *The Lion and the Unicorn: A Critical Journal of Children's Literature,* vol. 15, no.1, June 1991, pp. 1-26.

Reid, Ian. "Memory Loss and Retrieval." *Changing English: Studies in Culture and Education*, vol. 23, no. 2, June 2016, pp. 98-113. *Education Source*, doi:10.1080/1358684X.2016.1162965. Accessed 7 Apr. 2017.

Reisz, Matthew. "History in the faking." *Times Higher Education*, no. 1974, 18 Nov. 2010, pp. 44-6. *EBSCOHost*. Accessed 29 Aug. 2017. https://www.ebsco.com/.

Ringrose, Christopher. "A Journey Backwards: History through Style in Children's Fiction." *Children's Literature in Education*, vol. 38, no. 3, Sept. 2007, pp. 207-18.

Rochman, Hazel. "Core Collection: The Vietnam War in Youth Fiction." *Booklist*, vol. 102, no. 16, 15 Apr. 2006, pp. 62-64.

Rysick, Mary Taylor, and Brenda Rosler. "The Return of Historical Fiction." *Reading Teacher*, vol. 63, no. 2, Oct. 2009, pp.163-66.

"Searching for the Soul of Jewish Historical Fiction." *Moment Magazine*, vol. 40, no. 2, Mar./Apr. 2015, pp. 33-36.

Schwebel, Sara L. "Historical Fiction and the Classroom: History and Myth in Elizabeth George Speare's *The Witch of Blackbird Pond.*" *Children's Literature in Education*, vol. 34, no. 3, Sept. 2003, pp. 195-218.

Sepetys, Ruta. "Historical Fiction: The Silent Soldier." *ALAN Review*, vol. 42, no. 3, Summer 2015, pp.79-83. *Education Source*. Accessed 11 Mar. 2017. https://www.ebsco.com/.

Stevens, Anne H. *British Historical Fiction before Scott*. Palgrave McMillan, 2010.

Stone, Tanya Lee. "A Fine, Fine Line: Truth in Nonfiction." *Hornbook Magazine*, vol. 87, no. 2, Mar./Apr. 2011, pp.84-87. *EBSCOhost*. Accessed 30 Aug. 2017. https://www.ebsco.com/.

Travis, Madelyn. "'Heritage Anti-Semitism' in Modern Times? Representations of Jews and Judaism in Twenty-first-century British Historical Fiction for Children." *European Judaism*, vol. 43, no.1, Spring 2010, pp. 78-92. *EBSCOhost*, doi:10.3167/ej.2010.430106. Accessed 7 July 2017.

Trites, Roberta Seelinger. *Disturbing the Universe: Power and Repression in Adolescent Fiction*. U of Iowa P, 2000.

_____. *Waking Sleeping Beauty: Feminist Voices in Children's Novels*. U of Iowa P, 1997.

Vreeland, Susan. "Dip Into the Riches of Historical Fiction: A bestselling author offers an engaging overview of the genre and a step-by-step approach to getting started." *Writer*, vol. 124, no. 12, Dec. 2011, pp. 37-38. *EBSCOHost*. Accessed 30 Aug. 2017. https://www.ebsco.com/.

Wake, Paul. "'Except in the case of historical fact': History and the historical novel." *Rethinking History: The Journal of Theory and Practice*, vol.

20, no. 1, Mar. 2016, pp. 80-96. *Humanities International Complete*, doi:10.1080/13642529.2016.1134921. Accessed 11 Mar. 2017.

White, Hayden. "Historical Fictions: Kermode's Idea of History," *Critical Quarterly*, vol. 54, no. 1, Apr. 2012, pp. 43-59.

Widdowson, Peter. "'Writing back': contemporary re-visionary fiction." *Textual Practice*, vol. 20, no. 3, Sep 2006, pp.491-507. *EBSCOHost*, doi:10.1080/09502360600828984. Accessed 20 Aug. 2017.

White, Edmund. "More History, Less Nature."*Times Newspapers,* 25 Jul. 2003, no. 5234, pp. 11-13.

Williams, Wilda W. "The Great Escape." *Library Journal*, vol. 134, no. 7, 15 Apr. 2009, pp.22-24. *EBSCOHost*. Accessed 30 Aug. 2017. https://www.ebsco.com/.

Wilson, Kim. "The Past Re-Imagined: Memory and Representations of Power in Historical Fiction for Children," *International Research in Children's Literature*, vol. 1 no. 2, Dec. 2008, pp. 111-24.

Zamora, Lois Parkinson. *Writing the Apocalypse: Historical Vision in Contemporary U.S. and Latin American Fiction.* Cambridge UP, 1989.

Zheng, Yi. "The Prosaic and Provincial History of an Epic Revolution."*Journal of Language, Literature and Culture*, vol. 63, no. 2/3, Aug.-Dec. 2016, pp. 138-52. *Humanities International Complete*, doi:10.1080/20512856.2016.1244912. Accessed 3 Mar. 2017.

About the Editor

Virginia Brackett, Professor Emeritus of English, retired in 2016 from Park University where she directed the Honors Academy, the Ethnic Voices Poetry Series, and Poetry at Park, for which she received National Endowment for the Arts "Art Works" grant funding. In 2017, Brackett was selected to lead a discussion that focused on challenges to return to civilian life for military members as part of "Planting the Oar," funded by the National Endowment for the Humanities. She also serves as a member of the Kansas City Veterans Writing Team. Her fourteen books include a picture book, *What Is My Name?* (Reading Press, 2014), included on Renaissance Learnings' Accelerated Reading book list; *Critical Insights: Mary Shelley* (Salem, 2016), which she edited; *Mary Shelley: A Literary Reference to Her Life and Work* (Facts on File, 2012); *How to Write about the Brontës* (Chelsea, 2008); *The Facts on File Companion to 16th and 17th-Century British Poetry* (2008), named *Booklist* "Editor's Choice, Reference Sources, 2008"; *The Facts on File Companion to the British Novel: Beginnings to the Nineteenth Century* (2005); and *The Contingent Self: One Reading Life* (Purdue UP, 2001). Cited books include *Restless Genius: The Story of Virginia Woolf* (Morgan Reynolds, 2004), a recommended feminist book for youth by the Amelia Bloomer Project, 2005 (Feminist Task Force of the Social Responsibilities Round Table, ALA), PSLA YA Top Forty Nonfiction 2004 Titles, and "Writers of Imagination" series, Tristate Series of Note, 2005 and *A Home in the Heart: The Story of Sandra Cisneros* (Morgan Reynolds, 2004), included in PSLA YA Top Forty Nonfiction 2004 Titles and Tristate Books of Note, 2005. Her articles have appeared in *Selected Papers from the Eighteenth Annual Conference on Virginia Woolf, The Wildean, Mosaic: a Journal for the Interdisciplinary Study of Literature, Arachne, Women & Language, Notes and Queries,* and *Absolutism and the Scientific Revolution 1600-1720.* Her fiction includes the young adult novels *Angela and the Gray Mare* and *Girl Murders* in two versions, one with electronic interactivity, available at amazon.com.

Contributors

Amanda L. Anderson is an assistant professor of English at Delaware State University where in addition to teaching literature, theater, and writing classes, she also directs theatrical productions. Her article "Manufactured Maidens: Representations of Artificial Life in *Beauty and the Beast*" appears in *Critical Perspectives on Artificial Humans in Children's Literature*. She also recently directed an original hip-hop adaptation of Shakespeare's *A Midsummer Night's Dream*.

Steven T. Bickmore is an associate professor of English education at the University of Nevada, Las Vegas, in the Department of Teaching and Learning in the College of Education. He has served as an editor of *The ALAN Review* (2009-2014). He is also one of the founders and coeditors of *Study and Scrutiny: Research in Young Adult Literature* 2015 to the present. (https://journals.shareok.org/studyandscrutiny). He maintains a weekly academic blog on YA Literature: Dr. Bickmore's YA Wednesday (www.yawednesday.com). This academic blog offers a space for academics, teachers, librarians, and students to discuss scholarship and trends in young adult literature. His research interests include the induction and mentoring of novice teachers and how preservice and novice English teachers negotiate the teaching of literature using young adult literature, especially around the issues of race, class, and gender.

Danielle Barkley holds a PhD from McGill University where she specialized in nineteenth-century British literature. She has published in *Persuasions*, *European Romantic Review*, and *Victorians*, as well as numerous edited collections, including *Critical Insights: Mary Shelley*, edited by Virginia Brackett (Salem, 2016).

A former high school teacher, **Chris Crowe** is now a professor of English at Brigham Young University where he teaches adolescent literature, English teaching methods, and creative writing. He is the author of many academic articles, books for teachers, and fiction and nonfiction for young adults, including *Mississippi Trial, 1955*; *Getting Away with Murder: The*

True Story of the Emmett Till Case; and *Death Coming Up the Hill*. He has long had an interest in history and in historical fiction.

Amy Cummins, PhD, works as associate professor and English education coordinator in the Department of Literatures and Cultural Studies at the University of Texas Rio Grande Valley. Her scholarship about contemporary young adult literature has been published in venues including *The ALAN Review*, *Children's Literature in Education*, *Bookbird*, and *Dictionary of Literary Biography Volume 378: Novelists of the American Civil War*.

LuElla D'Amico is an assistant professor of English and co-coordinator of the Women's and Gender Studies Program at the University of the Incarnate Word in San Antonio, Texas. Her research focuses on early and nineteenth-century American women's writing, particularly on depictions of girlhood and girl culture during this period. She has edited a volume titled *Girls' Series Fiction and American Popular Culture*, and she currently serves as the vice president of the Harriet Beecher Stowe Society.

Christine De Vinne, professor of English at Ursuline College in Cleveland, Ohio, began her career in the middle school and secondary school classroom while earning her MA from the University of Notre Dame and then her PhD at The Ohio State University. She has served as faculty member and administrator at Ursuline College and Notre Dame of Maryland University in Baltimore. A past president of the American Name Society, she is currently book review editor and member of the editorial board for *Names: A Journal of Onomastics*. She publishes and presents on topics related to autobiography and life-writing, literary theory, names studies, and higher education.

Marta María Gutiérrez Rodríguez is a lecturer in English in the Department of English Studies at the University of Valladolid (Spain). She holds a BA and a doctorate in English. The theme of her doctoral thesis is the representation of the Salem Witchcraft Trials in nineteenth-century Anglo-American fiction. Her research focuses on the representation of this historical event in novels and plays written in the twentieth and twenty-first centuries. She has presented results of her investigation at conferences and has published academically on the representation of this historical event in different literary genres.

Jeffrey S. Kaplan, PhD, is an associate professor emeritus, School of Teaching, Learning and Leadership, College of Education and Human Performance, University of Central Florida, Orlando. He was President of ALAN, the Assembly on Literature for Adolescents (2012-13), the Research Connections Editor for *The ALAN* Review (2008-2013), and is currently chair of the Standing Committee Against Censorship (2014-2017), all affiliate organizations of the National Council Teachers of English. With Judith Hayn he coedited *Teaching Young Adult Literature Today: Insights, Considerations and Perspectives for the Classroom Teacher* (Rowman and Littlefield, 2012, 2016), *Young Adult Nonfiction: Gateway to the Common Core* (Rowman and Littlefield, 2015), and *Teaching Young Adult Literature: Integrating, Implementing and Re-Imagining the Common Core* (Rowman and Littlefield, 2015).

Christine E. Kozikowski is an assistant professor at the University of The Bahamas where she teaches a range of courses from the early British literature survey to popular fiction. Her research focuses on Middle English literature, where she examines medieval concepts of privacy and place. She published an essay entitled "Mary Shelley and Romantic Medievalism" in *Critical Insights: Mary Shelley*, edited by Virginia Brackett (Salem, 2016).

Sheng-mei Ma is professor of English at Michigan State University specializing in Asian diaspora / Asian-American studies and East-West comparative studies. His books in English include *Sinophone-Anglophone Cultural Duet* (2017); *The Last Isle* (2015); *Alienglish*(2014); *Asian Diaspora and East-West Modernity* (2012); *Diaspora Literature and Visual Culture* (2011); *East-West Montage* (2007); *The Deathly Embrace* (2000); and *Immigrant Subjectivities in Asian American and Asian Diaspora Literatures* (1998).

Natalie Neill teaches in the English Department at York University, Toronto. She specializes in Romantic literature, the Gothic, parody and satire, and film adaptation. Her recent publications include essays and book chapters about Gothic parodies, the popular culture commodification of *Frankenstein*, and the adaptation history of *A Christmas Carol*. She has also edited two rare early nineteenth-century comic Gothic novels for Valancourt Press and published an essay in *Critical Insights: Mary Shelley*, edited by Virginia Brackett (Salem, 2016).

Sara Rutkowski is an assistant professor of English at the City University of New York Kingsborough Community College. She is the author of *The Literary Legacies of the Federal Writers' Project: Voices of the Depression in the American Postwar Era* (2017), and has also published work on postwar American writers and the cultural and political contexts of twentieth-century global literature. She is currently working on a study of Ralph Ellison's fieldwork for the Federal Writers' Project.

Mary Warner is a professor of English and director of the English Credential Program at San José State University. She has taught English at the secondary and postsecondary level for more than forty-two years. Her areas of specialization include literature for young adults, the Bible as literature, and English education: she advises, prepares, and teaches seminars for future English teachers. In addition to numerous essays and book reviews, she is the author of *Winning Ways of Coaching Writing: A Practical Guide for Teaching Writing Grades 7-12* (1999); *Adolescents in the Search for Meaning: Tapping the Powerful Resource of Story* (2006); and coeditor and author of *Teaching Writing Grades 7-12 in an Era of Assessment: Passion and Practice* (2014). She is a member of the School Sisters of Notre Dame, an international congregation of women religious.

Jericho Williams earned his MA from the University of Alaska Fairbanks and his PhD from West Virginia University. He is an independent scholar whose current research interests include nineteenth- and twentieth-century American and African-American literature. He has published essays in *Critical Insights: The Harlem Renaissance* (Salem, 2015) and *Plant Horror* (Palgrave Macmillan, 2016). He is preparing one forthcoming essay about African-American slave narratives and another about Zora Neale Hurston and Harper Lee. He has taught American literature classes, as well as courses on science fiction and fantasy and literature of the supernatural.

Index

Bonaparte, Napoleon xix, 12
Bontemps, Arna 196, 202, 210, 211
Boston Massacre 27
Botkin, Benjamin 201
Bourcier, Richard J. 71
Boyce, Toby 169
Boyden, Joseph 22
Boyne, John 28
Bradbury, Ray 108
Brady, James 22
Brattle, Thomas 139
Brewitt-Taylor, Charles Henry 23
Brooks, Cleanth 27, 208
Brown, Joanne 167
Brown, Sterling 201
Bruchac, Joseph 28
Buck, Pearl S. 151, 155
Bull Run 166, 168, 169, 172, 173, 177, 179
Bumppo, Natty 122
Burns, Ken xxvi
Burton, Hester 112
Butler, Benjamin 173
Butler, Rhett 198
Butterfield, Herbert 68
Butterflies, the xvii, 212, 213, 214, 215, 216, 217, 218, 220, 223, 224, 225, 226

Cabral, Tomasina 217
Cadnum, Michael 93, 96
cannibalism 68
Canterbury Tales 96
capitalism 189, 196, 207
Caporael, Linnda R. 139
captivity narrative 127, 129, 132
Castle of Otranto, The 9, 10, 77, 78, 79, 80, 91

Castle Rackrent 86, 87, 90
Cather, Willa 22
Chandler, Alice 74
change bias 124, 133
character development 48, 147, 221
Chatterton, Thomas 7
Chaucer, Geoffrey 72, 76, 96, 97
Cheng'en, Wu 151
Chickering, Sara 39, 40
child prostitution 42
children's literature 25, 26, 107, 110, 114, 126
Chinese-American ethnic novel 163
Chinese American feminism 162
Chinese historical fiction 151
Chinese masculinity 81, 153, 155, 158, 159, 163
chivalry 63, 64, 68, 74, 88
Chong, Lin 153, 154, 157, 158, 160
Civil Rights Act 116
Civil Rights Movement xxv, 119
Civil War xi, xxiv, xxv, xxvi, xxvii, 5, 16, 19, 21, 27, 28, 30, 31, 85, 151, 162, 166, 167, 168, 169, 171, 173, 174, 175, 176, 177, 178, 179, 180, 183, 184, 188, 189, 195, 198, 199, 202, 206, 207
Clarissa 5, 6
Clark, Edward W. 130, 135
Clement-Davies, David 26
Clinton, Catherine xxvi
Cohoon, Lorinda B. 101
Coldfield, Rosa 209
Coleridge, S. T. 16, 29

Emmett Till case 114, 119
Enlightenment xv, 82
En, Shi 160
Erdrich, Louise xvii
Ernest, John 190

family xii, xx, xxiii, xxiv, 21, 38,
    40, 42, 43, 48, 49, 50, 51,
    52, 53, 54, 55, 56, 57, 77,
    79, 86, 87, 102, 117, 130,
    131, 132, 139, 141, 142,
    143, 145, 146, 152, 158,
    160, 166, 171, 177, 182,
    183, 184, 185, 187, 188,
    189, 190, 191, 193, 194,
    209, 213, 214, 216, 217,
    218, 219, 224
fantasy vii
Faulkner, William xxv, 22, 25,
    196, 205, 210
Federal Writers' Project xii, 201
Fei, Yue 162
femininity 37, 152, 153, 163
feminist criticism ix, 32, 33, 37,
    41, 42, 45
feminist lens 32, 34, 41
feminist theory 27
Ferns, Chris 63
fieldwork 201
filter x, 107, 109, 111, 115, 118
Finch, Isabel 34
Finch, Robert 35
Finkelman, Paul 173
Fitzwalter, Matty 103
Fitzwalter, William 103
Fleischman, Paul 166
Fletcher, Everell 123
Foer, Jonathan Safran 28

folklore xii, 92, 93, 95, 99, 100,
    201, 203, 205
Follett, Ken xvii
Foote, Shelby xxiv, xxvii
Forbes, Esther 25
Forrester, Viviane 38
Forrest, Nathan Bedford xxvi
fortune-telling 137, 138, 140, 141,
    142, 143, 144, 147, 217
frame story 217, 222
Franco, Pericles 217
Frank, Anne 28
Frazier, Charles 22
French Revolution 11, 12, 85
friendship 121, 125
Fuentes, Carlos 24
Fuller, Anne 82

Gabaldon, Diana xvii
Gable, Clark 197, 210
Gaines, Ernest J. xvii
Gao, Marshall 157
Garcia, Antero 27
García Márquez, Gabriela 24
Garrick, David 7
Gelfant, Blanche 198
Gettysburg Address 167, 178
ghetto 52
Ghost of Thomas Kempe, The xviii
Gibbon, Edward 7
Giovanni, Nikki 181
Goddard, Charley 166, 168, 180
Godwin, William 72
Gone with the Wind 22, 196, 197,
    198, 199, 200, 202, 205,
    209, 210
Good, Sarah 144, 146
Gordon-Reed, Annette xxvii
Gothic literature 11

Gottlieb, Jack 139, 150
Granger, Harlan 184, 187
Grant, Ulysses S. 172
Grapes of Wrath, The xx
Great Depression xii, 117, 182,
    183, 196, 210
Greenblatt, Stephen 17
Greenleaf, Marian 103
Gregory, Philippa xvii
gringa dominicana 217, 220, 224
Guanzhong, Luo 23, 151
Gupta, Rushir 24
Gustloff, Wilhelm 25

Hade, Daniel xxiv
Hahn, Steven 177
Hale, John 138
Hamnett, Brian 65
Hampton, Claudia xix
Han Dynasty 151
Hansen, Chadwick 139
Harclay, Sir Philip 80
Harlem Renaissance 181, 202
Harrison, Rebecca 224, 225
Hawksmaid 93, 102, 103, 104,
    106
Hawthorne, Nathaniel 20
Hearne, Betsy 99, 102
Heller, Joseph 22
Hemings, Harriet 27
Hemings, Sally 27
Hemingway, Ernest 22
Heng, Geraldine 68
Henry III 78, 80
Henry, John 116, 117
Henry V 81
Henry VI 80
Herbst, Josephine 207
Hersey, John 22

Herz, Dietrich 169
Hesse, Karen 26, 33, 45
heteroglossia 218
Higginson, Thomas Wentworth
    203
Hillburn, Hiram 118
Hill, Crag 27
Hipchen, Emily 224, 225
Hirsh, Esther 38, 40
historical context 112, 117, 118
historical romance 64
historicism 17
historiography 79, 83, 202
Hitler, Adolf 52
Holocaust ix, 28, 47, 48, 49, 51,
    52, 53, 55, 57, 58, 59, 219
Holt, J. C. 94, 102, 105
Hope Leslie 123, 128, 135
Howe, Katherine 137, 141, 147
Howells, William Dean 21
*How the García Girls Lost Their
    Accents* 212, 214
Hubbard, Betty 142
Huebner, Timothy S. xxv
Hugo, Victor 24
human trafficking 42
Hume, David 7, 78
Hunt, Irene 28
Hurd, Richard 80
Hurston, Zora Neale 201

identity 12, 36, 37, 38, 47, 48, 49,
    52, 54, 55, 57, 68, 69, 70,
    72, 73, 121, 137, 140, 148,
    160, 163, 177, 197, 200,
    201, 210
Iliad, The 23
In a Dark Wood 93, 96, 98, 105
Ink, Lynn Chun 217

Plantagenet, Richard 81
Pleasant Company xxiv
politics xxv, 16, 17, 72, 73, 85, 86, 89, 162, 163
Porter, Carolyn 199
Postmodern philosophy xvii
posttraumatic stress disorder. *See* PTSD 147, 168
presentism 238
Prévost, Antoine 5
Prince John 73, 102
Princess of Cleves, The 4
Prohibition 39
Promised Land 163
Prosser, Gabriel 202, 203
PTSD 147, 168
Puritanism 127, 128
Putnam, Ann 140, 141, 145, 146
Putnam, Joseph 143, 144
Putnam, Lucy 140
Pyle, Howard 99

Quakerism 128, 133
queer theory 27
Quirk, Thady 86

race 32, 34, 111, 122, 123, 127, 176, 181, 182, 187, 190, 193, 197, 199, 203, 223
racism ix, 39, 116, 117, 118, 171, 182, 191, 193, 199, 204, 209
Radcliffe, Ann 82, 83
Ransom, John Crowe 27
Rapin, Paul de 82
Reagan, Daniel 203
Realism 65, 67, 70, 77, 80, 87, 111, 206
Recess: A Tale of Other Times, The 82, 90

Reconstruction Era 184
Red Badge of Courage, The 230
Reeve, Clara 80
Reeves, Johnny 39, 41
Rehberger, Dean 65
repression 11
Richard Coer de Lyon 65, 68, 73, 75, 76
Richardson, Samuel 5
Rich, Charlotte 218
Rinaldi, Ann 26, 27, 29
Roberts, Kenneth 200
Robertson, William 7, 82
Robin Hood x, 73, 75, 92, 93, 94, 95, 96, 97, 98, 99, 100, 101, 102, 103, 105, 106, 153
Robinson, Jackie 115
Rogow, Sally M. 55
Roll of Thunder, Hear My Cry xx, 25, 117, 120, 182, 186, 187, 188, 194, 195
romance xxviii, 23, 63, 70, 72, 76, 78, 80, 82, 90, 134, 151, 225
Romanticism 19, 27, 80
Romola xvi
Roosevelt, Franklin Delano 201
Rose, Alan Henry 20
Rosenberg, Alyssa 198
Roth, Philip xvii
Rowland, Pleasant xxiii, xxiv
Rowlandson, Mary 130
Rushdie, Salman 24
Rye, William 169

sacrifice xii, 112, 157, 176, 182, 186, 187, 191, 193
Salem Witch Trials xi, 27, 147, 148, 149, 150
Scarlet Letter, The 20
